TELLING *the* OLD TESTAMENT STORY

Praise for *Telling the Old Testament Story*

"Why did the earliest followers of Jesus embark on mission to the Gentiles? It wasn't because they were Christians determined to convert the world to 'our religion.' It was because they were (initially) Jews, who knew the story they were in—namely, the story of their scriptures, the Old Testament as we have come to know it. For if the God of Israel has kept God's promise through the Messiah Jesus to open up the door of blessing to all nations, then they need to hear that good news. Brad Kelle's book reads the Old Testament with the grain of that great story, bringing out the canonical coherence of the narrative, even across the range of centuries, genres, and sources. In spite of some discomfort with texts and themes connected to the reality of God's judgment, his account spotlights the overarching motif of the mission of God to bring healing and blessing to his whole creation and all nations of humanity. This book is a welcome reminder that, if we are in Christ, this is our story too. Christian neglect of the Old Testament is a fundamental forgetting of the story we are in, which also explains the weakness of our engagement in God's mission. Tell the story. Live the story."

> —Christopher J. H. Wright, International Ministries Director, Langham Partnership, London, UK

"The story of God's mission? How can one see the Old Testament in those terms? In taking his readers through the Old Testament story, Brad Kelle demonstrates the way the beginning and the end (and the middle) of this story is God's missionary concern for the world. So this book is about the Old Testament story and about mission—and how they are interwoven. It also helps readers navigate much of the thinking of modern scholars who wrestle with the Old Testament texts and their interpretation."

> —John Goldingay, David Allan Hubbard Professor of Old Testament, School of Theology, Fuller Theological Seminary, Pasadena, CA

Brad E. Kelle

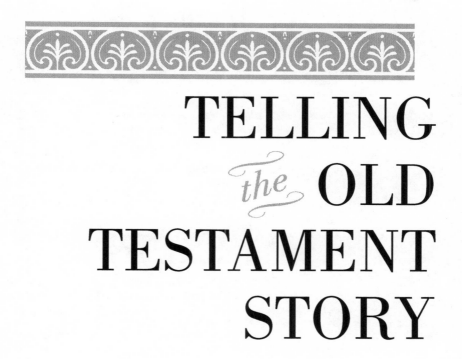

TELLING *the* OLD TESTAMENT STORY

God's Mission and God's People

Abingdon Press™
Nashville

TELLING THE OLD TESTAMENT STORY:
GOD'S MISSION AND GOD'S PEOPLE

Copyright © 2017 by Abingdon Press

Library of Congress Cataloging-in-Publication Data has been requested.

ISBN: 978-1-4267-9304-2

17 18 19 20 21 22 23 24 25 26—10 9 8 7 6 5 4 3 2 1
MANUFACTURED IN THE UNITED STATES OF AMERICA

For Tim Green,
professor, friend, mentor,
and the one who taught me to hear the story

Gather around
Give your ear
      To this stunning salvation story
            This soul-shaping and world-transforming story
            Irresistible adventure Unpredictable riches Wide-ranging wisdom
            A Shimmering Shining Scintillating shifting gears kind of Story
                  A story that rekindles the wreckages of the heart's true flame

Gather around
            This fascinating flame Give your ear
                      Give your heart
                          Give your mind
                              Give your all

—Dale C. Fredrickson, "Gather Around," in
Help Me Be: Praying in Poems

Contents

Contents

Preface

Not too many years ago, I remember seeing a television broadcast begin its coverage of a Major League Baseball World Series game with a commonly known Native American proverb, "Tell me a fact, and I will learn; tell me the truth, and I will believe; but tell me a *story*, and it will live in my heart forever." This promotional piece recast a championship baseball game as a gripping plot line that would make a lasting impact on those who watched it.

In our culture, stories have power. Good stories, told through literature, television, movies, journalism, documentaries, or other means can grab our attention, generate a range of emotions, and even move us to action. They can leave us in tears, fill us with joy, drive us to anger, or give us new ways to think about the events and realities that have unfolded in our lives and world. Whether the stories are fictional, historical, inspired by real-life events, or some other categorization, they give creative and powerful interpretations that have the potential to change the way we see the realities of our existence. And we don't even mind if we hear the same story told in different ways (just witness how often today's popular movies are remakes of older films from earlier eras or how young children often insist on hearing stories told many times, sometimes in different ways). It seems as though the ability to tell a story—to gather the pieces of information surrounding a particular person, event, or even fictional idea into a plot line that draws readers, hearers, or viewers into the narrative in a fresh way—stands at the heart of today's media culture. Telling stories has proven to be one of the most effective ways to help people engage significant facts and important ideas.

Story and the Old Testament

The Bible, particularly the Old Testament (OT), is full of stories. It certainly contains other materials such as poems, laws, and rituals, but even these seem to find their place within a larger plot line unfolding across the OT as a whole. In many ways, the OT seems like the perfect fit for a culture drawn to telling stories. Perhaps surprisingly, however, many students today, especially in introductory-level university and seminary courses, encounter the OT in a different manner. Rather than exploring the ways that the diverse writings of the OT might be viewed together as part of a larger story, introductory courses (and the textbooks typically used in them) are frequently an exercise in dissection. They isolate the individual books—and the smaller texts and older traditions within them—to analyze their historical and cultural backgrounds, processes of composition, layers of editing, literary features, and unique theological ideas. This is a necessary task that no study of the OT should neglect. Indeed, academic courses require more than simply asking students to read the Bible; they need to *introduce* students to the Bible as a complex, historical product that requires familiarity with these types of basic issues in order to read it in credible and appropriate ways. Especially for introductory or survey courses, however, there is a need to provide students with something more—some creative options for how to gather this dissected knowledge into a sense of the whole. And the power of storytelling in our culture provides an interesting opportunity.

This book is designed to serve introductory-level, nonspecialist students in Christian (especially Protestant) universities and seminaries, as well as similar types of readers in churches and nonacademic settings. It works as a companion to a standard introductory textbook on the OT. I've spent more than a decade teaching introductory survey courses on the OT within these settings, and I've been energized by the ongoing creative tension over the need for both analytical dissection and holistic understanding. In this book, I try to provide a supplement to (but not a replacement for) the typical approaches and textbooks that draws upon their insights but offers a way that one might read the OT, with all of its literary and historical diversity, as an overall story. I hope to show how one can identify this overall story and then consider what it might mean for contemporary readers to enter imaginatively into that story drawn from the OT texts.

My reading of the OT operates within several specific frames of reference that will be defined in the first chapter. Most notably, I write for Christians as a Christian. I hope that my insights might also serve a broader audience, but my focus is to offer a resource that most directly serves my own faith community. I try to write in a style that makes the book readily usable by beginning-level college and seminary students, as well as ministerial or lay-person studies in parish contexts. At the same time, I hope the interpretations offered here will be adequately informed and insightful so as to be useful to more advanced students and perhaps even some scholars.

Since the primary goal of this book is to consider how one might bring together the various elements of the OT texts into a theological reading of the whole, I don't attempt to provide a comprehensive introduction to the material or address certain questions related to the background or interpretive issues for each OT book. For example, I don't include explanations of the origins, composition, and editing of the individual books, the complexities involved in language and translation, or the social, liturgical, and ritual elements of ancient Israelite religion. Perhaps most noticeably in today's scholarly environment, I don't engage in the wide-ranging and often heated debates over the historicity of the biblical texts and how, if at all, the persons and events depicted in the OT relate to historical and archaeological evidence for ancient Israel's past. These discussions remain vital, and I've had a go at them in other settings, but they are not my focus here.[1] Still, the study of many of these more technical issues within biblical scholarship has produced resources that help with the reading of the OT as a whole, and insights from scholarship on these matters underlie what is presented here. I draw on these resources throughout, and I will, at times, say what is necessary to locate my interpretation. Readers wanting to dig deeper are invited to pursue the supplementary sources provided in the notes.

I'm also privileged to offer here an academic work that uses the The Common English Bible as the base translation for the biblical texts, a translation to which I had the good fortune of contributing. Readers may especially benefit from using *The Common English Study Bible* for supplementary and background information. The beginning of each chapter will list selected biblical texts that provide the focus for the discussion. Each chapter will then explore representative texts and key themes in the context of a macro-level story found across the OT books (sidebars will occur throughout the main chapters to raise related issues and offer further insights).

Acknowledgments

The writing of a book is never a solitary endeavor. I've been especially blessed with professional and personal support that sustained my work along the way. I'm grateful to my students at Point Loma Nazarene University and Fuller Theological Seminary who endured classes over the last decade and helped to shape the ideas represented in this book. Thanks are also due to the Wesleyan Center at Point Loma Nazarene University for a fellowship that provided support for the project in the fall of 2014. Thanks also to David Teel and the editorial team at Abingdon Press for their thoughtful work and good humor. I am especially grateful to my colleague Samuel M. Powell for taking time from his own impressive publication and research (and teaching!) tasks to read and help shape my work. Although he (nor anyone else) bears any responsibility for the shortcomings that surely remain here, every word of this book is better because Sam gave it his time and attention. Finally, and above all, I thank my wife, Dee, and our now seventeen-year-old son, Grayson, for their patience with yet again too many hours spent upstairs in front of the computer, where there are nice views of palm trees but too few views of family. I'm in their debt, as always.

Chapter 1

Introduction

Focus Text: Deuteronomy 6:10-25

A Story for the Next Generation

Telling a story can give people a new way to understand their lives. Consider an example from the Old Testament (OT). In an episode that occurs at a critical juncture on the journey of the people of Israel out of slavery in Egypt, Deuteronomy 6:20-25 describes Moses's instructions to Israelite parents concerning the next generation. Just before the people leave the wilderness, cross the Jordan River, and enter the land of Canaan, Moses instructs them on how they should respond in the future when their children ask them about the ways they live and the laws they follow: "In the future, your children will ask you, 'What is the meaning of the laws, the regulations, and the case laws that the LORD our God commanded you?'" (v. 20). Far from giving a list of rationales or threats to support a set of rules, Moses tells the parents to respond with something broader:

> Tell them: We were Pharaoh's slaves in Egypt. But the LORD brought us out of Egypt with a mighty hand. Before our own eyes, the LORD performed great and awesome deeds of power against Egypt, Pharaoh, and his entire dynasty. But the LORD brought us out from there so that he could bring us in, giving us the land that he swore to our ancestors. Then the LORD commanded us to perform all these regulations, revering the LORD our God, so that things go well for us always and so we continue to live, as we're doing right now. (vv. 21-24)

When confronted with a question that is ostensibly about rules and their justifications, Moses tells the parents to respond with a story. The parents' response is essentially to tell the story of what their God, YHWH,[1] has done for them because it is that salvation story that makes sense of the ways they live as a community. YHWH's demands on the people came only after and in response to his gracious deeds on their behalf. And those demands exist only to sustain the good life that the people received from YHWH's actions (v. 24). The story makes the system comprehensible.

Yet, the wording of the future children's question subtly suggests that this next generation doesn't yet identify with the laws or the God from whom they come. The children's words express a certain distance from the rules that govern their parents' lives, as they describe those laws as what "the LORD our God commanded *you*" (v. 20). Just as subtly, however, the words that Moses instructs the parents to use in response break down the presumed separation and include the children in the deliverance story: "*We* were Pharaoh's slaves in Egypt. But the LORD brought *us* out of Egypt with a mighty hand" (v. 21). In the literary setting of Deuteronomy, neither the parents whom Moses addresses nor the children he envisions as making the future inquiry were actual participants in the earlier events of YHWH's deliverance. The parents to whom he speaks were born in the wilderness as the second generation after the exodus from Egypt (Num 26), and the children represent generations to come. Yet, Moses uses first-person language that incorporates (the technical term is *inscripts*) both groups into these defining moments of the past, as if they had been there. Telling YHWH's story serves not only to render the people's practices intelligible but also to narrate new generations into that story and thereby shape their identity as members of the community.[2]

Starting Points

Taking a cue from Moses's words to the Israelite parents, this book is an effort to tell a story by gathering together the diverse narratives, poems, laws, rituals, and more that make up the OT—a story that can draw readers into those materials in new and imaginative ways. What I offer here is not a simple summary of the OT's teachings but a *reading* of the OT as one overarching story. In much the same way that one might attend a *reading* of poetry, where the presenter gives a particular expression of the poem's elements and discusses its possible meanings, in the pages that follow I try to give an interpretation that shows how the different OT texts come together to form a larger whole with broader significance. The OT as it now stands, especially in its present arrangement within Protestant Bibles, permits us to read it as a whole and tell it (or re-tell it) in the form of a larger story—a plot line within which many different dots connect. And as we connect the dots of this plot line, we will find that our understanding of the whole gives us new insights into the parts themselves.

The telling of the OT story that I offer in this book is an intentionally *Christian, canonical, narrative,* and *missional* telling. These terms (what I'll call "frames of reference") will be explained later in this chapter, but they yield a particular reading of the OT as a whole. *I attempt to tell the story of the OT as the story of God's mission in the world to restore creation to its divinely intended right-relationships, and the calling, creation, and formation of the people of Israel to participate as God's instrument in that mission.* The final chapter will briefly suggest how this story might continue into the New Testament (NT), as well as how the OT texts might draw us as contemporary readers into the story so that we begin to imagine in new ways who God is, what God is doing in the world, and what it means to be God's people who participate in God's mission.

This reading of the OT attends to what Walter Brueggemann has described as the "narrative rendering" of Israel's experience, testimony, and tradition that can be seen in the biblical texts.[3] Although the OT writings contain a rich variety of literary forms, including a significant amount of poetry, the ancient Israelite writers most often related the events and experiences of their past in a story mode—that is, in the pattern of a narrative plot line or sequence of events that moves from a beginning to a middle to an end. Even when these ancient writers preserved prayers, poems, and prophecies, they usually located them as moments within the larger unfolding story of Israel's life with God in the world.[4] This tendency of our biblical ancestors to communicate their experiences in a narrative mode invites us as contemporary readers to use *story* as a way to engage the diverse contents of the OT as a whole.

As I prepare to move through the OT in this way, let me highlight a few items that will define my approach. First, I acknowledge at the start that my telling is not the only way to envision how the OT works together in its entirety or how one might tell that story. Any particular reading of the OT, mine included, necessarily underemphasizes and even omits some elements, and other meaningful tellings are possible for readers who begin from different perspectives or emphasize different aspects. Still, my aim is to show how the OT provides the opportunity to tell a complex but coherent story drawn from its ancient and diverse writings. To borrow an analogy from Walter Moberly, I approach the interpretation of the OT as one might approach the interpretation of a musical score.[5] While the text of the musical score remains in some sense constant, there are different ways of interpreting the musical elements of the piece, and these interpretations can result in fresh performances that bring the piece to life in new and even diverse ways. Or, to use another example from the arts, any stage production of William Shakespeare's play *Romeo and Juliet* doesn't simply reproduce or repeat Shakespeare's dramatic text but brings the script to life in particular ways, performs it interpretively, and results in a unique presentation. What follows in this book, then, is not the only way to interpret the *musical score* or *dramatic script* of the OT, but it is one that hopefully gives expression to the text's elements in a creative and meaningful way.

Second, given my focus on viewing the diverse elements of the OT within a larger plot line, this book may serve best as a supplement to a more standard introductory textbook on the OT. I don't provide comprehensive introductions to the different OT books or try to address certain questions that result from academic study of the texts, their origins, or their translations. For example, I don't discuss the process through which the OT books came into being and later became part of the Jewish and Christian scripture.[6] Neither do I emphasize the ancient Near Eastern context of the OT writings or study them primarily by comparison with other compositions from that culture.[7] I also don't engage in the ongoing debates over the historicity of the biblical texts and how the persons and events depicted in the OT might relate to historical and archaeological evidence for ancient Israel's past.[8] Instead, I hope to capitalize on the "narrative rendering" of Israel's theological testimony that Brueggemann observed within the biblical writings and use a mode of reading that stays "inside the drama—inside the text itself."[9] Texts like those in the OT can communicate truth and meaning about God, humans, and the world in a variety of ways that need not be limited to questions of historical factuality.[10]

Third, my telling of the OT story stands in the line of several works of varying age and perspective that also attempt to consider the OT in terms of an overarching narrative concerned with God's purposes in the world and

Israel's participation in those purposes. H. H. Rowley's *Israel's Mission to the World* and *The Missionary Message of the Old Testament* were early examples.[11] Several more recent works have followed in the vein of holistic, often narrative-based readings of the OT, with varying starting points and results and sometimes employing the notion of God's and/or Israel's mission.[12] Many of these studies try to identify a unifying theme that, in their view, binds the OT (or all of Christian scripture) together around a single theological idea such as covenant.[13]

Three works resonate most closely with the approach taken in this book. Paul and Elizabeth Achtemeier's *The Old Testament Roots of Our Faith* is a Christian, popular-audience, and holistic reading of the OT.[14] Rather than seeking a unifying theme, they focus their reading of the OT on the promise given to Israel (especially in Gen 12) and Israel's mission in the world that flowed from it, exploring how the unfolding of this promise and its fulfillment provides the narrative shape to the biblical story. My reading owes much to their insights, but shifts the focus to God's mission (expressed initially in Gen 1–11) as the overarching framework for the story of Israel that follows. Robert Wall's and David Nienhuis's *A Compact Guide to the Whole Bible* is an attempt to read the entire Christian Bible as telling one scriptural story for the church.[15] They include several chapters on the NT and don't emphasize the notion of mission, but they proceed through the canon by suggesting how each major section contributes to the whole. Perhaps the most comprehensive treatment of the OT from the perspectives on which I focus is Christopher Wright's *The Mission of God: Unlocking the Bible's Grand Narrative*.[16] He uses the framework of a divine mission and Israel's participation in it as a means to read the whole OT. Many of Wright's insights underlie the reading offered in this book, yet he maintains a thematic rather than narrative or canonical approach that skips between major themes (e.g., creation, election, covenant) that appear in different parts of the OT writings.

In the spirit of these earlier studies, the chapters that follow will proceed by giving careful attention to representative biblical texts (rather than general themes), moving sequentially through the OT in the hopes of identifying one way to tell an overall story out of the writings, and reflecting on what it might mean for contemporary Christian readers in particular to enter imaginatively into that story. The beginning of each chapter will list selected biblical passages that provide the focus for the discussion (with all quotations drawn from the Common English Bible). Each chapter's discussion will then examine these and related texts in the context of a macro-level story found across the OT writings (with sidebars noting additional issues and insights). The goal throughout is to read the OT as the story of God's mission in the world to restore creation to its divinely intended right-relationships and in so doing to be drawn to new understandings of not only what God has done in the past but what God might be doing now.

Frames of Reference

As mentioned above, the telling of the OT story that I offer in this book is an intentionally *Christian, canonical, narrative,* and *missional* telling. To refer to my earlier analogy, just as an interpreter in a poetry reading gives his or her own expression of the poem and thus explores its meaning in new ways, these four adjectives (Christian, canonical, narrative, missional) refer to perspectives from which one may view the diverse contents of the OT and consider how they come together as different dots in a larger plot line.

I think of these perspectives as *frames of reference*. Within the field of physics, for example, a frame of reference is a framework that is used to observe and describe a physical phenomenon. It is a structure of views or values used to understand and evaluate data. (For example, imagine two people standing, facing each other on either side of a sidewalk. If a skateboarder rides down the sidewalk between them, for the person on one side of the sidewalk, the skateboarder is moving to the right; for the person on the other side, the skateboarder is moving to the left. The two people constitute two different frames of reference from which to describe the skateboarder's movement.) By placing data into a certain frame of reference, interpreters are able to describe it in a particular way. In fact, *reframing* a collection of data into different frames of reference yields new meanings that aren't necessarily visible from other frameworks. And if we place the same set of data into different frames of reference, we are often able to understand and describe it in more than one way.

For a nonscientific example, think about the ways that contemporary movies often take known facts about a historical person or event and reframe them within a storyline that gives them new dimensions of meaning. We might think here of the many movies made about the sinking of the *Titanic* cruise liner in 1912. One of the most recent of these movies, for instance, incorporated the names of historical persons involved in the events into a fictional, tragic love story of a romance forbidden by the social and economic class divisions of the time. This film creatively used various facts to tell a different story, and in the process left its viewers with new ways of imagining the personalities and actions of some of the real-life persons who experienced the actual event.

The point is that frames of reference are ways of gathering and viewing certain materials that bring out new dimensions of meaning. Whether physicists, moviegoers, or readers of scripture, observers can switch frames of reference and see different emphases and insights. As we'll see below, the production of scripture itself was a process of incorporating various earlier materials into new frames of reference, eventually resulting in the form of the OT that appears in Protestant Bibles today. And this is what we do every time we read the biblical texts. Even if we don't always realize it, we place the texts into frames of reference and see them from particular perspectives. My invitation in this book is for us to consider what meanings emerge from the OT when we read it within Christian, canonical, narrative, and missional frames of reference. Specifically, is there a bigger, overarching story revealed by these frames of reference that provides a framework for understanding the smaller, different stories and how they fit together?

The following sections briefly explain the specific frames of reference for my telling of the OT story. The naming of these frames of reference underscores that mine is a particular reading of the OT derived from specific contexts and that other meaningful tellings of the OT story are possible from readers who begin from different reference points or emphasize different aspects. However, the following sections explore some of the broader pressing issues that should be considered in any reading of the OT.

A Christian Telling

My telling of the OT story is a *Christian* telling. This book is written for Christians by a Christian (with the hope of a broader significance, as well). More specifically, I come to the OT texts and gather them together in ways deeply influenced by their present formulation in Protestant Bibles, the ways they have been read in the Christian tradition past and present, and the potential they may have for contemporary Christian belief and practice. As our postmodernist situation has reminded us, our interpretations of texts are influenced by the communities in which we encounter those texts. Far from being something to lament, this context-bound reality gives us creative and meaningful lenses to view the texts, celebrating the ways that such ancient and foreign texts take on local and particular significance. My aim here is to read the OT texts within a Christian frame of reference that remains attentive to other frames of reference. So, the discussion in this book will read the OT with attention to its ancient historical and literary context, but also with an eye to my own values and experiences and the communities in which I stand. Toward this end, the book will conclude by briefly sketching how one might see the OT story as told here continuing into the NT and how the OT story might shape contemporary Christian readers' understandings of God, humanity, and the world.

One issue for Christian readers is how to refer to the biblical writings under consideration here. The most common Christian label, *Old Testament*, has some problems. For example, *Old* might be taken to connote outdated or less important, so some interpreters have suggested we use titles such as *Hebrew Bible*, *Jewish Bible*, or *First Testament*.[17] These alternative designations capture important characteristics of the texts, including their historical nature as ancient Hebrew writings, their stand-alone validity and historical priority in relationship to the so-called *New Testament*, and their ongoing significance as scriptures that nourish contemporary Jewish faith communities. Far from quibbling over words, the terminology issue reminds readers that Christianity since its inception has wrestled with questions concerning how the OT texts function as part of a larger Christian scripture. And the designations *Old* and *New Testament* began to be used commonly and without clarification only in the fourth century CE.

I have chosen to keep using the label *Old Testament* out of convenience, since it's the most recognized label among Christians today. But other labels, especially *Hebrew Bible*, remind Christian readers that these texts originated as Israel's sacred writings, written in Hebrew (and Aramaic), edited, compiled, collected, and used before Christianity's emergence in history. On a related note, I will follow the common convention in today's scholarship and write the Hebrew personal name of Israel's God in the OT as YHWH, spelled without the vowels out of respect for the practice of the Jewish tradition both past and present, which honors the sanctity of God by not verbalizing the holy name.[18] Although most modern English translations replace YHWH with the words LORD or GOD (in all capitals), the use of a personal name for God within the OT is significant. It allowed Israel to distinguish its God from others believed to exist at the time ("YHWH is God"), and it communicates a sense of personal relationship that is missing from authoritarian titles such as "Lord" and "God."

A related issue for a Christian telling of the OT in today's context is the fact that the texts that Christians call the OT were and are Jewish texts. The long-standing Christian confession (see Rom 11) is that Christians have simply been invited to share in what originated as a Jewish story. The story the OT tells is not only God's story but also Israel's story, told most directly for them and historically by them. Additionally, it's important to remember that these texts continue to nourish the faith communities of Judaism today. So, the OT is a set of texts shared by Judaism and Christianity. A Christian reading, while certainly interpreting the texts in some unique ways, shouldn't ignore the Jewish origins and character of these texts or try to exclude Jewish interpretations. All of this is important precisely because of a history within Christianity that has, at times, denied the Jews their story or used the OT to harm the Jewish faith and foster anti-Semitism.[19] Christian interpreters today inescapably operate in the shadow of that history. Moreover, we now must offer our readings of the OT in the honest awareness of the Holocaust, an unimaginable brutality, abuse, and displacement suffered by the very community that has given us the texts that we seek to interpret.[20] Christian readings of the OT are credible and legitimate ways to understand these originally Jewish writings. But we bear the solemn responsibility to ensure that Christian readings attend to the Jewish character of the texts and their story and avoid claims that promote the rejection of Judaism (so-called *supercessionism*) or ignore the rich interpretation done by Jewish interpreters past and present.

A Canonical Telling

My telling of the OT story is a *canonical* telling—that is, a reading of the OT informed by the way it now stands as a collection of thirty-nine books in Protestant Bibles. The Christian use of the OT throughout history eventually resulted in an agreed-upon, authoritative list and arrangement of the biblical writings designed to shape the church's beliefs and practices. This list and arrangement of authoritative writings is referred to as a *canon*. To read the Bible in a Christian canonical frame of reference, then, means to approach the biblical writings in the way they have been received from the church and to think about them as *scripture* for the church—that is, sacred and authoritative writings that provide God's revelation to guide believers' faith and moral conduct. More importantly for our purposes, however, to read the OT canonically is to allow the arrangement of the canon to guide the meaning we find for the parts and the whole. We want to consider how the individual parts of scripture fit together in their present arrangement and how that bigger whole leads us to understand the individual parts.[21]

We should recognize that canons (like the one found in Protestant Bibles) are *frames of reference*. In the same way that I defined frames of reference above, canons are ways to gather and reframe a set of materials (in this case, the books of the OT) into certain structures that yield new meanings and insights for the parts and the whole.[22] In this book, I will introduce the OT writings according to their arrangement in the Protestant canon and explore the ways that the diverse traditions within the texts come together in this arrangement to form a larger story about God's mission to heal creation.[23] There are, however, several canons that developed throughout the history of Judaism and Christianity and that still today organize the books of the OT in different ways. Each of these canons reframes the biblical writings in a way that gives them some new dimensions of meaning not found (or at least not found entirely) in the other canons.[24] The arrangement in present-day Jewish Bibles, for instance, includes twenty-four or twenty-two books (depending on how one counts them) in a different order than that found in Protestant Bibles. The Jewish canon basically follows what we believe to have been the historical order in which the biblical writings were produced and finalized between the fourth century BCE and the first century CE. It begins with the *Pentateuch* (Genesis–Deuteronomy), followed by a collection of *Prophets*, and concluding with a group of *Writings* that feature poetic and wisdom texts.

In the centuries following their exile in Babylon in the sixth century BCE, however, Jews in various areas gradually produced another version of their scripture in Greek (sometimes called the *Septuagint*), alongside the version in Hebrew. This Greek Bible eventually adopted a different ordering for the biblical writings, as well as included a slightly larger list of books. These Hebrew and Greek collections of Israel's scriptures gave rise to the main arrangements found in Christian Bibles today. At first, early Christians seem to have relied on the Greek translation and ordering. Later on, divisions arose within the church. Today, Catholic and Orthodox canons of the OT tend to follow the Greek arrangement, including some of the additional books not found in the Jewish Hebrew canon (these books are sometime called the *Apocrypha*).

The Protestant OT canon, however, contains only the same books as the Jewish Hebrew canon but organizes them in an order closer to the Greek version and counts them in different ways to end up with thirty-nine books (for example, numbering 1–2 Samuel as two books rather than one and counting the Twelve Prophets as twelve individual books).[25] The Protestant OT canon begins with the Pentateuch but then moves to the historical books, followed by the poetry and wisdom books, and, finally, concludes with the prophets.

The point of observing these different OT canons is to highlight how the Protestant canon works as a whole to tell the bigger story of God's mission to restore creation and Israel's calling, creation, and formation as an instrument to participate in that mission. The Protestant canon begins with a storyline that runs from the early chapters of Genesis through the postexilic writings of Chronicles, Ezra, and Nehemiah. The storyline presents God's mission to restore a broken creation, Israel's emergence as a people called by God, and their rise and fall as two kingdoms through a time of exile and return. A series of poetic and wisdom books then provide theological reflections on the experiences of living as God's people in a variety of circumstances. Finally, the prophetic books close the OT by preserving theological commentaries on Israel's struggles to fulfill its identity as God's instrument of restoration and by envisioning an explicitly future-oriented dimension to the activity and mission of God and the people. A canonical telling of the OT story allows us to bring the diverse historical traditions in all the books into this kind of overall picture. We can highlight those voices and perspectives that are dominant within the Protestant canonical formulation, even while we acknowledge that other voices and perspectives are present within the books that may have had their own significant influence in ancient Israel's life and religion.

A Narrative Telling

My telling of the OT story is a *narrative* telling—that is, a reading that focuses on the OT as literature and especially explores the story-like elements and shape of the biblical texts, rather than questions of authorship, historical contexts, or stages of composition. Narrative reading is similar to canonical interpretation in that it can help readers perceive an overall story or plot unfolding across the collection of the biblical books as a whole. But narrative interpretation of the OT draws from ancient and contemporary theories for studying literature that might be used within university departments of literature. To use a common metaphor, narrative interpretation views the biblical text not as a window to look into historical times and places that stand behind the text, but as a mirror that creates meaningful interaction between the reader and the literary dimensions of the text itself.[26] Reading the OT in a narrative mode helps reveal an overarching story (consisting of many little stories), and interpretation becomes the attempt to tell that story faithfully.

This way of engaging the biblical texts seems to resonate with a deep love for stories and storytelling among many people, especially in contemporary western culture. Even casually, we often use stories to make meaning of events in our world and our lives, plotting them in a way that identifies a setting, problem, heightened tension, and resolution. But narrative interpretation also resonates with the practices of the biblical writers themselves. Our biblical ancestors seem to have gathered the various events, traditions, and memories shared by their community into a predominantly narrative rendering of their life as a people. Even the OT's poetic hymns (e.g., Exod 15; Judg 5) and major law codes (e.g., Exod 20; Deut 12–26) are embedded within the stories of God's great acts for Israel that constitute an unfolding biblical narrative. Of course, the construction of any such story always involves the selection and interpretation of particular experiences, so that every narrative is only a partial and particular way of giving account of reality. Yet, just as the biblical writers themselves selected and interpreted their community's experiences to create their stories, poems, and more, narrative interpretation invites us as contemporary readers to engage in narrative-making activity as we select and interpret the OT's various stories, poems, and more in order to gather them into new ways to tell the OT story as a whole.

An element of narrative interpretation that holds special significance for Christian readers of the OT involves what many have identified as the *formative* power of narrative. We often resonate with stories specifically because we can identify with the characters and experiences, in some sense finding ourselves drawn in to become participants in the plot. Stories become formative as they pull us inside their narrative and cause us to reimagine our world and our lives. We find our place within the narrative and accept new ways of making sense of our reality governed by the narrative's portrayal.[27] This way of thinking draws from earlier work that explored narrative not simply as a genre but as a concept and means for understanding and shaping the moral identity of persons and communities.[28] Narratives challenge their readers to locate themselves in the story and thus serve to shape how persons understand themselves, their world, and their place within it. We might think, for example, of how the stories told within Jesus's parables in the NT draw their readers into the story in ways that cause them to see themselves differently. Consider, for instance, how the story of the prodigal son (Luke 15:11-32) not only pushes its readers to examine whether they might be living a reckless, squandering life like that of the younger son, but also invites its readers to imagine God as a loving parent who waits eagerly for even the most irresponsible child to come home.

Building from these ideas, I offer here a narrative telling of the OT with the idea that scripture's story can shape the identity of those who read it. The shaping work of the OT begins when we start the process of interpreting any particular book or passage by first asking, "Where am I now in the overall story of OT?" The knowledge of what has preceded, what follows, and how a particular passage functions within the overarching story of the OT can open new insights into passages that often seem obscure or disconnected from the whole. From that point, we can begin to engage the OT as a story that has the power to draw us as contemporary readers into the story, urging us to become participants in the story of what God is doing in the world and to reconfigure our own lives in light of the narrative's terms for understanding reality. I propose that this narrative formation occurs as the overall OT story works to shape its readers' understanding of three questions in particular:

1) Who is God (and what is God doing in the world)?

2) Who are we as the people of God?

3) How should we live in the world (in light of who God is and who we are as the people of God)?

These questions are about *identity*—an understanding not only of who God is but who we are as individuals and communities. The various stories, poems, laws, and more that make up the OT work together to provide answers (often more than one) to these three questions and thus serve to shape the identity of those who read them. Telling the OT story functions not simply to provide information about these questions, however, but to draw even contemporary readers into new ways of imagining themselves and their lives as part of the larger story of God and God's mission in the world.

Even while emphasizing this identity-forming power of story, one word of caution is in order. Both the canonical and narrative frames of reference for telling the OT story share the danger of overlooking or even repressing the diversity of the biblical texts. Christopher Wright expresses well the tension felt by those who seek to engage the OT as a whole:

> It is of course not just a single narrative, like a river with only one channel. It is rather a complex mixture of all kinds of smaller narratives, many of them rather self-contained, with all kinds of other material embedded within them—more like a great delta. But there is clearly a direction, a flow, that can be described in the terms I have laid out.[29]

The OT texts were written by a multitude of different writers, in two different languages, and in a variety of historical, social, political, and religious circumstances, resulting in a genuine diversity not just of literary forms but also of theological ideas. We will notice, for example, that Proverbs seems to emphasize that a life of obedience to God will result in blessing that avoids the suffering that befalls disobedient people. However, Job seems to illustrate that even the righteous suffer, sometimes with no apparent reason for the suffering. Walter Brueggemann characterizes the OT as possessing a "multi-layered pluralism" of faith claims and perspectives, some of which provide different answers to the three main questions I highlighted above concerning the identity of God, God's people, and how God's people should live in the world.[30] As contemporary readers, we must attend to the diversity of theological perspectives among the biblical writings, even as we attempt to gather them into one particular telling. Perhaps we could use an art metaphor: the various texts and traditions within the OT are like different styles of art that portray the same object from different perspectives and methods.[31]

In light of these observations, I offer here a telling of the OT story that attempts to embrace and hold in tension the different theological perspectives found among the biblical writings, even while exploring how they might creatively fit together into a particular conception of the whole. I don't want to suggest that there is one grand, totalizing metanarrative that excludes all others—a mode of reading that has lost its power in the recognized realities of our postmodern context—or to lose sight of the many stories in light of a unifying one. I only aim to recognize that the present canonical formulation of the OT yields a particular plot line, with some narratives more dominant than others, and allows us to gather the OT texts into an overall story that includes different theological voices in dialogue over the key questions of the identity of God and God's people. In their diversity, these voices together advocate a particular understanding of who God is, what God is doing in the world, and what that means for the lives of God's people. Since my telling—as all tellings—remains a provisional construction that is based on particular frames of reference, it should be put into dialogue with other readings in a broader interpretive conversation.

A Missional Telling

As a final frame of reference, my telling of the OT story is a *missional* telling. I read the OT as the story of God's mission in the world to restore creation to its divinely intended right-relationships, and of the calling, creation, and formation of the people of Israel to participate as God's instrument in that mission. This reading stands in dialogue with new perspectives on Christian faith, scripture, and practice that have appeared most fully in recent years under the broad label of *missional* approaches.[32] These approaches grew out of an increased awareness of the declining influence of the church in the western world and the growth of the church's numbers in the two-thirds world. They also represent the blossoming of long-standing theological formulations about the activity of God in sending and working to accomplish the divine purposes in the world.

At the heart of the missional approaches to Christian faith and practice is a conviction about God's nature. In much of the modern history of Christianity, the term *missions* referred to the sending of missionaries seeking converts and performing other particular activities in specific times and places. But the earliest uses of the term *mission* in Christian theology referred to an attribute of God's nature evidenced in the doctrine of the Trinity and the notion of the sending of the Son by the Father and the sending of the Holy Spirit by the Father and the Son.[33] The phrase *Mission of God* (Latin, *missio Dei*) eventually (by the mid-twentieth century especially) came to designate this sending aspect of God's being, highlighting that the act of sending into and on behalf of the world is part of God's nature. Building on these theological formulations, recent so-called *missional* approaches focus on the notion of a divine mission underway in the world and the call for the church to participate in that mission. Seen in this way, mission is God's redemptive work in and with the world. The church participates as a sign and instrument of that work out of a faith conviction that refuses to accept the present state of the world as the true or final state and seeks to transform it by sharing in God's redemptive project already underway. Mission, then, is not primarily the activity of the church but an attribute and movement of God that includes the church as its primary but not exclusive means.[34] Mission refers not to a specialized activity but to the church's very identity as participants in God's larger work in the world, a work that may make use of other means as well.

What does it mean to read the Bible from this *missional* perspective?[35] Recently, so-called *missional hermeneutics* (interpretation) have followed several main "streams" or understandings.[36] One stream highlights how scripture's narrative tells the story of *God's* mission and the people who participate in it. The biblical texts provide the primary witness to God's missional nature and activity in history. The Bible itself came into being as the product of God's engagement with God's people in the world and is the revelation of God's purpose in human history. And missional approaches yield interpretive questions that can be addressed to individual texts. These include asking how a passage reveals God's mission in the world, illuminates the covenant people's role in that mission, or takes on a new meaning when read in light of God's larger purposes in history. A second stream in missional interpretation highlights how the biblical texts equip God's *people* to engage in God's mission in new and changing contexts. Just as narratives in general can draw readers into the stories, the goal of missional readings of scripture is to draw contemporary Christian readers into participation in the missional community described by the texts and thus into participation in God's redemptive mission in the world.

My telling of the OT story in the pages that follow uses the notion of God's mission and Israel's identity as participants in that mission to gather the ancient and diverse OT writings into a complex but coherent story of God's redemptive work in the world and the calling of God's people as instruments for that work. In the spirit of the missional approaches, this telling has a special interest in exploring how the OT texts might draw us as contemporary readers into the story so that we begin to imagine in new ways who God is, what God is doing in the world, and what it means to be part of God's people who participate in God's mission.

C h a p t e r   2

The Old Testament as Story

Focus Text: Nehemiah 9:1-31

The purpose of this chapter is to provide in advance a bird's-eye overview of the story the OT tells. I offer here my sense of the big picture of the OT writings as they now stand within the Protestant canon. The chapter is meant to give a convenient summary that can be kept in mind while exploring the details of the representative texts and themes in the following pages. As noted in the last chapter, however, we should remember at the outset that although the big, overarching story provides a framework for understanding how the smaller, different stories fit together, the construction of any such story necessarily represents just one way of narrating things and most certainly leaves out or, at least, underemphasizes some important elements.

Approaching the Old Testament as a Story

The OT doesn't look like a story. It doesn't consist of only a single writing or move smoothly through a singular plot line that proceeds from setting to tension to heightened tension to resolution in an uninterrupted fashion. It doesn't contain only narrative literature that revolves around major characters and events unfolding in chronological order. In fact, the OT is manifestly an anthology—a miniature library of discreet textual compositions (thirty-nine "books" in the Protestant canon), grouped mainly according to genre but coming from a wide range of writers, editors, and communities across various historical settings, generally between the eighth and second centuries BCE. On what basis and in what way, then, can we approach the OT as a story?

As mentioned in the preceding chapter, some things about the OT commend using the notion of story as a way to engage the diverse compositions as a whole. One of these elements is the previously mentioned "narrative rendering" of Israel's experience, testimony, and tradition given by the biblical writers themselves.[1] Although the texts contain a rich variety of literary forms that includes poetry, laws, and rituals, the biblical writers often use a narrative mode of shaping and plotting the experiences represented by these various literary forms. For example, several passages throughout the OT feature characters or a narrator who pauses the dramatic action and rehearses Israel's past up to that point in the form of a story that has unfolded across time. These passages provide narrative renderings or *story moments* of Israel's theological testimony (e.g., Deut 26:5-9; Josh 24:1-13; 2 Kgs 17:7-23).

One of these story moments appears in Nehemiah 9:1-31. The context is the Jewish community that had returned to Jerusalem following the city's destruction and exile and was struggling to rebuild the city and reconstitute their identity. The people gathered for an assembly of fasting and repentance, petitioning YHWH to see their difficult situation. As a part of that assembly, the Levites offered a prayer seeking forgiveness and reconciliation that rehearsed Israel's story from its beginnings with Abraham to the people's present situation in the postexile. Some English translations (such as the CEB) format the Levites' words here in poetic lines, emphasizing that they constitute a prayer that has a psalm-like quality. But the presentation of Israel's experiences in these words has a noticeable story quality, beginning with YHWH's actions as creator (v. 6) and moving through a plot line that features the major parts of Israel's life with YHWH before, into, and out of exile (vv. 7-31) (note that unlike the CEB, the NRSV prints the passage in narrative format). The Levites' prayerful telling of Israel's story begins with the call of Abraham (vv. 7-8) and then recounts the exodus from Egypt (vv. 9-11), the giving of the law at Mount Sinai (vv. 13-14), YHWH's provision and the people's rebellion during forty years in the wilderness (vv. 15-22), the entrance into the promised land and the period of the judges (vv. 23-28), disobedience and rebellion during the time of the kingdoms of Israel and Judah, including YHWH's patience with the people and gracious sending of the prophets as a warning (vv. 29-30), destruction and exile as divine judgment (vv. 30-31), and finally the present hardships of the postexilic community living under the dominance of the Persian Empire (vv. 32-37). The Levites looked back over the different episodes of Israel's past and saw a story whose plot line reveals the character of both YHWH and the people: "You have been just in all that has happened to us; you have acted faithfully, and we have done wrong" (v. 33).

For these postexilic priests, the dots of Israel's story plot connected and pointed to YHWH's faithfulness in the face of the people's continued unfaithfulness. This is, of course, not the only way to tell a story out of the experiences in Israel's past and, in fact, other OT texts tell a story with different emphases. The communal prayer in Psalm 105 is a litany of praise that retells Israel's story from the call of Abraham to the settlement in the land of Canaan in a way that emphasizes YHWH's constant goodness without mentioning Israel's disobedience. Psalm 106 is a communal confession of sin that presents the story of Israel from the exodus to the end of the Babylonian exile by emphasizing the people's faithlessness as the primary theme. Whatever their emphases, these kinds of biblical texts gather the various experiences in Israel's past into a story (narrative rendering) that not only gives new meaning to the events but calls for a response. For the Levites in Nehemiah 9, for instance, the telling of Israel's story moved them to both a petition and a confession of sin (vv. 32-37).

These kinds of story-making and story-telling moments within the biblical texts invite us to take a story approach to the OT as a whole. In some sense, passages such as Nehemiah 9:1-31 do exactly what I seek to do in the following chapters. They identify a plot line that stretches across and connects the experiences of the various ancestors, priests, prophets, and others who played significant roles in Israel's life as a people. Alongside these ancient tellings within the books themselves, however, there is another dimension of the OT as it now stands that provides additional impetus for us to take a story approach. That dimension is the way the OT has been arranged in the Protestant canon. As noted in the introductory chapter, my telling of the OT is a canonical telling—that is, a reading of the OT informed by the way it presently stands as a collection of thirty-nine books in Protestant Bibles. Notwithstanding the original diversity of the OT texts—coming, as they do, from a wide variety of writers, editors, and communities over the span of several centuries—the way that the OT has now been put together in the Protestant canon invites readers to engage it as one overall story of God, Israel, and the world (just as other canonical arrangements offer related but different ways of conceptualizing the whole; see introduction). Although books that stand next to each other in the canon—and in some cases even different parts within the same book—may have originated independently in settings separated by significant gaps in time, the present canonical arrangement begins with a main storyline that runs from Genesis to Esther. The storyline tells of the emergence of Israel as a people, their development into two kingdoms in the land of Canaan, their experiences of defeat, destruction, and exile, and their struggle to reestablish their life back in the land after those experiences. For the Protestant canon, this major storyline provides an overall framework within which to read the books that are grouped by genre in the remainder of the OT. Subsequent books of poetry and wisdom such as Psalms and Job explore various dimensions of living as God's people and understanding God's ways and the people's experiences in the world. The canon then concludes with the prophets, whose voices readers now hear as theological commentaries on the successes and failures, obedience and disobedience, triumphs and tragedies that marked Israel's main storyline. The placement of the prophets at the end of the canon also leaves readers with an explicitly future-oriented ending to the telling of God's activity in, with, and through Israel's experiences, suggesting that further divine action is to yet to come.

So, just like the story moments found in certain biblical texts, the present canonical arrangement in Protestant Bibles commends taking a story approach to the OT. This arrangement also provides a key starting point for beginning to envision what the OT story is overall. There is no doubt that the OT is most apparently and most simply about God and Israel. It's the story of Israel from their beginnings as a people, through their life as two kingdoms into defeat and exile, and into a phase of return and restoration. However, the Protestant canon (and, in fact, every current canonical listing) prefaces the story of Israel, which properly begins with the call of Abraham and Sarah in Genesis 12, with the broader story of God's intentions for and work within all creation in a universal way in the stories of Genesis 1–11. Stories about creation, the first human beings, worldwide sin and the flood, and the Tower of Babel give the OT a universal scope from the beginning. To illustrate from our culture, it would be as if someone began a book about the history of the United States with an opening section that discussed the origins of the universe and human life. Yet, this opening of the OT suggests that the story of Israel fits into and is a part of a larger story about God's intentions for all creation and God's efforts to bring those intentions to fruition in the world.

Even the specific telling of Israel's story in Nehemiah 9:1-31 underscores this broader scope. A less-than-careful reading of this passage can give the impression that the story to be told from the OT is simply or only about Israel. This misperception has, at times, led some contemporary Christian readers to dismiss the OT in favor of the NT, thinking of the OT as narrowly concerned with Israel and the Jews, but the NT as broadly concerned with all people regardless of ethnicity. As noted above, however, the opening lines of the Levites' prayer in Nehemiah 9:6, which goes on to tell Israel's story, begin with words that refer to something prior and broader: "You alone are the LORD. You alone made heaven, even the heaven of heavens, with all their forces. You made the earth and all that is on it, and the seas and all that is in them." The opening of the prayer places the story of Israel that follows into the larger context of God's creative work in and on behalf of the whole world. The OT features the plot line of God's relationship with Israel and Israel's life in the world as God's people, but that plot line stands within the larger story of God and God's relationship with all creation.

Reading the Old Testament as a Story

If we begin with these observations of Israel's narrative rendering of its own theological testimony in the OT texts and the present arrangement of the OT in the Protestant canon, how might we read the OT as one story? As a preview of what's to come in the following chapters, I here suggest that, taken as a whole, *the OT is the story of God's mission to restore creation, and the calling, creation, and formation of God's people to be the instrument to participate in that mission.* This story unfolds through five movements[2]:

1) The Introduction of God's Mission in the World (Genesis 1–11)

- *God's mission in the world is to restore creation to its divinely intended right-relationships.*

2) The Calling of God's People (Genesis 12–50)

- *God calls a people (the descendants of Abraham and Sarah) to be the instrument of blessing for all creation and thus to reverse the curse brought on by sin.*

3) The Creation of God's People (Exodus 1–15)

- *God takes Abraham and Sarah's descendants who have been called to be an instrument and creates them as God's own particular people.*

4) The Formation of God's People (Exodus 16–Deuteronomy)

- *God forms, teaches, and instructs those who have been called and created to be God's people (especially through the voices of Israel's priests and their Torah).*

5) The Life of God's People (Joshua–Esther)

- *The story of Israel's life as God's people in the land from their establishment in Canaan to their existence as two kingdoms to their experiences of defeat, destruction, exile, return, and restoration.*

a) The Voices of Israel's Poets and Sages before, during, and after Exile (Job–Song of Songs)

b) The Voices of Israel's Prophets before, during, and after Exile (Isaiah–Malachi)

These five movements tell a story in which God's good creation of right-relationships became distorted because of human sin, a distortion that resulted in estrangement among God, humans, and the created world. In response, God called a group of people, the manifold descendants of Abraham and Sarah, and created them to be a particular and peculiar people. God then undertook the long process of trying to teach, form, and mature them so that they could, as God's covenant partner, be the instrument for God to use to heal and restore creation back to the right-relationships intended for it.

Seen in this way, the various sections of scripture and episodes of Israel's story join together around God as the central character and God's purposes for creation. The key to this reading of the OT is the stories that open the canon in Genesis 1–11. These stories have a cosmic and universal character, portraying realities that unfolded before the emergence of Israel as a particular community. Moreover, they reveal God's purpose to heal and restore a creation that has become warped by human misdeeds. The stories of Abraham, Sarah, and their descendants that begin in Genesis 12 then reveal that God intends to accomplish this purpose by choosing the particular people of Israel to serve as God's instrument in the redemptive mission. In light of this movement from the opening stories in Genesis 1–11 to the introduction of Israel's ancestors in Genesis 12, we can think of the OT as including, so to speak, a smaller story that fits into and finds its meaning within a larger story. On a smaller level, the main subject of the OT story is God and God's relationship with Israel—that is, the promises of God to Israel and the struggle to see those promises fulfilled. Yet the OT introduces Israel's plot line into the broader story of God's mission to restore creation. The story of Israel fits into and is the vital part of the larger plot line of God and God's relationship with all creation in love and redemption. Given the origins and nature of the biblical texts, coming as they do from Israel's priests, sages, prophets, and scribes, Israel's story occupies something like 99 percent of the OT, but God's redemptive mission is the larger plot line within which the various dots of Israel's story told across the OT writings connect.

Let me preview the five elements of the OT story:

1) The Introduction of God's Mission in the World (Genesis 1–11)

The first eleven chapters of Genesis form the backdrop to the overall story of the OT and *introduce God's mission in the world to heal and restore creation back to the divine intentions for it*. The creation stories in Genesis 1–2 form the first part of this backdrop. They begin the OT story with portraits of God's good, intended creation of right-relationships. Humanity is created in the "image of God" (Gen 1:26), and all creation is characterized by right-relationships, with human beings living in right-relationship with God, each other, and the earth. The next section of the Genesis backdrop, however, introduces the crucial turn in the plot, beginning with the garden story in Genesis 3 that depicts humanity's disobedience and rebellion. The subsequent stories in Genesis 4–11 work together to portray the distortion of God's good creation as a result of humanity's rebellion. As the relationship of the first brothers ends in murder (Gen 4) and humankind's overwhelming violence causes God to send a flood of destruction (Gen 6–7), readers watch the intended right-relationships among God, humans, and the created world unravel toward chaos. The conclusion of the flood story in Genesis 8–9, however, introduces the divine mission in the world to restore creation back to the right-relationships and divine intentions that were portrayed in Genesis 1–2. Here, God surprisingly declares the divine determination never to destroy humankind again in response to their ongoing inclination toward evil (8:21). Instead, God becomes a covenant partner with humanity and all living beings (9:9-10), committing to the project of overcoming human evil and healing creation by engaging in a relationship with all flesh that will somehow turn out to be redemptive. God's covenant partnership will be the means by which the divine mission to overcome human evil and restore creation to its intended right-relationships will be accomplished.

2) The Calling of God's People (Genesis 12–50)

Only when the book of Genesis turns from the primeval tales in Genesis 1–11 to the stories of Israel's ancestors (Abraham, Sarah, Isaac, Rebekah, Jacob, Rachel, Leah, and Joseph) in Genesis 12–50 do we learn the specific form that God's covenant engagement will take. The divine mission to restore creation begins with *the calling of a people (who turn out to be the manifold descendants of Abraham and Sarah) to be God's instrument of blessing for all creation (Gen 12:1-3) and thus to reverse the curse brought on by sin.* God's calling of Abraham, Sarah, and their descendants constitutes the divine response to the distortion of creation brought about by human disobedience and rebellion. God chooses (elects) one group of people, enters into a (covenantal) relationship with them, and blesses them, so that through them the divine blessing may extend to all peoples of the earth. God bestows blessing on the descendants of Abraham and Sarah in order to enable all creation to experience the fullness of divine blessing once again.

3) The Creation of God's People (Exodus 1–15)

By the close of Genesis, Abraham and Sarah's descendants have come to reside in Egypt. The famous story of Israel's exodus from Egypt, told across the subsequent tales of Moses, Aaron, pharaohs, plagues, and the parting of the sea in Exodus 1–15, constitutes the crucial moment in which *God takes the loose group of Abraham and Sarah's descendants who have been called to be an instrument and creates them as God's own particular people.* By the time of their exit from slavery in Egypt, in fact, Abraham's descendants have been joined by a "diverse crowd" (Exod 12:38). There are now not just Hebrews, but a mix of people of different races and ethnic backgrounds, and the exodus event serves to bind them together as a new people. On the surface, the account of the Hebrews' miraculous escape at the sea is a deliverance story. But the symbols and language used in the telling make it into a creation story. As YHWH once more separates waters and brings forth life, what comes forth from the waters is a new people, called and now created to be YHWH's "kingdom of priests" and "holy nation" on behalf of the world (Exod 19:6).

4) The Formation of God's People (Exodus 16– Deuteronomy)

After leaving Egypt, the people do not proceed directly to the promised land of Canaan but spend the next forty years wandering through the wilderness—stopping and starting, obeying and rebelling—until a near-entirely new generation emerges to move into the next act in Israel's story. In these wilderness tales of Exodus, Leviticus, Numbers, and Deuteronomy, we encounter the OT laws. Especially at Mount Sinai (Exod 19–Num 10:11), Israel receives from YHWH several law codes designed to clarify the community's identity and govern how the people live in relationship to each other and the world. Through these laws, along with the other diverse traditions that comprise the remainder of the Pentateuch, God undertakes *the formation of those who have now been called and created to be God's people.* God works to teach, shape, and mature the people, and the laws, deeds, and experiences described between Exodus and Deuteronomy form the people's understanding not only of who God is but also who they are as God's people and how therefore they ought to live in the world as instruments of blessing to all creation.

5) The Life of God's People (Joshua–Esther)

Having been called, created, and formed, Israel enters the promised land of Canaan to begin their life as God's instrument of blessing and restoration for creation. The next sequence of books in the Protestant canon (Joshua–Esther) tells *the story of Israel's life in the land from their establishment in Canaan to their existence as two kingdoms to their experiences of defeat, destruction, exile, return, and restoration.* This large sequence includes numerous and differing perspectives and traditions—various dots on Israel's plot line—but the dots connect as the story of Israel's attempts to act in accordance with their understanding of who God is and who they are as God's people, and to live out their identity as God's people within God's mission in the world. However, the stories also portray the people's unfaithfulness to their calling and covenant and the steady deterioration of their life before God and with each other—a seemingly gradual slide toward destruction. That slide culminates with defeat and exile, yet the OT plot line moves beyond those experiences and nears its conclusion with a time of return to the land and the extended struggle to reconstitute the people back in Jerusalem in the following centuries. When the OT's main plot line of Israel's story comes to an end, there is a postexilic group back in Jerusalem working to rebuild their city and temple, renew their community, and reinvigorate their identity as God's covenant people, even as others of Abraham and Sarah's descendants struggle to maintain their identity and calling in foreign lands (see Esther).

The remaining sections of the OT in the Protestant canon, although grouped separately from the main plot line of Israel's life in the land, connect to that plot line as voices that spoke among and to the people during their existence before, within, and after exile. Although seemingly tangential to the OT's main story of God's mission and God's people, *the poetry and wisdom books (Job–Song of Songs) represent the voices and traditions of Israel's poets and sages* who offered theological reflections on the realities of the people's life, such as worship, wisdom, and family. And some of these writings, perhaps written during the crisis experiences of defeat and exile, give voice to a wide range of honest, human, and theological reactions to catastrophe and suffering, reactions that range from abrasive expressions of grief and anger to questions of God's justice to persistent hope for the future.

The Protestant canon then concludes the OT with the prophets. Like the poetry and wisdom writings, these books (Isaiah–Malachi) represent the voices and traditions of Israel's prophets who spoke to the people at various moments along their journey into and out of exile, often challenging them concerning their growing unfaithfulness to their identity and calling or offering hope that their identity and calling remain in the face of seeming evidence to the contrary. Prophets such as Isaiah, Hosea, and Amos spoke to the people about the path they saw as leading to destruction and exile. On the other side of destruction, prophets such as Haggai, Zechariah, and Malachi spoke to a community that had returned home from exile, urging them to renew their identity and calling as the instrument of God's mission to restore creation. Standing at the close of the canon, the prophetic books give the story of God's mission and people an open-ended and future-oriented quality. The ending of the OT story is a non-ending. The concluding words of the final prophet point to further work to come by God in and with Israel and on behalf of the world, a work centered on the healing of relationships within creation ("Turn the hearts of the parents to the children and the hearts of the children to their parents" [Mal 4:6]).

Engaging the Old Testament as a Story

So that is the telling of the OT story—or the general idea of it—I will offer in the chapters that follow. It is, as I commented earlier, one particular way of gathering the diverse narratives, poems, laws, rituals, and more that make up the OT and one way to envision how those texts works together as a whole and how one might construe and tell that story. Reading the OT as the story of God's mission in the world to restore creation to its divinely intended right-relationships and the calling, creation, and formation of the people of Israel to participate as God's instrument in that mission has the power to draw us as contemporary readers to engage these texts in new and imaginative ways. That kind of reading brings the OT story to life as something more than the story of an ancient people in a distant context. When we consider the plot line of the people of Israel within the broader story of God's mission introduced in the opening chapters of Genesis, we can find ourselves existentially engaged in not only what God has done in the past but what God might be doing now. And at the heart of this engagement is the recognition that within the larger and smaller stories of the OT, the many specific traditions, perspectives, and plot lines seem to address three primary questions that had significance for Israel in the past and continue to have significance for those who seek to live as God's people in the present:

1) Who is God (and what is God doing in the world)?

2) Who are we as the people of God?

3) How should we live in the world (in light of who God is and who we are as the people of God)?

As I mentioned in the last chapter, these questions are about *identity*. Both individually and collectively, the texts that make up the OT served Israel throughout the different phases of its existence as means to define identity—to offer different perspectives and portraits that provide understandings not only of who God is but who God's people are and should be. As Israel considered, reconsidered, and reworked their traditions and beliefs in light of experiences such as destruction and exile, their texts became instruments of identity formation. When we engage the story of God and Israel in the OT, this identity-making power of the story of God's mission and people can transcend the life of ancient Israel and make the three questions listed above relevant to us in fresh ways.

Note again how the voices of the prophets at the conclusion of the OT give the story an open-ended and future-oriented quality. Following from these voices, a Christian reading of the OT can imaginatively consider the ways that the story of God's mission introduced in the life of Israel continues into the NT, where God's people expands to include not just the ethnic descendants of Abraham and Sarah, but their spiritual descendants as well. The NT texts themselves describe Christians as branches that have been grafted onto the root of the covenant people of Israel (Rom 11:17). The church comes to share in Israel's identity and calling within God's ongoing mission. From this perspective, the OT provides the first part of a larger plot line that encompasses the whole Christian scripture. This plot line has an ideal beginning, a turn in the plot, a divine response in the formation of a covenant people, and, out of them, the Messiah in the person of Jesus of Nazareth, and an anticipated end with a renewed creation.[3]

Perhaps even more significantly, the open-ended quality of the story of God in the OT invites us as contemporary readers to become active participants in that ongoing story. As we watch the texts of the OT connect the dots of God's work, we are invited to reimagine our lives as if we are actors in God's ongoing story that transcends the limits of the Bible and to reshape our understanding of who we are as God's people and how therefore we are called to live in the world. As Timothy Green expresses the invitation: "Watch as the dots connect. Take a step back from the isolated parts, and explore the whole—the entirety of what God is up to. Become a participant in God's story, a character in the divine drama."[4]

Chapter 3

The Introduction of God's Mission

(Genesis 1–11)

Focus Texts: Genesis 1–3; 6–9

Location in the Old Testament Story:

1) The Introduction of God's Mission in the World (Genesis 1–11)

2) The Calling of God's People (Genesis 12–50)

3) The Creation of God's People (Exodus 1–15)

4) The Formation of God's People (Exodus 16–Deuteronomy)

5) The Life of God's People (Joshua–Esther)

  a) The Voices of Israel's Poets and Sages before, during, and after Exile (Job–Song of Songs)

  b) The Voices of Israel's Prophets before, during, and after Exile (Isaiah–Malachi)

Genesis 1–11 in the Larger Old Testament Story

Much like the sentiment expressed by the opening line of the famous *Star Wars* movies, "A long time ago, in a galaxy far, far away," the OT story, which will eventually revolve around Israel, begins at a place far removed

– 29 –

from that reality. As described in the last chapter, the OT tells the story of God's mission to restore creation, and the calling, creation, and formation of Israel as God's people to be the instrument of that mission. But the story begins before and beyond Israel. The opening of the OT takes us back to the cosmic and universal beginnings of God's creative work in the world and provides a broad backdrop to what will eventually become Israel's story. *The Bible's opening chapters in Genesis 1–11 form the first movement of the larger OT story as they reveal the need for God's mission and introduce what that redemptive mission will be.*

The first eleven chapters move from creation to Abraham, the one from whom Israel's story will emerge. Most importantly for telling the larger OT story, however, these opening chapters move toward the introduction of God's mission by first showing the initial picture of God's intentions for creation—a creation made perfect as an ideal existence marked by right-relationships of mutual blessing among God, humans, and the world. We then see the distortion of this divinely intended good reality by human misdeeds that lead to the introduction of God's mission to heal and restore creation.

This plot line unfolds in two sections within Genesis 1–11. First, the creation stories in Genesis 1–2 portray God's good, intended creation of right-relationships, with humanity created in the "image of God" (Gen 1:26) and all creation characterized by relationships of mutual blessing. Second, the stories in Genesis 3–11 introduce the crucial turn in the plot and explain the need for God's mission. They begin with humanity's disobedience in the garden in Genesis 3, and then portray the unraveling of God's good creation in Genesis 4–11. In the middle of this section, at the conclusion of the story of a universal flood sent in judgment against humanity (Gen 6–7), the OT storytellers introduce God's mission in the world (Gen 8–9). As we'll see, God's mission is to restore the originally intended right-relationships and blessing by becoming a covenant partner engaged in a relationship with all living beings that will overcome human evil and heal creation (9:9-10).

An additional note of introduction may be useful for reading the opening movement of the OT story. Genesis 1–11 stands at the beginning of the OT's first five books (Genesis–Deuteronomy), which are often collectively labeled the *Pentateuch* (Greek, *five scrolls*). These books share several themes, perspectives, and sources. Most introductory textbooks on the OT discuss the idea that the Pentateuch as it now stands (as well as each individual book within it) is a composite collection that was formed as a result of the work of many different authors and editors, with originally independent sources and traditions combined over time, and not always in a seamless way.

The Pentateuch and Its Sources

For nearly two centuries, biblical scholars have concluded that the first five books of the OT (Genesis–Deuteronomy) developed over time through the combination of originally independent sources. Various theories have tried to identify the specific contents, dates, and origins of these sources. The recognition of the presence of different sources side by side helps readers understand why some passages seem to contradict each other (e.g., the different numbers of animals that Noah takes on the ark in Gen 6:19 and 7:2). A helpful image for thinking about the Pentateuch and its sources is to think of the first five OT books as a *mosaic*—a beautiful picture made by the joining together of numerous, separate pieces.

For telling the OT story, this common understanding of the nature of the OT's first five books helps explain why, for instance, we find two different portrayals of God's original intentions for creation (Gen 1–2) and why there are multiple stories that depict the effects of human sin on God's good creation in different ways (Gen 4–11)—sometimes without a straightforward sequence. The writers of scripture's narrative have brought together multiple sources and accounts.

The multi-sourced nature of the Bible's first five books also helps us tell the OT story in another way. It reminds modern readers of scripture that these writings are ancient accounts that came from a different time and culture. As we'll see, the stories in Genesis 1–11 introduce God's creation, humanity's misdeeds, and God's redemption mission in ways that would've made sense to people living in the ancient Near East. They describe a type of *primeval* history—a sort of *world before time*—marked by idyllic gardens, talking animals, great floods, and divine beings who intermarry with humans. These descriptions are not usually the ways that we talk about the nature of the world and the origins of human life today (and they have little in common with what modern scientific study says, as well). However, as we move through the stories of Genesis 1–11 in light of their place within the larger OT story, we can see that the biblical writers have not just preserved multiple sources and ancient ways of speaking. They have also brought them together across the Bible's first five books in a way that invites us to see the different perspectives and portrayals as part of a larger story that begins with God's intentions, humanity's failures, and God's responses, and then carries on through the calling, creation, and formation of a people in the remainder of the Pentateuch.

For now, however, the opening stories in Genesis 1–11 not only introduce the OT's larger story, but they also provide the biblical writers' earliest testimonies to the primary identity-forming questions: Who is God? Who are we? And how are we called to live in the world?

Creation Made Perfect (Genesis 1–2)

The OT story begins with a remarkable portrait of God's original intentions for all creation, including humanity in its entirety. Genesis 1 and 2 open scripture's narrative with two accounts of the divine creation of the world and all that's in it. In a perhaps unexpected way, the biblical writers, who lived as members of the Israelite people with a sense of distinct identity and calling, chose to begin their telling of God's story with a cosmic scope, dealing with the world and humanity as a whole rather than focusing only on Israel or any particular race, nationality, or group. Even in the faithful imaginations of the ancient Israelite writers, the God whose story the OT tells is not a narrow God who works to the benefit of one group while excluding the rest of the human race. This beginning puts readers of the OT story on immediate notice: the story about to be told is not merely about Israel or even human beings, for that matter. The story begins before and beyond any single community of human persons. It begins with God—and singularly so: "When *God* began to create the heavens and the earth" (Gen 1:1). And throughout the remainder of the OT, the story of God and what God is doing in the world will provide the larger framework for the smaller stories of persons, communities, and kingdoms. As we'll see, even the portrayals of the anticipated culmination of God's mission given by the prophets whose words conclude the OT canon will imaginatively envision not just the redemption of humankind but the renewal of all creation.

As mentioned above, the two stories in Genesis 1–2 that depict God's original intentions for creation likely come from two sources or traditions. Genesis 1 (more precisely 1:1–2:4a) tells the story of the origins of the world and humanity from a *priestly* perspective, using language and imagery found in OT texts, such as Exodus and Leviticus, having to do with the priests and their activities (e.g., a well-ordered time scheme; the importance of the Sabbath). Genesis 2 (more precisely, 2:4b-25) seems to represent a different tradition (often called the *Yahwist* or *J* source[1]) that tells the story of creation in a flowing, almost folkloristic style, with an emphasis on humanity's personal interactions with God and the world. The two creation stories don't match precisely in their details or perspectives, but having them together as the opening of the OT story gives us more than one way to understand and express God's intended ideals for creation.

One other item is important for reading Genesis 1–2 as the opening of the OT story. Scholars have long noted that these chapters have similarities with other creation stories known from civilizations throughout the ancient Near East. This observation is important for telling the OT story because it helps explain why God's good, original creation is portrayed with some terms and images that seem foreign to us. These include references to chaotic waters, glassy domes, and idyllic gardens. Such terms and images appear because our biblical ancestors used ways of speaking about the origins of the world that were common in ancient Israel's broader cultural context.

Creation Stories in the Ancient Near East

Scholars have especially compared the language and imagery of Genesis 1–2 to creation stories from the civilizations of ancient Babylonia (for example, the *Enuma Elish*) and Egypt (for example, the Memphite Theology). Although creation stories from Israel, Babylon, Egypt, and elsewhere may appear radically different on the surface, closer examination reveals numerous similarities (but also important differences) in how these early storytellers conceived of the origins of their world.[2]

The OT writers used these ancient Near Eastern stories in various ways, but they have dramatically reinterpreted them, giving their elements new meaning within a story about Israel and its God. In so doing, the OT writers have done something similar to what happened later when Israel's own stories and poems were brought together into the canon of scripture (see ch. 1). Just like the later canonization of Israel's traditions into the larger OT story, the biblical writers placed some of the language and imagery of those ancient Near Eastern creation stories into a new context and reinterpreted the older material as part of a different story.

Even more importantly, the study of these other ancient Near Eastern accounts has revealed that creation stories in Israel's world were not first and foremost about what we might think of as scientific inquiry into the origins of the world. They were about *identity*—attempts to give the people a religious foundation that helped them understand the nature of their God, the purpose of creation, including humanity's place in it, and how that should affect their lives in the present.[3] So also Genesis 1–2. These chapters are the OT's first responses to the main identity questions for God's people that will continue to be present throughout the larger story. What do these creation stories say about who God is, who we are as God's people, and how, therefore, we are called to live in the world?

God's Creation and God's Image

The portrayal of God's originally intended creation in Genesis 1 begins with a striking image. Although many of us may be familiar with the traditional translation of Genesis 1:1 ("In the beginning God created the heavens and the earth" [NIV]), which pictures a nothingness into which God suddenly inserts created matter and space, a more accurate reading of the Hebrew provides a different, but no less striking, picture. The opening of verse 1 more literally says, "When God began to create the heavens and the earth—the earth was without shape or form."[4] Thus, the ancient storyteller begins this creation story not with an empty scene of nothingness but with a description of the condition of the world at the beginning of God's life-giving, creative work. At the inception of God's life-making actions, the earth was "without shape or form" (v. 2). The opening image of scripture, then, is that of "God's wind" (or "breath" or "spirit," Heb. *rûaḥ*) hovering over an unformed, disorganized, chaotic abyss of water and darkness. Contemporary readers trying to read this text within a scientific frame of reference will be frustrated by the lack of explanation of how this already-existing chaotic material came to be. But the biblical storyteller pays no attention to that modern question. Rather, the story of God's life-providing work opens with the image of life-denying chaos.

Translation of Genesis 1:1

The translation of Genesis 1:1 as a temporal clause ("When God began to create the heavens and the earth") has been the preferred translation at least since the Jewish rabbis in the Middle Ages. While modern readers often want to know what existed before the water and darkness with which the story begins, the rabbis creatively commented that the first Hebrew letter (the Hebrew *bt ēt*) of the first word of verse 1 has a shape that is closed to what would have come before it in a Hebrew line and is open to what follows it (like a capital *G* in English). Thus, they concluded that the text discourages us from thinking about what might have come before and pushes us toward what God makes out of this original material.[5]

The earth is a mess of dark and watery chaos with which God must deal. In the cultural world of ancient Israel and their neighbors throughout the ancient Near East, the sea was the symbol of the forces of chaos that prevent creation and deny life and to defeat and divide that sea was to bring life into being. The overcoming and ordering of chaotic waters was a common symbol for a deity's work of creation. Some surviving Canaanite texts about the god Baal actually portray the sea as another god ("Yam") that Baal defeats in combat in order to bring about life and fertility, dividing the sea and drying it up. Likewise, the Babylonian creation story, *Enuma Elish*, features the god Marduk's defeat of the sea monster Tiamat as the initial act of creation.[6]

And so in Genesis 1, into this situation of life-denying chaos, God begins to act in order to open up space for life. Beginning in verse 3, we encounter the primary way that God's creative activity takes place in Genesis 1—namely, God speaks something into existence and then uses it to separate the chaotic darkness or water. So, God speaks, "Let there be light" (v. 3). It is as if God then takes the newly appeared light and throws it into the chaos so that it divides the darkness (v. 4), beginning to make room for life to be brought forth. In a similar manner, God's room-making creative activity next turns to the chaotic watery abyss that marked the earth's condition. God calls forth a "dome" ("firmament" [KJV]), casts it into the waters, and separates the waters into two halves above and below the dome (vv. 6-7).[7] Through these opening creative activities, God brings order to a life-denying chaotic mess of darkness and water, dividing, organizing, and opening a space for creation to emerge right in the middle of chaos. In the storyteller's creative imagery, God has established a kind of island of order in a sea of chaos—a safe haven for life to be brought forth.

Then in verse 9, the priestly creation story begins a fast-paced roll, as God fills this carved-out, ordered space with life. Across the span of the next sixteen verses, at God's direction, dry land appears, and then plant life, fruit-bearing trees, and livings things such as birds, livestock, and wildlife all take their place within God's created space. Noticeable throughout these depictions is God's recurring evaluation of the created elements, "God saw how good it was" (vv. 4, 10, 12, 18, 21, 25, 31). In the context of this story, the adjective *good* (Heb. *tôb*) has a relational meaning. God evaluates that each element is *good* because it's appropriate for serving its intended divine purpose in relationship to the other elements of creation. The elements fit together in right ways according to God's intentions. Here, at the very outset of the OT story, we see a glimpse of the rightly-related creation that marks God's intentions for the world—everything existed and functioned together in mutually beneficial ways as God had designed.

By the time the story of Genesis 1 reaches the end of verse 25, all creation seems to be in place. God has separated and ordered the initial life-denying chaos of water and darkness, opened space for creation to emerge, and filled that space with life. Suddenly, however, God announces a new element, "Let us make humanity (Heb. *'ādām*) in our image (*ṣelem*) to resemble us so that they may take charge of the fish of the sea, the birds in the sky, the livestock, all the earth, and all the crawling things on the earth" (v. 26). There are many aspects of this verse that generate ongoing scholarly discussion.

"Let *Us* create" in Genesis 1:26

The plural pronouns in Genesis 1:26 have generated debate throughout the history of interpretation. In the context of the OT as a whole, the plural references here likely reflect the ancient Israelite notion of the divine council, "the assembly of heavenly beings believed to assist God in governing the world and communicating with the human race."[8] See 1 Kings 22:19-23; Job 1:6-7; Jeremiah 23:18, 22.

But special attention falls on what is said about humanity. God creates the human community to be his cooperative partner within all creation ("to resemble" and "to take charge"). The language of the following poetic lines v. 27) makes God's vision clear, as the lines proclaim that "in the divine image God created *them* [literally, '*it*' singular, referring to 'humanity']" and "male and female he created *them* [plural]." This combination of singular and plural references in Hebrew (humanity in the singular and male and female in the plural) envisions not merely individuals but a community of human persons created to partner with God to oversee the whole of creation and help maintain God's intended purposes for it. In Genesis 1, the Hebrew term *'ādām* ("humanity") refers to humankind as a species and not, as we'll see in Genesis 2, an individual human person. Timothy Green expresses the force of this creative moment well: "God puts into place a community of human beings who together, in cooperation with God, with fellow humans and with creation itself will 'be fruitful and multiply, and fill the earth and subdue it' (1:28)."[9]

Perhaps the most remarkable part of this creative act is the designation that God uses to describe humankind's intended nature and function. The human community (not merely individual persons) is created in and meant to serve as God's *image*. It's not immediately clear what this designation means.[10] Does it mean that humanity physically resembles God, has the ability for rational thought and a moral conscience, or possesses a special capacity for relationship with God? All of these and more have been suggested and might be helpful in their own ways. But how would our ancient Israelite ancestors who told and retold this story have understood what it meant for humanity to be this *image*?

The meaning of *image* used here for humanity comes at least partly from the domain of kings and kingship in the ancient Near East. When kings would conquer a new territory or exert sovereignty even over their own capital city, they would often make statues of themselves and place them in that newly conquered area (see Nebuchadnezzar's actions in Dan 3:1-7). The function of this statue was to represent the king and to remind all the inhabitants in that territory who ultimately ruled over them, even if that king wasn't physically present. In ancient Israel's context, that statue was designated by the very Hebrew word used to describe humanity in Gen 1:26—*image (ṣelem)*. Some OT texts actually use this term specifically to denote a statue of a god (usually an idol) that is an earthly representation of the divine (see Num 33:52; 2 Kgs 11:8; Amos 5:26). And elsewhere in the OT, Israel's language of praise and worship often describes YHWH as a king ruling over Israel and all the nations (see Pss 93:1-4; 97:1-5).

What does it mean, then, that God's original intentions at the beginning of the OT story link humanity with God's *image*? The ancient storyteller proclaims that the human race has a unique function to carry out in the midst of God's good creation. Like the statue that represents an ancient Near Eastern king, humanity's calling is to be the representative of the Creator's character and actions—to *image* the divine king within creation. As the human race lives together in right-relationships of mutual blessing with each other and with the world, all creation will see the presence and character of the divine king who has brought life out of chaos.

In this role as divine image-bearers, God calls humanity to "master" and "take charge of" (v. 28) the elements of creation. On the surface, this language might seem to suggest an exploitative disregard or abuse of nature by the human race for its own self-serving purposes. Indeed, the Hebrew terms used here connote the function of ruling with authority. However, the terms by themselves don't define the *way* in which that authority should be exercised, and different contexts in the OT show that they can describe either caring or harsh rule. What makes the difference for their meaning here is that humans, as the Creator King's representative in creation, must "master" and "take charge of" in the ways that the Creator would exercise that authority. When we look back over the Creator's actions described in verses 9-25, we see the picture of a God who doesn't act through coercion and domination but in empowerment and cooperation. Throughout these verses, God invited and empowered different elements of creation to participate in the act of bringing forth life. God invited, "Let *the earth* grow plant life" (v. 11) and, later, "Let *the waters* swarm with living things" (v. 20)—both phrases employing a Hebrew grammatical form used to express a wish or desire. Even the animals come into being as a result of empowering the earth's own creative activity: "Let *the earth* produce every kind of living thing" (v. 24). Through the Creator's empowerment, the earth itself gives life to plants and animals. In the reflection of this Creator King, then, to "take charge" means to empower all of creation to flourish together with the human community.

When we reach the end of Genesis 1, we've encountered some key elements for the larger OT story. We've heard the earliest responses that the story offers to the question, "Who is God?" The imagery of this priestly creation story reveals that the Creator God is the divine king who can conquer chaos and bring forth life out of the midst of life-denying disorder. As the rest of the biblical story will affirm, the Creator God undertakes this chaos-defeating, life-generating activity not just at one original moment in time but again and again throughout the moments when the people find themselves on the verge of being drowned by disorder and despair, even disorder of their own making. And although God is the chaos-conquering King, he is no coercive, manipulative, domineering tyrant. Rather, the way of this Creator in the world is one of partnership, working to bring about his purposes for creation through empowerment and collaboration. In keeping with this portrait of divine character, Genesis 1 also provides the first biblical testimony to the question, "Who are we as the people of God?" The story describes an identity that is not limited to Israel or any one group, but boldly proclaims that the entire human community has been created to *image* the Creator King, representing God's character and actions by living in cooperative, caretaking partnership with all the elements of God's world. As humanity faithfully represents the Creator's character, all creation will be able to flourish.

Perhaps most important for telling the larger OT story, however, the opening chapter of scripture reveals that this kind of flourishing world and image-bearing humanity were God's original intentions for creation. Here we see a divinely established world marked by right-relationships of mutual blessing. All the elements of the created world exist together in appropriate and beneficial relationships under the sovereignty of the empowering, life-giving Creator and the watchful care of the human community that *images* that Creator's character. What results is a creation marked by abundant life, being fruitful and multiplying together in harmony.

A Relational, Interconnected Creation

The second part of scripture's opening portrait of an original creation made perfect follows in Gen 2:4b-25. If Genesis 1 offered a broad portrait that was painted from a creation-wide, even cosmic point of view, Genesis 2 narrows almost all of its focus to the human race in particular. We find here a more specific picture of how humanity was intended by God to fulfill its calling to bear the divine image in the world. Humanity was formed to live in interconnected personal relationships marked by care, service, and mutuality, and these relationships were to result in abundant life for all involved.

Like Genesis 1, the story in 2:4b-25 begins with a description of life-denying chaos that the Creator must overcome. Verses 4-6 describe the earth at the outset of YHWH's ("the LORD God")[11] creative activity as a barren desert wasteland—a landscape devoid of plants, crops, and even the rain necessary to sustain life. Into the midst of that bleak scene, YHWH undertakes a series of quick actions (vv. 7-9) that transforms a barren desert into a flourishing garden. He creates a kind of oasis in the desert. If we picture the story's imagery in our minds, the opening action portrays YHWH as a potter who gets down into the dirt, shapes the "topsoil of the fertile land" (Heb. *'ădāmāh*) into the first "human" (*'ādām*) (v. 7), and breathes the divine "life's breath" into its nostrils to bring it to life. In this very first act, the story sets forth the intimate interconnected relationships that YHWH intends for creation. The "human" represents all humanity. The Hebrew term *'ādām* is the generic word for humankind. It's the term that was used in 1:26 to refer to the creation of humanity in general, both male and female.[12] But notice especially the similarities in the Hebrew terms for "fertile land" (*'ădāmāh*) and "human" (*'ādām*). The human is quite literally an *earthling* who is formed from the *earth*. In the Creator's vision for creation, humans share a deep connection with the ground. Yet, they are also intimately related to God through the divine breath that brought them to life.[13]

Once YHWH has transformed the barren wasteland into a luxuriant and life-sustaining garden (vv. 8-9), the imagery of the story further illustrates the relationships of mutuality intended by the Creator. YHWH places the human into the garden and appoints humanity "to farm" (Heb. *'ebed*, literally, "to serve") and "to take care of" (*šāmar*, literally, "to guard, protect, keep") the earth with which it shares an intimate relationship. The imagery here balances that in Genesis 1, so that we see the full picture of humanity's relationship with creation. With the two stories together, humans are called to rule *and* to serve the natural world. They are to represent the conquering king, but to do so through life-giving, caring relationships. Humanity's interconnectedness with nature means that human beings have power to affect the world (for good or ill), but are also dependent upon the earth for survival. In YHWH's good intentions for creation, humanity and nature exist in a right-relationship that allows both to flourish.

At this point in the story, in perhaps the most dramatic scene of the "relation-building Creator" working to construct a "relational image" for the human race to embody within creation,[14] YHWH for the first time acknowledges a deficiency in his good creation: "It's not good that the human is alone" (v. 18). YHWH's words express the fundamental conviction that humanity's very nature is to exist not in isolation but in right-relationships that sustain and nourish life together in the world. The Creator determines to give the human "a helper who is perfect for him" (v. 18). Even the words here indicate that YHWH's intentions are for humanity to exist in right-relationships of mutuality. The term *helper* (Heb. *'ezer*) doesn't necessarily carry the connotation of a lesser servant or assistant. Some OT texts actually use this term to refer to God as the one who provides the strength needed for the people's survival.[15] While *helper* doesn't refer to God here, neither does it imply a relationship partner who is less than equal. Moreover, "perfect for him" translates a Hebrew term that indicates *one who corresponds to/fits with/ is like* the other in an appropriate way. Far from being a reference to someone inferior or subservient, YHWH's description is of a partner who will provide intimate, equal, and nourishing relationship for the human.

YHWH's search for this relationship partner takes on an experimental tone in verses 19-20. For the Genesis 2 story, the creation of the animals occurs not prior to the creation of humans as in Genesis 1, but as part of YHWH's search for the right-fitting partner. The Creator once again shows his nature as one who works in cooperative relationship by empowering the human to name the animals. And the story stresses that the human and the animals are intimately connected, as the animals are "formed" from the very same "fertile ground" (*'ădāmāh*) out of which YHWH "formed" the human. Still, none of these animals provides the right fit for the human. It's only when YHWH takes part of the human and shapes it into another human (vv. 21-22)—the most interconnected relationship one could imagine—that the original human can burst forth into a song of right-relationship, "This one finally is bone from my bones and flesh from my flesh" (v. 23). The final words of the creation story give expression to these intimately connected human beings living in a supportive, open, and mutual right-relationship: "The two of them were naked, the man and his wife, but they weren't embarrassed" (v. 25).

God's Good Creation of Right-Relationships and Blessing

I've given some extended space to these two chapters at the Bible's beginning because of their significance for telling the larger OT story. Together, the creation stories in Genesis 1–2 form the opening movement of the OT's plot line and present the picture of God's original, good intentions for all creation that will be the centerpiece of the divine mission to unfold across the remainder of the OT story. To summarize that picture, from the very beginning, we see that God's purposes are not merely about Israel, although Israel will be vital and even indispensable to them. The humans in Genesis 1–2 are not yet called Hebrews, Israelites, or associated with any nationality or ethnicity. This is a broadly universal vision in which all humanity is called to image the Creator and is charged to care for creation and enjoy God's blessings. The creation stories also reveal that God's good intentions are not just for the well-being of humanity alone. He is the God of all creation in a cosmic and not just human-centered way. God declares all of his creative work "good" and establishes the whole creation in right-relationships of mutual flourishing, with humanity as the nurturing caretaker. It will be no surprise for us, then, when the larger OT story (and even the NT) later begins to envision God's full restoration of creation—the grand conclusion of God's redemptive work in the world—and describes that culmination not simply as a changed human race but as a new creation—a new heavens and a new earth marked by the blessing, life, and *shalom* (well-being) of God (e.g., Isa 65:17; 66:22; Rom 8:21-22; Rev 21:1).

Most important for telling the OT story, we've seen Genesis 1–2 portray *how* the human community is to *image* the Creator King. God's good intentions were for all humanity, and indeed all creation, to live at one with God and each other and thereby to experience abundant life. These stories imagine the divinely intended creation made perfect as a world of right-relationships that result in mutual blessing. As human beings live in right-relationship with God, each other, and the earth, all creation can flourish under God's blessing. The God who appears at the beginning of the OT story is the one who overcomes any and all chaos that threatens life and creates and sustains an abundant life through empowering partnerships with all creation. The human race is called to be the *image* of that God—to represent God's life-giving ways in the world through right-relationships that allow all creation to enjoy divine blessing and nourishment. So, as God intends the world, human beings have no need to fear for their own survival or try to establish their own security and well-being. They need only to live in right-relationships of care and mutuality and trust that God's goodness will then provide all the security and abundant life they need.

Creation Unraveling and the Need for God's Mission (Genesis 3–11)

Immediately following the remarkable picture of God's intentions for creation in general and humanity in particular, scripture's narrative introduces a crucial turn in the plot. If we're telling the OT story as it appears across the books in our Protestant Bibles, Genesis 3 introduces the need for God's redemptive mission that will occupy the remainder of the OT's plot line. Allowing virtually no time for readers to bask in the glorious abundant life of humanity living as God's image within the right-relationships of a good creation, the story reveals "the great human crisis" that threatens to undo God's intentions for the world and that constitutes the problem that God's mission will seek to address.[16]

What appears in this famous story in Genesis 3 is not just an act of disobedience to a particular set of God's instructions, but *a self-serving move made by humanity out of a sense of distrust and fear and in an effort to secure its own control, survival, and well-being.* Here we see human beings who give in to dissatisfaction and fear in the face of their calling to *image* the creator, live in mutual right-relationships in creation, and trust that doing so will provide them with the safe and flourishing life they desire. The humans attempt to seize moral authority over the right and wrong of their lives, but also to ensure for themselves their ability to survive and even thrive in the world. In this way, Genesis 3 introduces a theme that will appear throughout the next several biblical chapters: *the blurring of the line between human and divine.* Beginning in the garden and recurring throughout the following stories, God's created image-bearers struggle to be satisfied or secure with just being the representative of the divine king and relying on mutual right-relationships; they want to be the sovereign over their own survival, security, and destiny. This human grasp for control has the effect of distorting and fracturing all the life-giving right-relationships that were established to nourish creation. The fracturing of these relationships begins in Genesis 3, but the stories that follow across Genesis 4–11 recount a series of episodes that portray the slow unraveling of God's good creation of right-relationships into rebellion, violence, bloodshed, and destruction.

A Crisis within God's Creation

The story of the first human beings in the garden (Gen 3) introduces the need for God's mission that will be the central focus of the rest of the OT story. The garden narrative continues the story that began in Genesis 2, but grabs our attention through the sudden appearance of a new character: an intelligent talking snake (v. 1).

The Snake in Genesis 3

It is only in later Christian interpretation (for example, in the book of Revelation) that the snake in Genesis 3 is identified with Satan. The Genesis story simply identifies it as another one of the "wild animals that the LORD God had made" (v. 1). And some ancient Near Eastern stories such as *The Epic of Gilgamesh* from Babylonia also feature a snake that prevents human beings from achieving immortality.

Much could be and has been discussed about this foundational story. The chapter has generated long-standing questions and played a role in the construction of whole theological systems within Christianity, especially concerning understandings of sin and salvation. But what interests us the most for telling the larger OT story is the humans' disobedient act and its effects on God's good creation that was depicted in Genesis 1–2. The serpent's first words to the human couple[17] raise the primary question with which God's people will struggle throughout their entire story: Can God really be trusted to provide his image-bearing people with the survival, security, and abundant life that they need? Can human beings safely and trustingly surrender control over their own lives to the direction and provision of this Creator? "Did God *really* say..." the snake prods; "You won't die! *God knows...*" (vv. 1, 4-5). The snake's words intimate that YHWH is holding back on humanity and might not be the trustworthy Life-Giver pictured in the creation stories.

Although the woman actively debates the snake (vv. 2-3), the message gets through: with survival and success on the line, humans might be better off taking control of their own lives and determining their own means to create, provide, and flourish rather than depending on the divinely intended relationships of interdependence and mutual blessing that the Creator has established. Along these lines, the snake's words describe the effect of the disobedient act of eating from the forbidden tree with these telling words: "you will be like God, knowing good and evil" (v. 5). Although the theological debates over the meaning of these words have been (and remain) wide-ranging, the implication is clear. The human community that was created to be the image of the divine king can make itself king instead. The Hebrew root word for *knowing* (*yāda'*) carries more than the meaning of *understanding* or *recognizing* good and evil. Elsewhere in the OT, "knowing good and evil" seems to refer to acquiring the capacity to decide right and wrong, whether as a child who comes to the age of responsibility or a ruler who hands down decisions to subordinates (e.g., Deut 1:39; 2 Sam 14:17).[18] And when the snake pairs the promise that the humans can *know* good and evil in this way with the assertion that they will "be like God," it becomes clear that the temptation presented to the humans is for them to *determine* (*yāda'*) for themselves what counts as good and evil.

According to scripture's narrative, here is the great dilemma of the human community that will appear throughout their story and will necessitate God's redemptive mission in the world. Those created to serve as the image that points to the chaos-defeating, life-giving King and to live in right-relationships that yield mutual blessing for all creation are tempted to turn inward toward themselves. Out of fear for its own survival and pride in its possible new position, humanity grabs for self-sovereignty: We will be God; we will make the rules! We will determine our own good and evil; we will ensure our own survival and provision! The human race begins to blur the line between human and divine, being unsatisfied and insecure as the image that reflects and desiring to be the sovereign who determines. In later moments within the OT story, some of the prophets will apply this same imagery and language to specific individuals, especially those who are already in positions of power such as princes and kings. The sixth-century Judean prophet Ezekiel, for example, proclaims a stinging divine judgment on a power-hungry ruler, the "prince of Tyre," accusing him of a pride and self-interest that claims for himself the position of God: "In your arrogance, you say, 'I am God...' Though you claim to have the mind of a god, you are mortal, not divine" (Ezek 28:2; see also Isaiah's judgment on the "king of Babylon" in Isa 14:12-13). In light of the garden story at the opening of the OT, however, we can recognize that these individual rulers are just particular embodiments of the broad human temptation to overstep the line between human and divine and grasp for self-sovereignty and self-sufficiency.

The humans' actions in the garden introduce a fundamental change in the cooperative partnership between the Creator and the human community that was intended to bear God's image in the world. While humanity remains under its divinely appointed vocation to *image* the life-giving Creator, the rest of Genesis 3 begins to depict the fracturing and disintegration of the divinely intended right-relationships. Immediately upon their disobedience, the humans hide from the very God they were created to represent (vv. 8-10). And when they finally engage with YHWH, they blame one another (and the snake) for their actions (vv. 12-13). Perhaps most tragically, however, the narrative reaches its climax in a series of divine punishments (vv. 14-19). YHWH's words in these curses express sad realities that seem to be very far from the Creator's original intentions for the human race and how it should live together in harmony with the elements of its world. YHWH speaks of animosity and violence between humans and animals, pain-filled struggle required for both the woman and man to carry out their primary roles of child-bearing and farming, and a ground that is no longer readily fruitful but often cursed with weeds and thorns. Perhaps the clearest sign that God's original intended right-relationships have been fractured, however, is that one gender now grabs a position of dominance over the other, as the one who was "perfect for him" (2:18) now becomes one "he will rule over" (3:16).

The effects of the humans' disobedience in Genesis 3 clearly involve much more than just the relationship between humanity and God. Humankind's grasp for self-sovereignty has brought curse rather than blessing not just upon the humans' relationship with God and one another, but also upon the processes of life, the products of the ground, and the whole created order. As Timothy Green puts it, the "routine interaction of humanity with God's creation" has fundamentally changed to "head-crushing enmity and thorn-bearing brokenness" and the divinely intended "relational nature of the image-bearing human race" has fractured.[19] Christopher Wright also summarizes the sweeping nature of the distortion of God's divinely intended good creation: "It is not just that every human person is a sinner. It is also the case that the totality of our social and economic relationships with each other, horizontally and historically, and of our ecological relationships to the earth itself have all been perverted and twisted."[20] All creation has been affected, and all creation needs to be restored.

When we read the divine curses in verses 14-19 within the larger context, it becomes clear that the biblical writers were not saying that these realities are what God wants for people and the world both then and now. YHWH's words are descriptions but not prescriptions. The broken realities and disrupted relationships reflected in these words do not prescribe the way that the Creator orders the world to be. Rather, they describe what results if and when humanity refuses to live as the image of God and instead attempts to overstep the line between human and divine and assert its own self-sovereignty. All of the alienation and brokenness described in these verses are under curse—they are not what YHWH intends for his image-bearing community's life together in the world (note, for example, that it's only under curse that the man makes the woman subordinate to him). Instead of trusting in YHWH's provision to allow them to survive and flourish, the temptation is for humans to grasp for control and security. And the garden story says that human mistrust, pride, and rebellion disrupt every originally good relationship with God, each other, animals, the land, and the whole of creation.

In summary, Genesis 3 introduces the crisis that will plague God's good creation in the OT story. By placing this story at the beginning of the OT before Israel has even emerged as a unique, chosen people, the narrative of scripture gives it a significance that goes beyond the actions of the two individuals depicted in the narrative. The struggles God's people will have throughout the rest of the OT to live out faithfully their identity as obedient covenant partners with God are not merely Israelite struggles. In light of Genesis 3, we should see these struggles to come, which will include Israel's worshipping other gods, making sacred cows, seeking security through human kings and alliances, and more, as embodiments of what is actually the basic dilemma of the human race as a whole—namely, the temptation to give in to fear and to grasp for sovereignty and security. Reading the story in Genesis 3 is like looking into a mirror. Standing as it does at the opening of the OT, when the scope remains universal, even cosmic, and the people are presented simply as humans rather than Israelites or some other particular ethnic group, the story of the first humans in the garden represents the story of all humanity that happens again and again in the world. This temptation to self-sovereignty, mistrust, and blurred lines between human and divine is the great dilemma of the human race. And here in the garden, we see the dilemma in its broadest form. This human grasp for self-sovereignty and self-sufficiency creates the crisis in God's good creation, as it wrecks the divinely intended right-relationships of mutual blessing that were established at the beginning of the OT story.

The Unraveling of God's Good Creation

Just as the garden story in Genesis 3 *introduced* the need for God's mission to restore creation to its intended right-relationships, the series of stories in Genesis 4–11 *illustrates* the need for that redemptive work. As readers of the OT story, we follow the first human couple out of the garden and encounter the lives and actions of their descendants, beginning with their two sons, the first two human siblings, Cain and Abel (Gen 4). Across the next eight chapters, we witness God's good creation of right-relationships steadily disintegrate into pride, violence, and bloodshed. To grasp what's being portrayed, we might think of a large fabric quilt with a loose thread hanging from one side. If we pull that thread, part of the stitching begins to unravel. The more we pull, the more the stitching unravels, until what was once a clear and pleasant design has unraveled into a set of jumbled, disconnected strings.

In the same way, the stories in Genesis 4–11 depict God's good creation of right-relationships among humans, God, and the earth slowly unraveling back to chaos marked by division, disorder, and death. There is an overall pattern to each of the major episodes in these chapters. Each major story begins with a sinful event or bad act, which is then followed by a divine judgment and, subsequently, by an act of grace done by God to help the humans involved. The recurring movement of sin-judgment-grace shows a steady escalation of human wrongdoing alongside marks of divine judgment and grace. As this movement unfolds across these stories, the breakdown of the cooperative partnership between the Creator King and his image-bearing human race continues and steadily comes to distort and pollute creation itself.

In the first episode (4:1-15), for example, the sinful action takes place as Cain murders his brother, Abel, and the divine judgment follows, as Cain is banished as a fugitive from his people and land. Yet, God's grace marks Cain with some sort of sign for his protection. So the pattern begins. But so does the unraveling of God's good creation of right-relationships. The story of the first siblings ends in violence, as one brother kills the other—an act soon followed by another in which one who is merely wounded takes murderous vengeance on the wounder (4:23-24). The next major story (6:1-4), just prior to the catastrophic flood, continues the pattern. The sinful act occurs as divine and human beings blur their line because of sexual desire, and the earth itself becomes corrupted with violence and death. This strange description of the intermarriage of "divine beings" and "human daughters" has often been seen as out of place, and scholars have searched for parallels in various ancient Near Eastern mythological texts.[21] But in its context here, the episode represents the ultimate line-crossing of the human and divine and results in such a ruined condition for the world that it calls forth the most devastating divine judgment yet.

Genealogies and Lifespans

Within Genesis 4–11 there are several lists of ancestors (genealogies) that provide family histories. Some of the ancestors in these lists have exceptionally long lifespans, especially those who lived before the flood. The long lifespans of pre-flood people is a well-known feature in ancient Near Eastern texts outside the Bible. The lifespans of some of the rulers in Mesopotamian king lists were even longer, with pre-flood rulers living an average of 30,000 years.[22] In Genesis, many of the major pre-flood figures lived almost one thousand years each (see 5:1-32). While the historicity of these figures and numbers remains uncertain, the long lifespans generally function to depict the pre-flood era as an ideal beginning age from which humankind slowly declined.[23] Hence, the lifespans in Genesis 11:10-32 for those who lived after the flood steadily decrease. In the context of the larger OT story, the decrease in lifespans after the flood symbolizes humankind's steady loss of their intended, ideal nature and identity.

Across these first few stories, the biblical storytellers portray the earliest era of human history before the flood as a time of failure. As the human community turns inward toward its own desire and survival, humanity loses its created identity as God's image-bearers called to right-relationships that allow for mutual blessing. Just after the ultimate line-blurring act of divine and human intermarriage, YHWH's words in Genesis 6:5-6, 11 give a climactic summary of what has become of his good, intended creation: "The LORD saw that humanity had become thoroughly evil on the earth.... The LORD regretted (Heb. *nāḥam*, repented for) making human beings on the earth, and he was heartbroken.... [And] the earth had become corrupt and was filled with violence." In the span of six chapters, humanity's propensity toward mistrust and self-sovereignty has not only wrecked their relationship with the Creator but ruined the creation itself.

In response, the divine judgment takes its most severe form in a world-destroying flood (Gen 6–8). Standard introductory textbooks on the OT typically note that numerous ancient Near Eastern flood stories appear in texts such as *The Epic of Gilgamesh* from Babylonia, and that the biblical flood story bears both similarities and differences to those texts.[24] These comparisons show that in line with some of the common imagery of their day, the biblical storytellers do more than just present the flood as an act of divine destruction. Marshalling images we've already seen in the OT narratives, the writers portray the flood as a reversal of God's original creation. Israel's storytellers describe the onset of the great flood in 7:11 by using the very same language and imagery as the creation story in Genesis 1: "the springs of the deep sea erupted" and "the windows in the skies opened." Just as God's initial creative act on the second day (1:6-8) established a dome to restrain the life-denying chaotic waters above and below the earth, the flood is depicted as God's undoing of creation, reversing those restraints, allowing the chaotic waters to return, and casting the earth back to the shapeless disorder with which it began. Rather than a physical, geological, or geographical description, the biblical writers use the meaning-filled language of the OT story itself to offer a symbol of comprehensive divine judgment: God un-creates creation. And the message in the context of the larger story is clear. When human beings refuse to live as God's image and instead attempt to blur the line and become their own sovereign, all creation is thrown back to chaos.

When the chaotic waters surge to their highest point over this undone creation, however, God's grace brings about a turning point: "God remembered Noah, all those alive, and all the animals with him in the ark" (8:1). True to the broad scope of God's intentions for creation, the new beginning after the flood emerges not only from God's commitment to humankind but also from the Creator's concern for the animals! The Israelite storytellers once again use the language and imagery of the priestly creation story in Genesis 1 to depict the ending of the flood as a new act of creation (or re-creation) by God. The Creator sends a "wind" (Heb. *rûaḥ*) over the water-covered earth, pushes back the chaotic waters, and closes the windows to the waters above and below (8:1-2; compare 1:2, 6-7).

God created; humanity caused the undoing of that creation; but God has re-created. In some sense, it feels like this could already be the happy ending of the OT story, as Noah and his family exit the boat to reboot life on the earth. Surprisingly, however, YHWH's first words after Noah has left the boat reveal that even after the great flood and a re-creation, absolutely nothing has changed with the human condition! Strikingly, YHWH pledges never again to make the "land" suffer because of humankind, but acknowledges that "the ideas of the human mind are evil from their youth" (8:21). This is the same language that was used to describe humanity's condition before the flood (6:5). Ironically, YHWH's dramatic un-creation and re-creation moves only God to act differently. The human dilemma remains, as those created to be image-bearers continue with an inclination to mistrust, self-sovereignty, and violence. And if the human dilemma remains, then so, too, does the danger that human mistrust and disobedience will wreck even this post-flood new creation.

This despair-filled acknowledgment leaves a question hanging over the OT story: *How can God deal with a humanity inclined to evil if he has determined not to destroy it?* For readers of the OT story, this might seem like an impassable roadblock. Yet, already in the creation stories of Genesis 1–2, the biblical narrative has answered the question, "Who is God?" by portraying a chaos-conquering, life-giving Creator who engages in cooperative partnership with creation. And this committed, relational, and dynamic character of God turns the seemingly despair-filled roadblock moment in the OT story into the starting point for imagining something new and for introducing God's mission in the world.

The Introduction of God's Mission

The answer to the lingering question posed at the conclusion of the flood story comes in Genesis 9 in the form of a single, destiny-altering divine act that puts a new reality into place for God, humanity, and all creation: covenant. This is the decisive turning point for my telling of the OT story because this is where God introduces his redemptive mission in the world. In 9:1-17, the Creator embarks on a new beginning for the future of creation. No longer will God respond to the evil-inclined image-bearers with sweeping judgment and devastating destruction. Rather, God now commits to a new way to bring humanity and all creation back to the blessing and flourishing (fruitful multiplying) originally intended (9:1, 7). On the other side of the flood, God declares that he has determined to invest in a long-term commitment—a covenant relationship—that will somehow turn out to be redemptive for all creation: "I am now setting up my covenant with you, with your descendants, and with every living being with you" (9:9-10).

This is the first of four covenants God will make in the OT (later covenants will involve Abraham, Moses, and David). Just as in the creation stories, once more here the God of scripture's narrative is revealed as a relationship-making, partnering God who works in dynamic cooperation to accomplish the divine purposes in the world. Now, the choice to enter explicitly into covenant relationship becomes the decisive divine act that will open a new future for the creation that had unraveled due to human sin and rebellion. The Covenant-Maker's words here reveal that this initial, decisive divine engagement and partnership includes more than just Israel or even the human race. It extends to "every living being with you—with the birds, with the large animals, and with all the animals of the earth" (9:10).[25]

For my telling of the OT story, this post-flood covenant commitment introduces God's mission as the divine effort to restore creation back to the mutually flourishing right-relationships with which it began (see 9:7-11). The language in Genesis 9 makes explicit that God's mission going forward—and the purpose of his becoming a covenant partner—is to restore creation. The divine commission and blessing given to Noah ("be fertile, multiply, and fill the earth," 9:1, 7) parallel the language addressed to humanity in the first creation story (1:28). In fact, chapter 9 is the first time we hear of God's blessing of creation after chapter 1, and it's presented as the goal that God's covenant commitment to all living beings is designed to achieve. For the biblical writers steeped in Israel's priestly tradition, Genesis 9 envisions a return to the original conditions of blessing, fertility, and flourishing described in Genesis 1—a universal redemptive promise for all of creation.

At this point, we know that God's mission is to restore creation by becoming a covenant partner. But we don't yet know the exact form that God's redemptive covenant partnership will take in this mission. Before the OT story reveals that next element, however, the final episodes within Genesis 1–11 remind us that the human dilemma (and its effects on God's good creation) remains. The first interaction among humans after the flood (9:18-28), for example, consists of a bizarre encounter in which Noah's son, Ham, commits some sort of disgraceful act toward his father, who has become drunk and lies exposed in his tent. It's difficult to determine the precise nature and meaning of the actions involved, and interpreters have offered many speculations, including possible sexual misconduct or disregard of proper duties toward a parent.[26] But the story emphasizes the consequences for Ham's son, Canaan, who is cursed to be subservient to his relatives. While the narrative may be a historical justification for the Canaanites later serving the Israelites (see 11:10-30), in the context of the larger OT story, it shows that the human dilemma of broken relationships and domination remains even after the flood. God's mission to restore creation through a covenant commitment is only just beginning.

Similarly, the final two chapters in the OT's opening section underscore that the image-bearing human race continues to struggle with the temptation to mistrust, self-provision, and self-sovereignty. The listing of Noah's descendants in Genesis 10 shows the expected spreading of the nations in fulfillment of God's post-flood command to "multiply, and fill the earth" (9:1). Suddenly, however, chapter 11 presents a contradictory picture, as humankind reverts back to its fear for survival and desire for power. United by one language (v. 1), all humanity decides to settle in one place, as one homogenous group, and build a "city and a tower" (v. 4), an action that God disrupts by confusing their languages and scattering them across the earth (vv. 5-9). Here is another example of the human temptation to pride and sovereignty, to overstepping the line between human and divine. The people aim "to make a name for themselves" (v. 4), and YHWH worries that they grasp for power to do whatever they wish (v. 6).

At the same time, the so-called Tower of Babel represents another moment when the image-bearers who were called to trust in YHWH for their flourishing yield to fear for their survival.[27] They expressly state their reason for building, "So that we won't be dispersed over all the earth" (v. 4). Their concern to hunker down together and create their own well-being flies in the face of God's intentions for his human image-bearers stated at the very beginning (1:28) and reiterated after the flood (9:1, 7): to trust in divine provision, multiply, and fill creation with variety and difference. In some ways, the people's fearful words and actions here resemble the common aspirations of empires, one of the realities of ancient Israel's world and a reality known to us in the form of powerful nation-states in today's world. Both then and now, empires and nation-states try to ensure security and prosperity by controlling resources, repressing differences, and pushing people to conform to a particular culture and language. It is as if the biblical narrative at the conclusion of these opening eleven chapters indirectly raises the question of whether such imperial ways and means might resolve the human crisis of a misaligned creation and a mistrusting image. Do great empires (like those of ancient Assyria and Babylonia) represent the means by which God's covenantal commitment to restore creation will play out? The OT answers no. The story in Genesis 11 ends by dispersing both the people and any such notion. Scripture's narrative leads us to anticipate that the specific form of God's covenantal mission to restore creation will begin with something more local, particular, and modest.[28]

Toward the Beginning of God's Mission

The Bible's opening stories in Genesis 1–11, which form the first movement of the larger OT story, have revealed the need for God's mission and the nature of that mission as God's commitment to engage as a covenant partner in order to restore creation. God's original intentions were for a creation made perfect as an ideal existence marked by right-relationships of mutual blessing among God, humans, and the earth. But God's rightly-related world with faithful human image-bearers has become an unraveled creation in need of restoration. At the conclusion of Genesis 1–11, all humanity, which once was together in one place, has now been scattered all over the earth, as those created to be God's image-bearers continue to struggle with the temptation to self-sovereignty and self-reliance. Hence, a question hangs over this critical moment in the OT story: What is to be done with this human inclination to rebellion and this unraveled creation?

As we've already seen, after the flood (Gen 9) God introduced a new, long-term commitment to restore creation back to the right-relationships with which it began. The final verses of Genesis 11 hint at the specific form that God's covenantal mission of restoration will take. These verses lead us down the generations of Shem's descendants (vv. 10-31) until we encounter two seemingly obscure people named Abram and Sarai who are on their way from Ur of the Chaldeans to the land of Canaan (vv. 26-31). When the OT story begins its next section in Genesis 12, we'll see that out of all those scattered peoples, YHWH will call out this one group of Abram, Sarai, and their descendants to enter into a special relationship with them and to use them as an instrument to carry out the divine mission by blessing all nations.

C h a p t e r   4

The Calling and Creation of God's People

(Genesis 12–50) (Exodus 1–15)

Focus Texts: Genesis 12:1-3; 17; 22; 50;
Exodus 3–4; 13–14

Location in the Old Testament Story:

1) The Introduction of God's Mission in the World (Genesis 1–11)
2) **The Calling of God's People (Genesis 12–50)**
3) **The Creation of God's People (Exodus 1–15)**
4) The Formation of God's People (Exodus 16–Deuteronomy)
5) The Life of God's People (Joshua–Esther)
   a) The Voices of Israel's Poets and Sages before, during, and after Exile (Job–Song of Songs)
   b) The Voices of Israel's Prophets before, during, and after Exile (Isaiah–Malachi)

The Calling of God's People (Genesis 12–50)

When I was a child growing up in my local church, I regularly attended Vacation Bible School—the annual, weeklong, summertime event for young children that included Bible lessons, activities, and, of course, silly songs. One of those songs was "Father Abraham," an entertaining little ditty that combined a simple melody with high-energy motions. The lyrics were brief and repetitive: "Father Abraham had many sons; many sons had Father Abraham. I am one of them, and so are you, so let's just praise the Lord." What the song lacked in gender inclusive language, it made up for in activity. As each repetition of the tune went by, we were encouraged to add the movement of a certain limb ("right arm!" "left arm!"), until the whole body was in motion while singing.

In spite of the song's intentional silliness, "Father Abraham" captures some of the plot of the next major section of the OT story in the remainder of the book of Genesis. Here, God works with one person, who then expands into a multitude of descendants, for the purpose of participating in God's redemptive work in the world. In the light of the human dilemma, its effects on an originally good creation, and God's determination to engage in covenantal mission, Genesis 12–50 provides the next movement of the larger OT story as God calls a people—not for its own sake, but to participate as an instrument in the accomplishment of God's mission for the sake of humanity and the world.

Genesis 12–50 in the Larger Old Testament Story

The preceding section of the OT story (Gen 1–11) introduced God's mission in the world. It drew our minds back before and beyond Israel to the broadest horizons of all humanity and even all creation. It depicted God's creation made perfect—the divinely intended right-relationships and mutual blessing, with all humanity being at one with God, each other, and the earth. But the stories also portrayed the subsequent unraveling of God's intended creation due to humanity's tendency toward mistrust, fear, and self-sovereignty. In the face of that dilemma, the opening chapters of scripture's narrative introduced God's mission to restore creation to the originally intended, life-giving right-relationships. God has committed to become a covenant partner with all living beings (Gen 9) in a way that will somehow turn out to heal and restore a fruitful and flourishing existence for all creation.

At this point in the OT story, then, we know that God's mission is to restore creation by becoming a covenant partner, but we don't yet know what specific form that mission will take. *The stories of Israel's earliest ancestors in Genesis 12–50 now reveal the specifics: God calls a particular people, who begin with Abraham, Sarah, and their descendants, to enter into a special relationship with them so that they become the instrument of life-giving blessing to the world.* As noted at the end of the last chapter, when we reached the conclusion of Genesis 1–11, we saw that all humanity, which once had been together in one place, was scattered over the earth, as those created to be God's image-bearers continued to struggle with the temptation to self-sovereignty and self-reliance. And a question hung over that critical moment in the OT story: What is to be done with this human inclination to rebellion and this un-raveled creation in light of God's commitment to a redemptive, covenant mission of restoration? The final verses of Genesis 11 then led us down the generations of Shem's descendants (vv. 10-31) until we encountered two seemingly obscure people called, at that time, Abram and Sarai, who were on their way from Ur of the Chaldeans to the land of Canaan (vv. 26-31).

Beginning in Genesis 12, this seemingly unremarkable couple takes center stage in the OT story. What has so far been a story about the whole human race, and even the entire cosmos, narrows its focus to the particular group that will become the people of Israel. But coming as they do after the opening section of scripture's story in Genesis 1–11, the stories of Abram, Sarai, and their descendants don't overshadow the bigger picture of God's life-giving concern for humanity and all creation. Instead, out of all those scattered peoples at the end of Genesis 1–11, YHWH calls out one group for a special status and task—not for its own sake but for the sake of the healing of the whole world. YHWH's commitment to covenant engagement with all living beings in order to restore life-giving blessing will take the form of working with and through a specific covenant partner—the descendants of Abram and Sarai who eventually become the people of Israel—on behalf of all creation.

Here at the outset of this next movement in the larger story, we're reminded of who the God of the OT story has already been shown to be—the life-giving Creator who most characteristically works to accomplish his work in the world not through coercion, domination, or overwhelming displays of power but through cooperation with human covenant partners. We also see at the outset that the story of Israel—the group that will dominate the remainder of the OT as God's special, chosen people—stands as a smaller story within a larger story. Remarkably, the Israelite writers themselves make clear that they understand their own status and calling in just this way—not as some exclusive privilege but as part of God's larger intentions for all humanity and the divine effort to heal creation.

God's Missional Calling of a People (Genesis 12:1-3)

The first part of my discussion of God's calling of a people will focus on the specific divine call of Abram and Sarai in Genesis 12:1-3, since it's the primary articulation of the particular form that God's redemptive mission will take in the world. In these pivotal verses, the God who has a mission calls forth a people who have a mission. But the revelation of the specific form of God's redemptive mission in the world comes as an out-of-the-blue surprise. Without warning in Genesis 12:1-3, YHWH calls out to the elderly, childless couple who had been traveling around the Fertile Crescent[1] at the end of Genesis 11. In these opening divine words, YHWH mixes commands with promises. He commands them to leave their present location and extended family for a journey toward a place they don't yet know. He then declares his intention to enter into a special relationship with this particular couple and their descendants so that they may become the instrument used to restore the life-giving blessing that God had originally intended:

> The LORD said to Abram, "Leave your land, your family, and your father's household for the land that I will show you. I will make of you a great nation and will bless you. I will make your name respected, and you will be a blessing. I will bless those who bless you, those who curse you I will curse; all the families of the earth will be blessed because of you." (12:1-3)

For my reading of the OT, the divine call in 12:1-3 is perhaps the single, most defining passage for understanding the identity and role of God's people within God's mission to restore creation. While I see YHWH's covenant-making commitment to all living beings after the flood (Gen 9) as the most important biblical tradition for reading the OT as the story of God's redemptive mission in the world (see ch. 3), I agree with some other interpreters who have referred to the divine call in 12:1-3 as the "launch" of that mission, the actual "beginning of God's answer" to the human dilemma, and the "foundation" for our understanding of the remainder of the OT's overall story.[2]

The divine call for Abram (the name he has in the narrative at this point; see Gen 17) to leave the place and company of his extended family in order to journey to an as-yet-unknown destination contains three specific promises from YHWH that will be a part of the journey, if Abram is willing to make it: (1) a land in which to live, (2) a line of descendants that will become a great nation, and (3) divine blessing. These divine promises are immediately remarkable within the context of the unfolding larger OT story for how they replace curse with blessing. The emphasis is clear, as the term *bless* appears five times in verses 2-3 alone. This term carries special meaning against the background of thorn-filled ground, infertile barrenness, and destructive violence that resulted from humanity's disobedience. As we saw across the stories in Genesis 4–11, the human actions of mistrust and rebellion in the garden resulted in a creation living under curse, an existence marked by alienation and strife. Within this larger story, blessing, then, represents the undoing of sin's curse and the restoration of creation to the abundant, flourishing life described by God's covenant words at the end of the flood: "Be fertile, multiply, and fill the earth" (Gen 9:1).[3] At the inauguration of the divine mission to restore creation, YHWH promises the opposite of curse in the form of life-giving blessing for both Abram's family and, through them, all the people of the world.

Yet, for readers of the OT story, these promises are also curious in many respects, especially the promise of children and other descendants that will lead to a great nation. Verse 4 indicates that childless Abram is already seventy-five years old at the time of YHWH's call. And even more strikingly, the introduction of Abram and Sarai at the conclusion of Genesis 11 mentioned what is in some sense the main plot problem for their whole story across Genesis 12–25, namely, that Sarai was unable to have children (11:30). In an unexpected way, then, God's mission to restore creation begins not with mighty empires or powerful leaders, but with a woman and her womb, as YHWH promises to work through the unlikeliest of life-denying situations in order to bring life-giving blessing to all the world. And although the wording of verses 1-3 is most directly addressed to Abram, as the episodes unfold over the following chapters, it becomes increasingly clear that YHWH's calling and promises are just as much about Sarai as they are about Abram (see especially Gen 16).

Even so, the following chapters will also reveal that both Abram and Sarai (as well as the later generations of their descendants) will struggle with the call to trust these unlikely sounding divine promises of land, descendants, and blessing. The plot of the stories of Israel's ancestors in the rest of the book of Genesis will revolve around the tension between promise and threat—can the mothers, fathers, and children of this newly called-out human community trust YHWH to fulfill these promises and provide life, especially when the promises appear to be threatened by the circumstances in which they find themselves? What do you do when you're living under promise but there are threats to that promise? Readers of the larger OT story will recognize across the stories of Israel's ancestors in Genesis 12–50 the same struggle that marked the dilemma of humanity as a whole in Genesis 1–11: the tendency toward mistrust and fear that breeds the temptation to self-sovereignty and self-provision.

Before any of that, however, YHWH's promises in verses 2-3 especially bring into focus the nature of the calling of this soon-to-be community and its role in the larger plot of scripture's story. First, although the divine call and promises are directly addressed to Abram in the singular, YHWH's focus is already on the future generations that will come to be a special people and to play a role in YHWH's blessing of all creation. Abram and Sarai are the initial ancestors that represent a community of people that will become a "great nation" (v. 2). And in the language of verse 2 and throughout the stories of their descendants in the rest of Genesis, YHWH extends the call and promise to each new generation, ultimately revealing that the calling to be YHWH's instrument of blessing is a corporate not individual calling. YHWH seeks a *people* who together will model the Creator's life-giving ways and channel those blessings to the world. YHWH talks to Abram, but calls a people.

The divine words in the remainder of verses 2-3 then emphasize that YHWH is calling this people not simply to be in a special relationship with him and receive blessing for themselves but to be the instrument he can use to restore creation back to the right-relationships of life-giving blessing for which it was created. At the end of verse 2, YHWH expands the promise that he will bless Abram (and the future community of people who will come from him) to indicate explicitly that Abram and his descendants will be an instrument of blessing. Although often translated as a simple declaration ("you will be a blessing"), YHWH's words are actually a command (an imperative in Hebrew): "Be a blessing!" The flow of the sentence is somewhat awkward, but this command at the end of verse 2 matches the command (another Hebrew imperative) at the opening of verse 1 ("Leave your land"). YHWH's call to those who will become his chosen, promised, and blessed people is literally a two-part command to govern their life: "Go...bless!" Moreover, in Hebrew grammar, a sequence of two imperatives typically communicates that the second command is meant to be understood as the purpose or result of the first. Seen in this way, YHWH actually calls Abram and the future community of his descendants toward a new land, nation, and identity specifically for the purpose of being a blessing to others ("Leave... [in order to] be a blessing!").

The opening phrase of verse 3 seems difficult to reconcile with the idea that YHWH is calling this people to be the instrument of his mission to restore creation. Here, YHWH promises to bless those who bless Abram but to curse those who curse him. Some interpreters have made the case that we should read the threat of cursing here only as YHWH's noting a possible exception with which he may (or may not) have to deal. YHWH *intends* to use Abram's descendants to bless others, but "should there be one" who attempts to curse (bring death rather than life to) them, YHWH will respond in kind to preserve those chosen to carry his blessing.[4] In other words, YHWH doesn't call Abram and his descendants *in order to be* instruments of divine cursing, but YHWH warns that those who mistreat them will forfeit the life-giving blessing that YHWH aims to deliver through this chosen people. This interpretation seems to fit with the force of the imperatives that we noted as defining the purpose of the people's calling in verses 1-2 ("Leave... [in order to] be a blessing!"). In essence, YHWH states his purpose to extend restoring blessing to all people, but once more reveals his dynamic, cooperative, relational way in the world. While all are intended to receive this blessing, their participation will be determined by how they live in relationship to YHWH's people. As we'll see throughout the rest of the OT story, the biblical writers often use this notion to explain not only the rise and fall of kingdoms and empires, but even the fates and fortunes of those within Israel.

The final phrase of verse 3 provides the climax of YHWH's calling of a people and makes abundantly clear that they are called not for their own sake but to be the instrument YHWH can use to restore the blessing of creation: "all the families of the earth will be blessed because of you." Here we see the wide scope of YHWH's redemptive mission. The Hebrew term (*mišpǝḥôt*) used is even broader than "families," often appearing elsewhere in the OT to denote large subgroups (clans) or even whole peoples related as kinship groups. Thus, YHWH declares his intention to extend blessing to "all" the various people groupings that make up the human population, with none left out in favor of another. As Christopher Wright observes, the implication is not that "every individual human being" will automatically or ultimately receive YHWH's blessing, but that the divine mission is intended to extend to creation on the whole and as a whole.[5] All human life will now have the possibility of experiencing the life-giving blessings of a creation becoming "very good" once again.

"All the Families of the Earth Will Be Blessed" (Gen 12:3)

The Hebrew verb in the final phrase of Genesis 12:3 can be translated in various ways. The most common translation, "will be blessed," implies that Israel's blessing will overflow and be the means by which all the families of the earth will also be blessed. Another translation, "will bless themselves," suggests that Abraham's blessing and well-being will be the standard by which other peoples will ask for a blessing ("May we be blessed as Abraham was").

The last words of verse 3 reiterate that all these families will have this possibility on account of YHWH's new image-bearing community that will come from Abram and Sarai ("because of you"). The Hebrew in these final words can be read in various ways (e.g., "by you"; "in you"; "with you"). The overall context of YHWH's call of Abram in verses 1-3 and its place in the larger OT story thus far, however, suggest that the Israelites will not be the ones with whom the blessing originates and will not always be the ones who actually perform the blessing. YHWH will be the source of the blessing and the agent who bestows it, but Israel will be the instrument ("through you")— the means through which the life-giving, life-restoring blessing reaches all humanity.[6]

The Implications of God's Missional Calling

In Genesis 12:1-3, YHWH calls a particular group of people—who will turn out to be the manifold descendants of Abram and Sarai—to enter into a special relationship with them, to bless them, and to use them to be the instrument of blessing as part of the larger divine mission to restore creation to the life-giving relationships with which it began. Here, then, is the turning point where the specific form of God's covenant, redemptive engagement with creation, which was announced after the flood, comes into view. The biblical testimony is that God has chosen to conduct his mission in the world by working in and through a special relationship with one group of people. From this point forward, then, the OT story will be predominantly given over to telling the story of the people of Israel (including their interactions with other nations). Israel's story makes up something on the order of 99 percent of the subjects of the OT writings. Yet in the context of the whole OT, Israel's life is the smaller plot line that stands within the larger plot line of God's mission to restore creation. God's more narrow work with one couple, family, and nation finds its meaning within the divine effort to use them as an instrument of blessing on behalf of all nations and all creation.

The role of Israel within God's larger mission sheds light on the often-noted theme of *election* (Israel as God's chosen people) within the OT. The biblical testimony is that Israel has a special status as the divinely chosen (elected) people out of all the nations of the earth. Since the OT writings are ancient Israelite texts, it has been tempting for interpreters throughout history to see this as a self-serving claim made by the Israelite writers or as a divine choice that implies a narrow, clique-ish favoritism by God at the expense of the devaluing or even rejection of the other peoples of the world.[7]

The Chosen People

Modern interpreters have sometimes used a narrow, exclusivist interpretation of Israel as the chosen/elected people to justify actions that subordinate and disenfranchise certain groups. Some recent biblical scholarship has challenged such exclusivist interpretations, with regard to their contemporary implications. For example, Robert Allen Warrior's "Canaanites, Cowboys, and Indians: Deliverance, Conquest, and Liberation Theology Today" rereads the OT's exodus and conquest stories from the perspective of the Canaanites who were displaced from the land and sees similarities with the experiences of Native Americans throughout United States history.[8]

Although there are many possible dimensions of meaning to the notion of Israel's election and Genesis 12:1-3, reading this idea and passage within the canonical context of Christian scripture suggests that we should understand Israel's election in the *instrumental* terms described above.[9] The story of God's creation-wide purposes for all humanity told across the preceding chapters of Genesis 1–11 clarifies that Israel has been chosen to be special not as an end in itself but for the missional purpose of being an instrument of blessing for the benefit of all the families of the earth. In OT terms, to be *elected* means to be chosen *for a purpose on behalf of others.* As we'll see in the next section of the OT story, on this definition, election equals holiness. Soon God will work to form the people he's called into a *holy* nation—a people set apart with a particular character for a specific purpose (see Exod 19:1-6).

Living as a Divinely Called People: Israel's Fathers and Mothers (Genesis 12–50)

From the moment when YHWH calls Abram, Sarai, and their descendants to be his instrument of blessing—the moment when the plot line of the OT turns the vast majority of its attention going forward to the story of the people that will come to be known as Israel—we begin to encounter two elements together. Throughout the story of the covenant God and his covenant people, we'll see God's missional efforts to bless and restore creation continually at work in the world. Yet, at the same time, we'll see the human community, which was created to be divine image-bearers, repeatedly struggle with mistrust, fear, and rebellion, often distorting or even thwarting God's life-giving purposes. We will see both these positive and negative elements in the people and forces that surround the Israelites (some of whom sustain and support them, while others oppress and enslave). But we'll also see both positive and negative elements in the ways and deeds of the divinely called covenant people themselves, who will often give in to distrust, disobedience, and self-preservation in ways that harm themselves and others. At times, we'll struggle to understand how Israel's character and actions described in the OT fulfill their role of blessing others, but at other times we'll see very positive examples of the divine restoration mission unfolding in and through them.

Abraham and Sarah: A Tension-Filled Journey

This tension is visible right away in the stories of Abram and Sarai's journeys in response to God's call in Genesis 12–25. Across the tales of Israel's founding father and mother that begin when they set out for an as-yet-unidentified promised land (12:4), the biblical storytellers give early glimpses of the struggle to live out the identity of being a promise-trusting and blessing-bringing people. Their story is a microcosm (small-scale representation) of Israel's story to come. Where we might expect to find an idealistic depiction of Abram and Sarai, since they are the ancestors of the very Israelites who wrote and preserved these stories, we instead find portrayals of surprisingly flawed persons who often seem hesitant to trust YHWH and all too ready to act for their own benefit.

The Character of Abraham

Many contemporary Christians think of Abraham as something like a perfect super-saint, who always trusted and obeyed God (perhaps because of the NT description in Heb 11:8-19). But Abraham's actions (especially with Isaac in Gen 22) have received a wide variety of interpretations from ancient to contemporary times in Jewish, Christian, and Muslim traditions, and among central thinkers of the modern western philosophical tradition (such as Immanuel Kant and Søren Kierkegaard).[10]

As noted above, their story revolves around the three strange-sounding, unlikely divine promises (land, children, blessing) given in the midst of barrenness. But their story also includes the ongoing struggle for Abram and Sarai to trust the promises and the promise-giver, especially when the promises seem threatened, and resist fearfully taking matters into their own hands to assure their own self-preservation through their own ways and means. We find in the surprising, sometimes disturbing, stories of these first ones to live as part of YHWH's called people moments when they trustingly live out their calling to be instruments of blessing and become life-givers to those with whom they interact. Yet, we also see other moments when their fear and self-interest make them life-taking instruments of harm, even to one another.

Before the first chapter of the couple's journey has ended, for example, a famine threatens their survival in the promised land of Canaan and pushes them toward Egypt for refuge (12:10-20). Seemingly consumed by fear for his own survival, Abram tells Sarai to deceive the Egyptians by saying that she is his sister and not his wife. The struggle to trust YHWH for provision, protection, and fulfillment begins right away! And when the pharaoh desires to marry Sarai, thinking she is unmarried, Abram richly benefits with material possessions. But the text soon makes clear that Abram's fearful efforts in self-preservation bring harm rather than blessing—they take life rather than give it—as Sarai, the one proclaimed by God to be the mother of the promised-child-to-be, finds herself married off into the harem of a foreign ruler, and Pharaoh, along with his entire household, find themselves suffering under severe plagues that bring to light his unintended sin in marrying Sarai. In the end, YHWH intervenes to rescue Sarai and get the couple back on their journey.

In contrast to this unexpectedly disappointing beginning to the founding ancestor's story, however, Abram's next actions show his ability to summon trust and courage and act to give and protect life (13:1–14:16). He and his allies rescue his nephew, Lot, who had been taken captive in the military raids of a coalition of kings. On the way home from the rescue, Abram becomes the blessed and the blesser (14:17-24). God (here called *El Elyon*, "God Most High," vv. 18-20) compels the priest, Melchizedek, to bless Abram, even as Abram becomes an instrument of blessing by giving one-tenth of the material goods recovered to the priest and offering the remainder to those who were with him.

The remaining episodes of Abram and Sarai's journey under YHWH's promises illustrate this same tension between fear and trust, life-taking and life-giving. In Genesis 15, YHWH acts as the covenant-making God once more (see the covenant with Noah and all living beings in Gen 9), as he makes a formal but one-sided covenant commitment to Abram as a means of dramatically reaffirming the divine promises and calling Abram to continue to trust. Yet this elderly couple continues childless chapter after chapter—now more than ten years on (see 12:4 and 16:16)—with no evidence that YHWH will give the needed land, provisions, and descendants. Immediately after YHWH's covenant-making moment, Sarai and Abram fall victim once more to the temptation to take matters into their own hands in self-provision (16:1-6). In the process, they again act as instruments that take away life, dignity, and personhood, as Abram impregnates an Egyptian servant girl named Hagar, Sarai resents her, and together they expel her out into the wilderness alone. Yet, the promise-making God once more intervenes, calling Hagar by name in the wilderness and even expanding the divine blessing to her future son, Ishmael, and his descendants (16:7-16). YHWH refuses to allow the promise, calling, and journey to end in death and despair. In fact, in the very next chapter, YHWH enacts another covenant with Abram (Gen 17). Perhaps originally a duplicate version of the covenant in chapter 15, although from a different source (see the introduction to the Pentateuch in ch. 3 above), in the present arrangement of scripture's canonical story, chapter 17 now portrays the determined, persistent, covenant God reiterating his commitment and trustworthiness immediately after Abram and Sarai's failure with Hagar. And this second divine covenant ceremony with Abram is even more dramatic, as God symbolizes the dependability of his commitment by renaming Abram as "Abraham" ("father of a multitude," v. 6; Sarai also received the name "Sarah," v. 10) and instituting circumcision—a permanent mark in the flesh (vv. 10-14)—as the perpetual sign of the covenant relationship.

Over the final episodes of Abraham and Sarah's travels—now more than twenty years after YHWH's original calling and promise (see 17:1)—we continue to see the tension between fear and trust, life-taking and life-giving that will mark the entire story of the covenant people. In one moment, Abraham passionately pleads with YHWH to spare some in the land of Sodom (18:16-33); and in another moment, he again gives in to fear for his own survival and deceives the king of Gerar into marrying Sarah (remember 12:10-20), who has once more been deceitfully passed off as his sister rather than his wife (20:1-18).[11] Just as before, Abraham is the opposite of a life-giver, putting the unsuspecting king in danger of a divine death sentence (vv. 3-5) and bringing a curse of barrenness on all the women in the king's household (vv. 17-18). Even so, YHWH continues to work with this called-out couple, pushing their journey with his promises forward. And finally, in Genesis 21:1-7, after ten chapters and twenty-five years (see v. 5), fulfillment happens. Sarah gives birth to the long-awaited promised child, Isaac, the sign of God's covenant-keeping faithfulness and the beginning of the people who will be God's instrument in the divine mission to restore creation.

This seemingly happy-ending moment is short-lived, however. In Genesis 22, without warning, God demands that Abraham sacrifice the long-awaited promised child and the future of God's covenant people. Perhaps much to our surprise given what we've seen from Abraham along the way, he begins to carry out the divine demand. In another surprise, however, God's messenger stops Abraham's sacrifice of Isaac—seemingly at the last possible moment—with another divine address: "Don't stretch out your hand against the young man....I now know that you revere God and didn't hold back your son, your only son, from me" (v. 12). "I *now* know," God says, remarkably! This is presented as new knowledge that is gained by God at this moment! What might seem like a strange notion at first becomes clear when we embed it into the plot line of the OT story and what we've already learned about who this promise-making God is. The God of the OT story is not a manipulative puppeteer who chooses robots pre-programmed to be reliable. As Abraham and Sarah's story has shown, he is a determined but cooperative covenant partner who works in a dynamic relationship with human partners who are asked to respond in particular ways—but they may (and as we've seen, sometimes do!) choose otherwise. The calling of Abraham and Sarah appeared in the OT story as God's first attempt to bring specific form to the divine mission to restore creation that was announced after the flood. Now, at the end of the rocky journey across Genesis 12–22, it seems as if God remained uncertain about whether he had found the people that could be the instrument of blessing to participate in that mission. So God "tested" Abraham (22:1). Abraham seemed to pass. God learned that Abraham could be faithful. The missional story could continue.

The Promise and the Call Continue

At the end of even a brief survey of Israel's earliest ancestor couple, we've learned more about who God is and who God's people are and are called to be. The people called to be instruments of blessing are certainly not perfect super-saints. Contrary to what we might have expected, even Abraham and Sarai struggled with the human dilemmas of mistrust, fear, and self-sovereignty, at times becoming instruments of harm rather than blessing.

Israel's Fathers and Mothers

It's possible that the less-than-perfect portrayals of Israel's patriarchs and matriarchs in Genesis 12–50 were intended to be encouraging models for even the ancient audiences of these stories. As Frank Frick explains, "The author intends the readers of the text, who see themselves as the descendants of the characters in the narrative, to see themselves mirrored in the life and faith of their forerunners. Thus, the fathers and mothers of Israel are pictured as 'real people,' *not* as idealized human beings or picture-perfect 'saints' who had an unfaltering faith."[12]

Yet, these ancestors' story turned out to be more about God's faithfulness than their righteousness. Abraham and Sarah were faithful in a very human manner—with doubts, failures, and wrong actions along the way. Yet, the calling, covenanting God remained committed to protecting the promise, sustaining the calling, and bringing into being a people who can be the instrument of God's restoration mission for creation.

The rest of the book of Genesis (chs. 25–50) tells the story of the generations of descendants (Isaac, Jacob, Joseph, and their families) that come from the unlikely source of the elderly, childless couple called out by God in chapter 12. The tales of these ancestors continue the plot line introduced with Abraham and Sarah, as each new generation struggles to live out their identity as God's called people and to see the divine promises of descendants, blessing, and, especially, land fulfilled in tangible and complete ways. Moreover, the same tension between fear and trust, life-taking and life-giving that we saw in Abraham and Sarah's journey appears here as well. The biblical writers recount the tales of Isaac finding his wife Rebekah among his mother's extended family back in Aram. They tell of Jacob deceiving his older brother Esau in order to take the inheritance birthright, marrying Leah and Rachel, and then seeing the birth of twelve sons (who will give their names to the twelve tribes of Israel as the generations unfold; Gen 29:31–30:24). They describe Joseph being sold into slavery in Egypt, rising to unexpected power, and finally relocating his elderly father Jacob and eleven brothers (with their families) there as well.

In and through these tales appear key moments—usually at the transitional point when the ancestor of the next generation first journeys out on his own—in which YHWH reaffirms and passes on the identity-marking promises he has given to this chosen, covenant people. As Isaac flees a famine to settle in Gerar (26:3-5), as Jacob sleeps at Bethel and dreams of a staircase between heaven and earth (28:13-16), and even as Joseph lies on his deathbed in Egypt (50:24-25), the text sounds YHWH's commitment to keep his word and bless them with a line of descendants and a land in which to live. We repeatedly hear words like these spoken to Jacob, "I am the LORD, the God of your father Abraham and the God of Isaac. I will give you and your descendants the land on which you are lying. Your descendants will become like the dust of the earth" (28:13-14). And we see more and more fulfillment of the promises, as the stories provide long lists of growing generations of Jacob's (Israel's) sons, who dwell for a while in the promised land of Canaan before moving to Egypt (e.g., 46:8-27), and even references to Israelites "blessing" other peoples such as the Egyptians (e.g., 39:5; 47:10). In these reaffirmation moments, YHWH not only passes on the promises he has made but also extends the calling for this particular people to be instruments of blessing to all peoples. At the transitional moments when YHWH meets Isaac and Jacob and grants to them his same commitment to deliver the blessings of descendants and land, he also places his ongoing call upon them: "Every family of earth will be blessed because of you and your descendants" (28:14; see also 26:4). Across the generations of its founding ancestors, Israel remains a people called to participate in YHWH's mission to restore creation to the life-giving right-relationships with which it began.

Perhaps surprisingly, when we reach the end of these founding generations at the close of Genesis, YHWH's missional calling of the Israelites to be the instrument of restoration blessing seems a long way from coming to fruition. Notice the last two words of the book of Genesis in 50:26—"in Egypt" (CEB). Joseph dies and is buried in Egypt, and all of Abraham's descendants remain living there, outside of the promised land of Canaan. Abraham, Isaac, Jacob, Joseph, and their families lived through journeys filled with doubts, frustrations, wrestling, weeping, hope, and faith, but YHWH seemingly has more in store for this called people. Experiences await that will create them into something new.

The Creation of God's People (Exodus 1–15)

Up to this point in the OT story, God has introduced the divine mission to restore creation back to the right-relationships with which it began by becoming a covenant partner with all living beings. As the specific form of that covenant engagement, God has *called* a people (the manifold descendants of Abraham and Sarah) to be in a promise-filled relationship with him and to be the instrument of life-giving blessing as part of the divine mission. *In the stories, language, and symbols of the next major section of scripture's narrative (Exod 1–15), God now takes this called group of descendants and creates them as a distinctive people—a national community—who will soon be given a special character and task to define how they are to be the instrument within God's mission to restore creation.* As we'll see, two particular things will mark this newly created community that will emerge on the other side of the exodus from Egypt: (1) this community will include a diverse group of different races and ethnic backgrounds now joined together with Abraham's descendants (Exod 12:38), and (2) this people will have YHWH as their fundamental, life-defining reality because he delivered and provided for them in a decisive way (Exod 14:30-31).

Enslaved People and the God of Freedom

The story of the creation of God's people begins with an account of deliverance in the biblical narratives of Moses and the Israelites' exodus (departure, escape) from slavery in Egypt. These narratives have attracted much attention in popular American culture over the years. Creative depictions appear in funny cartoons (Moses portrayed as a lifeguard who annoyingly parts the swimming pool's water), animated movies filled with inspirational music (*The Prince of Egypt* from DreamWorks Pictures, 1999), epic Hollywood action blockbusters (*Exodus: Gods and Kings* from 20th Century Fox, 2014), and more. Contemporary audiences resonate with some of the iconic images from this section of scripture's story: baby Moses floating in a basket on the Nile, the voice of God speaking out of a burning bush in the desert, and piled-up walls of water at the sea. Yet, the context for these stirring narratives and their images is the ongoing journey of Abraham and Sarah's descendants, who had settled in Egypt at the end of Genesis.

When the book of Exodus begins, this called group of descendants remains in Egypt, outside the land that YHWH had promised them. But their situation has changed dramatically. In Exodus 1, Jacob's immediate descendants, who had gone down to Egypt being about seventy in number (v. 5) have now grown to fill the land (v. 7). And when a new king comes to power in Egypt (v. 8), the Egyptians begin to see the Israelites as a threat. The remainder of the opening chapter of Exodus describes the tragic and horrifying measures the Egyptians then take to try to reduce the number of Israelites—making them forced-labor slaves, ordering the midwives to kill male babies at birth, and finally summarily executing all boys by drowning in the Nile. In short, the people once called to be instruments of life-giving blessing now find themselves enslaved in a life-denying, death-dealing circumstance that threatens to bring an end to both their existence and YHWH's calling to use them as his instrument.

From this beginning, then, the next fourteen chapters recount the story of Moses, who begins as an endangered baby, escapes death to be raised in Pharaoh's court, flees as a fugitive to the desert of Midian, receives a call from YHWH for him and his brother, Aaron, to return to Egypt, and then attempts to bring about YHWH's will and lead the Israelites out of slavery toward their own formation as a community living in the promised land of Canaan. These stories are full of literary and historical features that illuminate different dimensions of their meaning.[13] For my purposes, however, within the stories of God's call of Moses in the desert (chs. 3–4) and the ten plagues on Egypt (chs. 7–12) that lead up to the decisive and defining moment at the crossing of the sea (chs. 13–14), there are several elements that bring forth the OT's plot line of God's mission to restore creation and to use Israel as the instrument in that mission.

The first moment in which the OT's divine plot shines through actually occurs even before YHWH calls Moses from the desert to return to Egypt and set the Israelites free. In what seems like a passing comment, just when Moses has settled into a new life far away from the death-dealing circumstances of the Israelite slaves in Egypt, the biblical storyteller relates the turning point that sets YHWH's call of Moses into action:

> A long time passed, and the Egyptian king died. The Israelites were still groaning because of their hard work. They cried out, and their cry to be rescued from the hard work rose up to God. God heard their cry of grief, and God remembered his covenant with Abraham, Isaac, and Jacob. God looked at the Israelites, and God understood. (2:23-25)

After years of oppression, violence, murder, and despair, this ground-shifting moment brings us back to the commitment and promises of the covenant God who has called Abraham's descendants and now reinvigorates the larger mission and their part in it. At the end of the reign of another oppressive pharaoh, the enslaved Israelites raised their voices in a "cry" (Heb. *zāʿaq*—a cry not just of grief, but of protest). Perhaps surprisingly, their cry wasn't even explicitly directed to God. They didn't cry out "to God"; they just cried out. It's as if the weight of their oppression was so great that they couldn't even think to pray; all they could manage was just to *zāʿaq*. Yet, the text says, God heard it. God recognized that the covenant people he had called were crying out. The language might seem strange to us, as God "remembered" his covenant; but it's also striking, as God looked again upon the Israelites and "understood" (Heb. *yādaʿ*, "knew, comprehended, acknowledged" the situation). And as the story moves forward, we realize that this cry motivated God to act. Immediately after this moment, chapters 3–4 recount God's calling of Moses to return to Egypt, free the Israelites, and push the mission of the divinely called people forward. Here is another remarkable portrait of the nature of this covenant God—a life-giving Creator who can be moved to action by the cries of human suffering, even cries not explicitly directed to him.

When we place this transitional moment into the ongoing plot of the larger OT story, the Israelites' deliverance from Egypt comes into a new focus. The people called to become a great nation with a special land and to serve as the instrument of blessing to others (Gen 12:1-3) find themselves in a bondage that prevents any such things. But the missional God remains committed to the covenant relationship into which he has called the people (Exod 2:23-25). So, in response to their cries of despair, YHWH takes action. Across chapters 3–4, YHWH appears to Moses in a burning bush and calls him (four times!) to return to Egypt to lead the Israelites to freedom. True to the nature of this covenant God who works in dynamic relationship with human partners, YHWH patiently responds to Moses's (several!) objections, even giving Moses a deeper and more intimate insight into the divine character by explaining God's special name ("I Am Who I Am," 3:14) and allowing Aaron to work with Moses on his task (4:10-16).

God's Special Name

God's personal name given to Moses in Exodus 3:13-15 ("I Am Who I Am") is based on the Hebrew verb meaning "to be." It could also be translated, "I Will Be Who I Will Be." The name YHWH (usually translated as "Lᴏʀᴅ" in English versions) is the third-person form ("He Is/Will Be"). The name both reveals and conceals God. It promises that the divine presence will be with Moses and God's people ("I Will Be"), but it maintains that God will be present in the ways that God alone chooses ("Who I Will Be").

Within the call of Moses, the plot line of the divine character and mission especially shines through in YHWH's opening words to Moses from the burning bush. In 3:7-10, YHWH emphatically states that he is fully aware of Israel's suffering in every way—seeing, hearing, knowing intimately—and is also taking action (coming down to deliver). In Hebrew, YHWH's words are thick with first-person repetition and emphasis (*"I've* clearly seen... *I've* heard... *I* know... *I've* come down"). This opening divine declaration reiterates that for the larger OT story, the redemptive mission belongs to God's initiative and consists of God's actions. Yet, in just the way we've come to expect concerning how this covenant God works in the world, YHWH's opening declaration makes clear that the divine redemptive action will occur through human agents. YHWH has fully known and come to rescue, but he commands Moses, "So get going. I'm sending *you* to Pharaoh" (3:10).

YHWH's first responses to Moses's objection that follows this opening declaration point to the larger plot unfolding in God's mission in another way. YHWH states that Moses will lead the Israelites out of Egypt and bring them back to the holy mountain on which he now stands (3:12). Verse 1 calls this mountain "Horeb," but other traditions in the OT use the name "Sinai."[14] The point of YHWH's deliverance is not simply to set the people free from Egypt. It is to bring them as a community to the holy mountain where they will receive instructions on how they are to live as the people called to participate in the divine mission to restore creation (see Exod 19). The larger mission is in view even before the people are freed from Egypt.

When Moses and Aaron return to Egypt, the story moves into the depiction of a series of ten plagues that YHWH sends against the land (Exod 7–12). Interpreters often note that the primary message of these stories is to demonstrate the divine power of YHWH as the true sovereign and expose the false claims to sovereignty and divinity by the pharaoh and the gods of Egypt. Seen in this way, the plague narratives portray a contest between YHWH and Pharaoh, but with Pharaoh being thought of in terms of what he represented in ancient Egypt—not merely a human ruler, but one who was considered semi-divine while alive and fully divine after death, and one who symbolized the entire collection of the Egyptian gods.[15] Thus, we are asked to imagine a deity versus deity (not God versus human ruler) showdown—the way that someone living in ancient Egypt might have imagined.

The Hardening of Pharaoh's Heart

Readers have sometimes been troubled by the references throughout the plague stories that YHWH "hardens Pharaoh's heart" ("makes him stubborn," CEB; e.g., 4:21; 7:3; 9:12; 10:1, 20, 27; 11:10; 14:8, 17). These references make it seem like Pharaoh is the object of a sinister game. Even some early Christians saw these references as divine arbitrary control of a particular person (Rom 9:14-18). But sometimes Pharaoh hardens his own heart (7:22; 8:15, 19, 32; 9:7) and the plague stories in Exodus 7–12 seem to imagine the pharaoh as a deity (the way he would've been viewed by the ancient audience) in a contest between two gods. When Pharaoh is seen in this way, YHWH's ability to harden his heart is meant to show which deity is truly God—that is, the one who can control the actions of the other "god" is truly God. The texts are likely not meant to say anything about how YHWH treats individual human persons.

The contest is over who has true divine power and what the character of that sovereign deity is. Is the true sovereign the God of the systems and structures that enslave people or the God who sees, hears, knows, and rescues the oppressed? The plagues that fall upon various areas of life—the elements of nature, health of the body, and even life and death—constitute an unmasking of Pharaoh's supposed sovereignty. And some of them seem to demonstrate YHWH's control over specific aspects of nature that were associated with particular gods in Egypt (e.g., the Nile [7:14-24] and sun [10:21-23]; see also 12:12).[16]

Within these dramatic, tension-filled encounters between Moses and Pharaoh, the larger OT plot line of Israel as the instrument of God's mission within all creation shines through. On several occasions, YHWH announces that the purpose of all that's happening in the plagues and on behalf of Israel is that Pharaoh and all the Egyptians "will come to know [*yāda'*] that I am the LORD" (7:5, 17; 8:22; 9:14; 14:4, 18).[17] In these contexts, "to know" likely means not simply to "become aware" but to willingly "acknowledge" (see 5:2). And at one point, YHWH also declares that his purpose in these actions is even wider than Egypt, as he aims to make his name "known [acknowledged] in the whole world" (9:16). These words draw the specific events unfolding with Israel in Egypt back into God's larger plot line. The ultimate goal of God's mission—and therefore of God's efforts to liberate the people called to be his instruments—is that all creation will come to know/acknowledge him. Previously, YHWH's actions with and for Israel were portrayed as means to send forth his life-giving blessing. Now, those actions are portrayed as a kind of ancient learning platform for all people designed to make accessible the knowledge of who YHWH is and what YHWH is doing in the world.

Deliverance and Creation at the Sea

At the conclusion of the ten plagues, Pharaoh allowed the Israelites to leave, but immediately changed his mind and pursued them. And this led to the climactic moment of the story of God's people thus far—the miraculous, sea-crossing escape in Exodus 13–14. Trapped between a body of water and the approaching Egyptian army, the Israelites watched as YHWH miraculously parted the sea. They crossed on dry ground, and the waters returned to sweep away Pharaoh and his chariots and soldiers.

There's no doubt that this exodus narrative is one of the most dramatic deliverance stories in scripture. The delivering God ended the plot line of captivity, which had forced this promised people to play the roles of pyramid builders for oppressive kings and temple builders for foreign gods, even to the point of seemingly losing sight of the larger covenant and calling of which they were a part (see the discussion of Exod 2:23-25 above). Overcoming the death-dealing power of chariotry, cavalry, and empire, YHWH reopened a future of hopeful possibilities. He set the divinely called-out people free to resume their faith-filled journey toward the fulfillment of the promises that they will be a nation of blessing-bringers in a land of their own. The impact of these life-giving acts called forth a very fitting song of praise from Miriam, as she and the other women stepped out of the sea and danced to the rhythm of tambourines, singing, "Sing to the LORD for an overflowing victory! Horse and rider he threw into the sea" (15:21).

For the OT storytellers, the divine intervention to free the Israelites is the decisive demonstration that YHWH is the true God and the definitive display of that God's character. The covenant God, who is determined to restore creation, is one who fully comprehends the suffering of the oppressed and uses his divine power to save and liberate. Seen in this way, the exodus story is not simply about Israel; it's the broader paradigm (model) of how God seeks to work redemptively in the world. The life-giving Creator works on behalf of the oppressed to set them free in tangible ways—political, social, economic, and more. All across the remainder of the OT, biblical storytellers, poets, lawmakers, and prophets repeatedly refer back to the exodus story as the pivotal revelation of God's character that undergirds the divine call on the people and that provides the model for how they should live as God's people in the world (especially in the laws that YHWH gives to form the people and guide their patterns of life in the next section of the story). Even more, YHWH's liberating actions for the oppressed in the exodus provide a definition for the "blessing" that Abraham's descendants are called to bring upon all the families of the earth. As defined by the God of the exodus, to *bless* is to bring about freedom from bondage and oppression, especially for those who are poor, weak, and vulnerable. If the exodus is the model, then the mission in which Israel is called to participate is an "*exodus-shaped*" mission of redemption that seeks to bring life and not death to all creation.[18]

There is an additional way that we might understand the meaning of what is portrayed in this pivotal story and how it relates to God's calling of Israel to be an instrument in the divine mission of restoration. On the surface, the exodus narrative is a deliverance story. But on the symbolic level, it's a creation story. While describing the Israelites' journey from Egypt to the water, Exodus 13:18 identifies a specific location, the "Reed Sea" (*yam sûp*).[19] When the biblical storytellers offer their recounting of YHWH's dramatic parting of the water in chapter 14, however, they repeatedly label the object of YHWH's miraculous action simply as the "sea" (*yam*, see especially vv. 21-23, 26-29). There is a clear emphasis on YHWH's power not just over Pharaoh and the death-dealing Egyptian oppressors but over the sea itself, which is split in two by YHWH's "wind" (*rûaḥ*, "breath," v. 21). As I mentioned in reference to Genesis 1, in the cultural world of ancient Israel and their neighbors throughout the ancient Near East, the overcoming and ordering of chaotic waters was a common symbol for a deity's work of creation. The sea was the symbol of the forces of chaos that prevent creation and deny life and to defeat and divide that sea was to bring life into being. Some surviving Canaanite texts about the god Baal actually portray the chaotic sea as another god ("Yam") that Baal defeats in combat in order to bring about life and fertility, dividing the sea and drying it up. Likewise, the Babylonian creation story, *Enuma Elish* (see ch. 3 in this book), features the god Marduk's defeat of the sea monster Tiamat as the initial act of creation. We've seen some of this imagery in Genesis 1, with God's separating of the waters. But various hymns of praise in the Psalms explicitly use the imagery of YHWH splitting the sea and shattering the heads of sea monsters in his role as creator (see Ps 74:12-15). In the symbolic language of Israel and its neighbors, when a god divided waters, a new creation emerged—a dry land, a new space for life.

This long-standing tradition gives a new perspective on the exodus story. Through the narrative's language and symbols, the biblical writers cast God's deliverance at the sea as another act of divine creation that overcame chaos and brought forth life—the creation of a new people. One more time, just as at the beginning of scripture's story, God separates the waters and creates a new reality. But this time what God creates is not the heavens and the earth, but a newly constituted people who will soon receive a renewed call to covenant relationship and to a special status and task. In other words, the biblical storytellers proclaim that what really happened at the sea that day wasn't just deliverance; it was a creation. YHWH created the particular community that would go forward toward the promised land and the full experience of YHWH's calling and promises. And why was it necessary for YHWH to *create* the people he had already *called*? Couldn't we imagine Israel's creation as a national community taking place earlier in Genesis when Jacob gave birth to twelve sons who then developed into twelve tribes before coming to Egypt (Gen 29–35)? Remember, however, that from that time until this point in the OT story, these Israelites had been a loose and sometimes scattered group of descendants. Moreover, Exodus 12:38 reveals that it wasn't just Israelites who left Egypt with Moses and Aaron. It was a "diverse crowd" of freed slaves—a mixture of different races and ethnicities—now joined together with Abraham's descendants and following the lead of Israel's God. At the sea, the storytellers say, YHWH took this mixed multitude and created a new people, grafting all of them together into a national community.[20]

Some of the words that appear in the texts following the deliverance at the sea make clear that something new has come into being for the people that had previously been called to be the instrument of blessing to the world. Whether they were originally part of Abraham's line or some of the diverse crowd of others, they now stand together as a new community. And the narrator concludes the exodus story by indicating that the members of this newly created people have attached themselves to YHWH in a profound way. As they looked back on the closed-up sea and their now-perished oppressors, the "people were in awe of the Lord, and they believed in the Lord and his servant Moses" (14:31). Likewise, the poetic hymn of praise that follows in Exodus 15 affirms a newfound, *personal* attachment to YHWH, as Moses and the Israelites now proclaim, "This is *my* God, whom *I* will praise, the God of my ancestors, whom *I* will acclaim" (15:2). Through the events at the sea, a new community has emerged for whom YHWH is more than just the God of their ancestors; he is their God, too.

From the opening of the book of Exodus through the hymnic celebration of the crossing of the sea, God has taken the group of Abraham's descendants that he had called (along with others who've been drawn into the work of this liberating Life-Giver) and created them as a distinctive people—a national community. YHWH is this people's fundamental, life-defining reality ("my

God") because he has delivered them in a decisive way. And when they leave Egypt, they move into the next stage of their journey. YHWH will lead this people that he has called and created into the wilderness in order to teach them how they should live and form them into a community with a special character that can serve as a particular kind of instrument within the divine mission to restore creation.

Chapter 5

The Formation of God's People

(Exodus 16–Deuteronomy)

Focus Texts: Exodus 19:1-6; 20:1-17; 34:6-7; Leviticus 19;
Numbers 13–14; Deuteronomy 6:4-5

Location in the Old Testament Story:

1) The Introduction of God's Mission in the World (Genesis 1–11)
2) The Calling of God's People (Genesis 12–50)
3) The Creation of God's People (Exodus 1–15)
4) The Formation of God's People (Exodus 16–Deuteronomy)
5) The Life of God's People (Joshua–Esther)
   a) The Voices of Israel's Poets and Sages before, during, and after
      Exile (Job–Song of Songs)
   b) The Voices of Israel's Prophets before, during, and after Exile
      (Isaiah–Malachi)

The Formation of God's People in the Larger Old Testament Story

"Follow the yellow brick road." In L. Frank Baum's novel *The Wonderful Wizard of Oz* (later made famous by the 1939 film adaptation, *The Wizard of Oz*), these words provide the directions given to Dorothy for how to find the

Emerald City and the Wizard who can help her (and her little dog) get home to Kansas. As one who grew up seeing versions of this novel in movies, plays, and musicals, I remember that these words mark the beginning of a journey that Dorothy takes with various companions she meets along the way. I also remember that the story itself is really more about the journey than the destination. The road is filled with trials, hardships, and obstacles. *The Wizard of Oz* portrays the most dangerous parts of the path as a wilderness—a haunted forest complete with animated trees and evil flying monkeys. But perhaps the biggest thing I recall about this story is that it was this journey—with all of its danger and distress—that made Dorothy and her friends into who they really needed to be. Through this journey, the Scarecrow, Tin Man, and Cowardly Lion all became the very things they thought they weren't (smart, compassionate, and courageous), and Dorothy realized the true value of the life she had at home.

For those who grew up reading and watching the journey of Dorothy and her friends, the biblical storyteller's first line after the Israelites' victorious exodus from Egypt may bring the adventures in Oz rushing back to mind: "Then Moses had Israel leave the Reed Sea and go out into the Shur desert" (Exod 15:22). After crossing the sea to escape Egypt, this band of freed slaves doesn't proceed immediately into the land of Canaan that YHWH promised to Abraham as a home for his descendants. Rather, Moses leads them into the desert (or "wilderness," see NRSV) through which they will travel for the foreseeable future and beyond—a journey that will take up the remainder of the books of Exodus, Leviticus, Numbers, and Deuteronomy. But how does this fit into the larger OT story that has unfolded to this point?

As we saw in the last chapter, the deliverance at the sea made clear that something new had come into being for the people who began as the descendants of Abraham and Sarah. Up to this point in the overall story, we've seen that God's good creation of right-relationships has become distorted because of humanity's mistrust, fear, and self-sovereignty. We've also seen the introduction of the divine mission to restore creation back to the intended, life-giving right-relationships, as God committed to become a covenant partner with all living beings (Gen 9) in a way that will turn out to be redemptive for them. As the specific form of that covenant engagement, God *called* a people (the descendants of Abraham and Sarah) to be in a promise-filled relationship with him and to be the instrument of life-giving blessing to the world. Then, on the banks of the sea, God took that group of descendants that he had called (along with others who'd been drawn into the work of this liberating Life-Giver) and *created* them as a distinctive people—a national community (see discussion of the exodus in ch. 4).

Now, God's people move into the next stage of their journey. Throughout the rest of the Pentateuch, *God will lead this people that he has called and created into the wilderness in order to teach them how they should live and form them into a community with a special character that can serve as a particular kind of instrument within the divine mission to restore creation.*

The Wilderness Journey as the Way of Formation

Seen in this way, the wilderness section of the OT story that spans Exodus 16 through Deuteronomy and recounts the people's journey from Egypt to Sinai to the edge of the promised land possesses a special significance within scripture's narrative. Unfortunately, contemporary Christian readers often ignore or even disparage large parts of this section, not least because so much of these books consists of law codes and other behavioral instructions that seem so foreign today. These codes talk repeatedly and sometimes confusingly about animal sacrifices, food regulations, skin diseases, worship buildings and their decorations, and proper crop tending. But putting the wilderness journey and its laws into the context of the overall story of God's mission and Israel's calling to be the instrument of that mission invites us to see this section from a different perspective. Israel's time in the wilderness is for them what we might call a *liminal* period. This term refers to a period when a person (or group) is between two life stages—a transitional period between significant boundary crossings and destination points. It's the between-time, the meantime—the time when one is betwixt and between point A and point B.

Liminality

The notion of a *liminal* (or transitional) period comes from the anthropological category of *liminality*, which refers to the uncertainty or disorientation that occurs in the middle phase of a ritual or practice. In this phase, a person or group no longer possesses their former status but does not yet have a fully new status.

And these liminal periods are often marked by hardship and trial. Yet, these are also the times when a person's (or group's) identity gets forged, as people discover who they are and mature into adulthood. Even today, some non-industrial cultures know this experience as the time when a young child reaches a certain age, is sent into the jungle to survive on her or his own for a period of days, and returns to be acknowledged as an adult. In American culture, some people describe the experience of college in this way, as a student crosses a graduation platform at the end of high school and, typically, four years later crosses another graduation platform to mark her or his entrance into the professional world.

Jesus in the Wilderness

It's possible to think of the account of Jesus's temptation in the wilderness (Matt 4:1-11) as a liminal period. At the start of his ministry, Jesus endures forty days of trial in the wilderness and when he returns, he begins his ministry in earnest and with power.

In the story of the people of Israel, the wilderness journey between Egypt and the promised land functions in just this way. On the way out of Egypt, the Israelites crossed a body of water to enter the wilderness. Later in the OT story, near the beginning of the book of Joshua, they will cross another body of water (the Jordan River) to exit the wilderness and enter Canaan. Now, however, they are betwixt and between. YHWH leads them into the wilderness—a time of hardship and trial—in order to forge their identity (that is, their understanding of who they are and how they should live) as those called and created to participate in the divine mission to restore creation. As the canonical story will show, YHWH didn't intend for this formation journey to last forty years; that duration was the result of the people's disobedience. Even so, the story indicates that YHWH intended to bring the people into the wilderness (for a positive experience) for about a year. It's no wonder, then, that this section of the OT story contains law codes and behavioral instructions. As we'll see, these are YHWH's attempt to reveal to Israel more fully and specifically the content of the three major identity questions we've found to be at the heart of scripture's narrative: Who is God? Who are God's people? And how, then, should God's people live in the world in light of who God is and who God's people are supposed to be?

Into the Wilderness on the Way to Sinai

The wilderness section of the OT story contains three main kinds of material. First, there is an ongoing narrative plot line—the story of the Israelites as they travel from Egypt, through the wilderness, and to the land of Moab just across the Jordan River from the promised land. Second, along the way, some texts recount defining moments, both good and bad. Perhaps the most significant of these moments occurs as the people camp at Mount Sinai (Exod 19:1–Num 10:10), the holy mountain where Israel most clearly learns the nature of their God and their calling. Third, especially in the context of the people's stay at Sinai, texts from this section of the story describe the law (better, "instruction;" Heb. *tôrāh*) that God gives to govern how the people live.

But the coverage of the different parts of this wilderness section is very uneven. Most noticeably, Exodus, Leviticus, and Numbers devote over fifty chapters to the events of a single year of the journey—the people's stay at Mount Sinai. The overall structure of this wilderness section of the OT story features a large Sinai-block of material at the center:

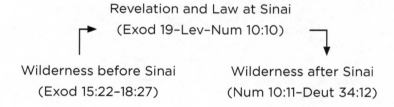

Revelation and Law at Sinai
(Exod 19–Lev–Num 10:10)

Wilderness before Sinai   Wilderness after Sinai
(Exod 15:22–18:27)   (Num 10:11–Deut 34:12)

This overall structure, with its obvious focus on Sinai and what happens there, highlights once again that this section of Israel's story is about formation. The preservers and compilers of scripture's story placed a clear emphasis on the instruction (*tôrāh*) that these texts give to God's people—past and present—about identity, as the events and laws at Sinai provide crucial revelation about who God is that should form who God's people are and how they ought to live in the world.

The wilderness section of the OT story begins with the first few episodes of the people's journey out of Egypt and toward Mount Sinai (Exod 15:22–18:27). Right away, it becomes clear that this newly created community of freed slaves will wrestle with the same tension that has appeared throughout the story of the covenant God and his covenant people. Just like the human community in general, which was created to be divine image-bearers, the Israelite community on the wilderness road immediately wrestles with mistrust, doubt, fear, and rebellion. Here and throughout the rest of this wilderness time, the people often lose heart in fear or turn to self-provision in rebellion. From the outset, it's clear that the wilderness experience will be both a positive and negative time for the Israelites and their relationship with YHWH. It'll be a time of YHWH's provision and protection, but also a time of the people's complaining and rebellion.

The Wilderness Tradition

Israel's wilderness journey from Egypt to the promised land (told in the books of Exodus to Deuteronomy) became a prominent tradition in ancient Israel and appears in later books in the OT, especially the prophets. In keeping with the mixed portrayal of the experience in the Pentateuch, these later texts refer back to the wilderness time in different ways. Jeremiah, for example, describes the wilderness as a positive time—a kind of honeymoon when Israel was devoted to YHWH like a "young bride" (Jer 2:1-3). But Ezekiel remembers the wilderness as a time of rebellion, when Israel already rejected YHWH's life-giving instructions (Ezek 20:10-17).

This reality becomes evident right away, as the newly created community faces an immediate series of crises in the barren wilderness (Exod 15:22-27; 16:1-35; 17:1-17). The people awake their first morning of freedom to the realities of hunger and thirst and the fear of survival. And once more YHWH responds. Divine provision shines through in each crisis, and the God who calls, delivers, and creates becomes the God who provides on the journey. YHWH miraculously makes undrinkable water drinkable and brings low-flying quail for the people to have meat. The hungry Israelites also see thin flakes of something glistening in the morning dew and ask, *"Manna?"* (literally, "What is it?"). Finding it to taste like "honey wafers" (16:31), they come to understand that this is the bread that YHWH will give them to eat throughout their journey. And soon their worrisome thirst is quenched again by water miraculously flowing from a rock. YHWH's initial provisions for the people culminate with special divine protection against an attack by the Amalekites (17:8-15).

However, laced throughout these initial episodes of YHWH's provision and protection are the people's complaints and rebellion. In nearly every episode, they raise their voices in fear, mistrust, and despair and put the future of their life as YHWH's special people at risk: "Oh how we wish that the LORD had just put us to death while we were still in the land of Egypt. There we could sit by the pots cooking meat and eat our fill of bread" (16:3); "Why did you bring us out of Egypt to kill us, our children, and our livestock with thirst?" (17:3). Even in the face of YHWH's promise that enough bread would be provided each day so that no one needed to take extra and keep it overnight, some feared the scarcity of provisions, untrustingly horded supplies, and then watched as the horded heavenly bread became worm-infested by morning (16:16-21). The people's fear-driven struggle to trust YHWH seems to culminate in Exodus 18, when their complaints and quarrels become so numerous that Moses has to set up a judiciary to hear them all.

A New Dimension of the People's Identity (Exodus 19:1-6)

Out of the see-saw struggle between divine provision and protection and human complaint and rebellion, the Israelites arrive at Mount Sinai in Exodus 19. Here they will remain for the rest of Exodus, Leviticus, and the first ten chapters of Numbers. And here, YHWH will once more make a covenant (this time through Moses) with the Israelites, describing his gracious deeds toward them in the past and calling them to particular actions in response.[1] The details of the response for which YHWH asks will appear in the various laws across the remaining chapters of Exodus, Leviticus, and Numbers. Before giving these identity-shaping laws, however, YHWH's first words to Moses at Sinai (19:1-6) constitute one of the defining moments along the wilderness journey, perhaps even the moment that allows us to understand the significance of all the covenant instructions that follow. And these words add further definition and a new dimension to the people's identity.

The story thus far has said that the Israelites have been specially called and created to be the instrument of the divine mission to restore creation. But how, specifically, do they participate in YHWH's redemptive mission and what does their calling and identity have to do with the rest of the world, especially those who are not part of this unique covenant community? The call of Abraham and Sarah in Genesis 12:1-3 shed some initial light on these questions, as YHWH called this people to be the instrument of blessing for all the families of the earth. Now, at this pivotal moment in the larger story, the writers and preservers of the tradition in Exodus 19, who probably came from circles of priests within ancient Israel, expand the answers to these questions with priestly language and imagery.[2] They recount what YHWH instructed Moses to tell the people:

> You saw what I did to the Egyptians, and how I lifted you up on eagles' wings and brought you to me. So now, if you faithfully obey me and stay true to my covenant, you will be my *most precious possession* out of all the peoples, since the whole earth belongs to me. You will be a *kingdom of priests* for me and a *holy nation*. (vv. 4-6)

Here, YHWH reveals his desire to take this people that he has called and created and form them into a community with a special character that can serve as a particular kind of instrument within the divine mission to restore creation. First, it's important to note that everything YHWH asks of the people is here identified in advance as only a response to what YHWH has already graciously done for them in divine deliverance and provision ("You saw what I did. . . . So now, if you faithfully obey" [vv. 4-5]). From that perspective, the specific terms within Exodus 19:1-6 express the special character and particular kind of instrument that YHWH envisions for the covenant people. The passage first describes their character and role as a "most precious possession" (Heb. *sagullāh*). The imagery here is that of a treasured part of a larger whole specifically chosen to fulfill a unique task. It is not a statement that YHWH has favored one people group to the devaluing or exclusion of all others but that precisely because all peoples belong to him ("since the whole earth belongs to me" [v. 5]), YHWH has given one particular portion a special charge to carry out within and for the sake of the whole.[3]

The passage's other two descriptions of Israel make this idea explicit: "kingdom of priests" and a "holy nation." YHWH defines Israel's calling to be a holy community that fulfills a priest-like role for all the peoples of the world. At the most basic level, priests in ancient Israel's world were "go-betweens"—messengers or intermediaries between YHWH and people. They stood in the middle and represented YHWH to the people and the people to YHWH. Timothy Green notes that in keeping with this role, priests had three specific tasks.[4] First, they were required to maintain a higher standard of holiness that allowed them to help others live holy lives by offering sacrifices on behalf of the community, overseeing worship, and distinguishing between what was pure and impure among the people. Second, they had the responsibility of providing the community with the instructions given by YHWH. Third, and perhaps most importantly in the context of the OT story, priests had the task of pronouncing blessing upon the people—to be means of bringing life, flourishing, and hope to people, places, and circumstances.

Priestly Blessing

One of the most well-known examples of priestly blessings upon the people appears in Numbers 6:24-26: "The LORD bless you and protect you. The LORD make his face shine on you and be gracious to you. The LORD lift up his face to you and grant you peace." The words of this blessing appear in a Hebrew inscription on silver amulets found in Jerusalem that date from the seventh century BCE.

So here, at the beginning of the formative period for the people, YHWH establishes a unique covenant with them and declares the special character into which he seeks to shape them: the covenant people are to have a priestly identity and role with regard to all creation. Just like the Israelite priests were a special portion of Israel, called to a higher standard of holiness and charged to be instruments of YHWH's life-giving ways and blessing to the covenant community, so now YHWH calls Israel as a whole people to practice that holiness and perform that priestly, go-between role to all the world.[5] Throughout the remainder of the stay at Sinai that is described from Exodus 19 through Numbers 10:10, YHWH will provide the laws, rituals, and practices that serve to shape the people into this new identity and equip them for this priestly role. But YHWH's fresh articulation of Israel's character and function in Exodus 19 keeps the bigger divine mission in view. The identity and role of this called and created people is articulated in light of YHWH's unwavering commitment that "the whole earth belongs to me" (v. 5). As Christopher Wright explains, YHWH's formation of Israel that begins at Sinai and extends through the wilderness journey unfolds as a part of the "wider mission of blessing the rest of the nations" and represents a "fresh articulation of the original seminal covenant that God made with Abraham," explaining what it will mean for them "to live within the framework of the Abrahamic covenant as a national community."[6] Readers of the larger OT story might also note that the fresh articulation in Exodus 19 connects not only to the calling of Abraham and Sarah's descendants to be an instrument of blessing but also to YHWH's original covenant with all flesh in Genesis 9 and the divine commitment to restore creation to the right-relationships of life-giving blessing with which it began.

Law and Formation at Sinai

Following the new articulation of Israel's priestly character and function in Exodus 19:1-6, the remainder of Exodus, Leviticus, and the first ten chapters of Numbers are devoted to the laws, rituals, and practices that YHWH gives at Mount Sinai to govern how the covenant people should live out this identity within their own community and in relationship to the rest of the world. The Sinai block of material (Exod 19:1–Num 10:10) describes nearly a full year of instructions at Sinai.[7] In their current form, the texts present most of those instructions as words delivered to Moses as the primary lawgiver for the people, and they appear as several now-identifiable law collections, although the biblical books, as well as the laws codes and other materials within them, may have originated independently in different times and places in ancient Israel.

The Old Testament Laws

Although people often casually refer to the OT "law" as a singular entity, at least six different law codes appear within the Pentateuch. The precise textual boundaries of the codes aren't always clear, but the canonical story locates all but one (Deut 12–26) as part of the divine revelation at Sinai:

The Ten Commandments (Decalogue) (Exod 20:1-17; cf. Deut 5:6-21)
The Book of the Covenant (Covenant Code) (Exod 20:22–23:19)
The Ritual Decalogue (Exod 34:10-28)
The Priestly Code (Lev 1–16; Num 1:1–10:10)
The Holiness Code (Lev 17–26)
The Deuteronomic Code (Deut 12–26)

On the surface, the purpose of these laws was to govern different areas of ancient Israel's life in its cultural context (e.g., worship, rituals, festivals, personal injury, sexual relationships, animal and property ownership, slaveholding, economic fairness toward workers, care for the poor). But within the larger context of the overall OT story, the purpose of these laws is to form the covenant people's identity. Practicing these laws will be the means by which YHWH is going to form Israel into the special character and function that he has called and created them to embody. The instructions and practices move Israel to a fuller understanding and embodiment of who YHWH is, who they are, and how they are called to live in the world, especially as an instrument of blessing, holy nation, and priestly kingdom within YHWH's mission to restore creation. This larger purpose of formation for the laws shines through in various moments, as some texts explicitly state that the motivation for obedience to the laws is that Israel can then be a witness and example of YHWH and his ways to the surrounding nations (see Deut 4:6-8; 28:9-10).[8]

So how might those of us who are paying attention to scripture's larger narrative read the laws in this formational way? Initially, there are some obstacles to overcome. As I mentioned previously, in spite of the significance (and size!) of this Sinai section of the OT story, contemporary Christian readers in particular have often struggled to see its importance within scripture as a whole. Not only is there a somewhat understandable lack of interest in reading ancient law codes about sacrifices, farming, sexual relationships, and proper building techniques, but there is an undeniable strangeness for today's readers to both what is said in some of these texts and how, raising the vexing questions of which laws remain relevant throughout time and in what ways. There is a sense among some Christians that the OT laws are no longer relevant at all in light of God's further revelation in Jesus Christ.[9]

We can begin to overcome these obstacles and recognize the OT laws as part of the formation of God's people if we first understand that within the context of scripture's larger narrative, obedience to the law is a response to what YHWH has already, graciously done for Israel. The laws enter the story only *after* the grace-filled deliverance in the exodus. YHWH first acts to deliver the people, and only then are the people asked to take up the question, "Now then, how should we live?" The laws have the flavor of asking, "How do we act in accordance with what YHWH has done for us?" Or, "How do we maintain the relationship that YHWH has initiated with us?" For our biblical ancestors, the laws given at Sinai were a divine gift to be celebrated, given by YHWH specifically to allow the people to remain faithful to the relationship that YHWH had established. They aren't presented as a means for the people to *establish* a relationship with YHWH (or earn salvation).[10] Rather, they are YHWH's concrete answers to the response-oriented question, "How do we live as YHWH's people, now that we've been redeemed?"

In keeping with this insight, modern biblical scholarship has long noted that the Sinai covenant and its accompanying laws resemble the patterns of certain kinds of political treaties known from the ancient Near East (especially the conditional treaties between a more powerful king ["suzerain"] and a less powerful ruler or people ["vassal"]).[11] One characteristic of many of these ancient political treaties is that they begin not with a set of demands but with an opening prologue that first recounts the benevolent acts that the suzerain has done for the vassal as motivation for why the vassal should serve loyally. Then, only after that recital, the treaties detail the specific stipulations for obedience placed upon the vassal, with blessings promised upon obedience. As we've seen, the Sinai covenant and its accompanying laws are set up the same way. YHWH's opening words at Sinai in Exodus 19:1-6 didn't begin with specific laws or demands for obedience, but with a rehearsal of the gracious acts that this delivering, sovereign, divine King has done for Israel ("You saw what I did to the Egyptians" [v. 4]). Only in that context, then, did YHWH ask for obedience ("So now, if you faithfully obey" [v. 5]) and begin to give specific laws (ch. 20 and following).

Another way that we can see the OT laws as part of the formation of God's people is by focusing not so much on the specific cases and regulations but on what might be the underlying principles, functions, and goals of the particular commands and practices. These underlying elements usually go unstated in the texts. Another insight from biblical scholarship, often noted in introductory textbooks, sheds some light on this question. The OT laws found in Exodus through Deuteronomy contain similarities (sometimes even to the point of exact parallels) to laws known from Israel's neighboring ancient cultures. These ancient Near Eastern law codes come especially from Mesopotamian civilizations such as Sumer, Babylon, and Assyria, and range in date from ca. 3000 to ca. 500 BCE.[12]

Code of Hammurabi

Perhaps the most famous ancient Near Eastern law code studied in comparison to the OT laws is the so-called Code of Hammurabi. Written in cuneiform, this code originated in ancient Babylon around 1750 BCE and is named after a Babylonian king. It is the largest currently known collection of ancient Mesopotamian law. The code bears several striking resemblances to biblical laws found in Exod 20:22–23:19, especially the laws pertaining to a goring ox (21:28-32) and the law of retribution ("eye for an eye") (21:23-25).

In spite of the high number of such legal texts that have been discovered, scholars remain unsure about many issues related to why and how the law collections were made (especially in light of the many similarities among them) and how exactly they functioned. Other surviving documents indicate that the law collections themselves were rarely referred to in actual court proceedings. Overall, it seems that these law codes weren't comprehensive legal systems but mostly examples of actual or hypothetical cases and judgements meant to illustrate more general principles. And perhaps most importantly for us, just like many of the OT laws, the general principle that might underlie a particular law usually goes unstated in these ancient Near Eastern collections.

The point is that since the biblical laws, like their ancient Near Eastern counterparts, often don't state the underlying general principles or functions at work in the specific cases, those of us reading the OT as a part of the narrative of Christian scripture may struggle to see how the particular things addressed in these laws transcend Israel's ancient context or have a larger purpose. At first glance, they don't seem to have a broader significance as a way to form the identity of a people who can participate in a wide-ranging and long-term divine mission to restore all creation to the right-relationships for which it was created. What do regulations governing who must dispose of a discovered animal carcass (Exod 21:33-34) or which kinds of seeds can be planted together (Lev 19:19) have to do with being an instrument that God can use to bless (give life to) all the nations of the earth? But the characteristics of these laws suggest that we can see their broader function as means of formation if we focus not just on the meaning that specific regulations may have had in their original cultural contexts but especially on what might be the underlying principles or goals expressed by the various laws. It is these underlying principles (and not necessarily the literal laws themselves) that might transcend the cultural context of ancient Israel and reveal the kind of identity that the instructions and practices seek to form. As we read one of these ancient biblical laws in Exodus through Deuteronomy, we might ask, "What's the underlying principle that this law expresses and how could that same principle be embodied and enacted in a different context, with different cultural and material realities?" What, for instance, is the underlying principle of a law that required an Israelite who happened upon an enemy's lost ox or donkey to return it to that enemy (Exod 23:4)? What is the underlying principle of a law that required every fiftieth year ("Jubilee" year, Lev 25) to be a time when slaves were freed, debts were canceled, and purchased land was returned to its original owners? Moreover, what would these underlying principles look like if practiced in different societies not characterized by the ownership of oxen, donkeys, or slaves?

To put it another way, if we inquire into the underlying principles of the instructions and practices that YHWH gives at Sinai, we might conclude that the OT law in the context of scripture's larger story is not ultimately about "dos and don'ts," but about providing concrete ways of living individually and collectively that form a particular kind of people and community. Each part of YHWH's instruction invites the question, "What kind of people/community does this law or practice envision and try to bring into being?" And there is perhaps the most important point for reading the laws at Sinai in the context of the larger OT story of God's calling, creation, and formation of a people: the laws are like rules given to children during their upbringing. The rules themselves, while important, are not the point of moral formation. Moral identity is not achieved when the child learns to do (or not to do) what the parent says. The purpose of the rules is to help the child develop patterns of behavior that can be applied to many different instances. The goal is that the mature person will no longer have to reference—or even need—the specific rules because they will embody the moral identity that the rules expressed.

So it is with the laws that appear at Sinai on Israel's wilderness journey. Their goal is to form the people whom YHWH has called and created into the instrument of blessing for the world and, more specifically, into a holy community that can serve as priests for all people. In other words, the laws aim to form a community that is purposefully distinct—on purpose and for a purpose.[13] Many of the laws function to establish an alternative religious and social order that contrasts in some important ways with Israel's surrounding environment and is characterized by right-relationships with YHWH and others. The Sinai instructions challenge idolatry and call for wholehearted devotion to YHWH alone as Israel's creating, providing, and covenanting God. But they also put into place laws and practices that create a just society marked by fair and life-giving social and economic practices that protect and provide well-being (*šālôm*) for the poor, immigrants, widows, and other vulnerable people. Readers of the whole OT story will recognize that the identity these laws aim to form reflects the very character of the life-giving, covenant-making, restoring God who calls, delivers, creates, provides, and protects. Moreover, if Israel lives out this holy and priestly identity, the covenant community will be a snapshot of what God's restoring work actually looks like in the world. In the wilderness, the divine Torah aims to form a community—even though bound to a particular time and culture—in which one might see a glimpse of the right-relationships that God had intended for creation and continues to try to restore for all peoples, times, and cultures.[14]

Calvin's Third Use of the Law

The notion of the OT law as a positive means of grace and formation resembles John Calvin's (1509–64) so-called third use of the law (expressed in his *Institutes of the Christian Religion*).[15] In addition to convicting people of sin and curbing societal evil, Calvin thought the law helped believers learn what God's will is and inspired them to follow it. The law is what the people of God should look like.

A People Commanded to Right-Relationships (The Ten Commandments)

Space doesn't permit an examination of all the specific laws and instructions that appear in the texts after the people's arrival at Sinai in Exodus 19. Just a few samples of YHWH's Torah given to Israel at Sinai, however, illustrate how the various laws try to shape Israel into a holy, priestly community by forming them to be a people who live in right-relationships with God, each other, and the world—the very kinds of right-relationships that God originally intended for creation.

The very first set of commands that YHWH gives at Sinai—the so-called Ten Commandments (Exod 20:1-17)—provides a ready example of the law as a means of forming a holy, priestly community living together in life-giving right-relationships.[16] Even the structure of this famous collection illustrates the nature and function of the law for the people. Before giving any commands, the passage begins with a preface that recounts YHWH's gracious acts: "I am the LORD your God who brought you out of Egypt, out of the house of slavery" (v. 2). YHWH doesn't simply appear and begin making demands. Rather, this opening reminder of the larger story situates all the laws that follow as a response called forth by YHWH's previous saving deeds for the people. In a sense, the first thing YHWH asks the covenant people to do at Sinai is to remember! This is the motivation for accepting a new vision of who they are and how they should live in the world.

The divine commandments that follow call the people to live in life-giving right-relationships with God, others, and the world. The first part of the list (vv. 2-7) focuses on right duties to God. And no commandment is more fundamental to Israel's identity than the first: "You must have no other gods before me" (v. 3). Note carefully the words. This commandment doesn't assume monotheism (the philosophical belief that only one God exists). Israel, like its ancient Near Eastern neighbors, largely assumed the existence of multiple gods (polytheism). Rather than calling Israel to a new philosophical belief, this command calls for action that is perhaps even more striking—obedience to *one* God before and above all others. In a setting where other options were believed to be genuinely available for worship and allegiance, YHWH asks Israel for single-minded devotion (obedient *action*, not philosophical belief). And the reason for that total fidelity comes from the opening preface (v. 2). YHWH is the God (and not any other) who has created and delivered them; *therefore*, he (and not any other) should be the sole object of their devotion. This opening commandment introduces a major element of the identity into which YHWH is trying to form the people—an element that will appear repeatedly throughout the rest of the OT's story of Israel's journey in the wilderness and life in the promised land. At the heart of who the people are called, created, and formed to be is the notion of *undivided loyalty* or *wholehearted devotion* to YHWH. Throughout the story to come, leaders like Moses, Joshua, and Samuel will echo this call to fully devoted reliance and obedience, even as the biblical storytellers recount the people's tendency to put their trust in loyalties such as other gods, sacred statues, human kings, political alliances, and social institutions.[17] The undivided loyalty of having no other gods before YHWH means that YHWH alone should be the fundamental reality that defines the people's identity. In a world full of forces, institutions, and people who will seek to be Israel's identity-shapers, YHWH begins the formation of the people by declaring that the covenant God who calls and creates should be the principal reality that defines who they are and how they live.

But the identity of the set apart priestly kingdom is not just about how they live in relationship to YHWH. The second part of the Ten Commandments (vv. 8-17) focuses on divinely commanded duties to others. Laws that prohibit murder, adultery, theft, and more are ways of forming a people who carry out basic personal and social obligations to one another and resist death-dealing actions that rob people of their selfhood and negate the dignity of human life. One of these commandments is especially interesting for considering the formation of a people characterized by right-relationships. The command to keep the Sabbath day (vv. 8-11) institutes a day each week set aside to rest from all work as a reminder that life is a gift of divine grace and that a person's worth is not determined by what she or he can produce. Moreover, it establishes this as the people's duty to both human and nonhuman creation. The command calls Israel to extend this life-giving practice of rest to immigrants, servants, and even animals (v. 10).

Overall, then, the Ten Commandments provide the first glimpse of what YHWH's holy, priestly, life-giving community might look like. In reflecting on the kind of people that these first Sinai laws envision, Walter Brueggemann emphasizes their setting in the context of YHWH's great act of salvation and liberation in the exodus. In that context, he concludes, the theological aim of this first and most basic set of divine laws is to "institutionalize the Exodus: to establish perspectives, procedures, policies, and institutions that will generate Exodus-like social relationships."[18] These exodus-shaped relationships mean a community marked by life-giving practices that nourish, provide, and protect neighbors, immigrants, and even animals. On a broader scale, then, the covenant people are called to provide a snapshot, albeit limited and context-bound, of what a restored, rightly-related creation might look like.

A People Who Carry God's Presence

As the people remain at Sinai, YHWH continues to provide instruction. Along with other law collections (e.g., Exod 20:22–23:19), the second half of the book of Exodus offers another uniquely priestly way of describing who YHWH is forming Israel to be and what that means for how they live in the world. With only one brief interlude (chs. 32–34), the last fifteen chapters of Exodus are devoted to the priestly building of the sanctuary (or tabernacle, meaning "dwelling") in the wilderness.[19] Chapters 25–31 recount very detailed instructions from YHWH on how to build the sanctuary; then chapters 35–40 describe the people meticulously carrying out those divine instructions and building the sanctuary. This portable worship structure will provide a meeting place with YHWH throughout the rest of the people's journey in the wilderness. But how does all this attention to the tabernacle's instructions and construction fit into the formation of the people's identity at Sinai?

The wilderness sanctuary symbolizes the ongoing presence of YHWH in the midst of the people. In the book of Exodus, not only does YHWH rescue the Israelites, join them to himself in a covenant, and begin to instruct them on how to live within that relationship; he also comes to dwell among them in an ongoing way. *Another dimension of Israel's identity is that they are the people who have YHWH's living presence in their midst.* As YHWH describes the tabernacle to Moses, "They should make me a sanctuary so I can be present among them.... There I will meet with you" (25:8, 22). This tabernacle will be the place where YHWH will consistently come to meet with Moses and the Israelites in the wilderness, and it represents the reliable promise of YHWH's presence with them throughout their journey. The priestly writers in Exodus use the phrase "the glory (Heb. *kābôd*) of the LORD" as their dominant way of talking about YHWH's presence among his people.[20] The Hebrew word *kābôd* ("glory") literally means "heavy" or "weighty," signifying the overwhelming uniqueness and powerfulness of this God and his presence among them. Often using language of blinding light and consuming fire, the Sinai texts describe this *kābôd* as engulfing the holy mountain (24:9-18). But now, that same weighty, overpowering presence will come to dwell continuously in their midst wherever they travel (40:34-38).[21] This element of Israel's identity makes their God distinct in a particular way. The deities most familiar to ancient Israel's world typically resided on a mountain, remained there, and required their followers to travel there for worship.[22] But the story of the building of YHWH's wilderness sanctuary marks Israel and its God differently. Throughout scripture's narrative so far, we've seen this covenant God accompany the first humans out of the garden, journey with Abraham, Sarah, and their descendants, and meet the Hebrew slaves in Egypt. Once more, the wilderness tabernacle announces that YHWH is a God who goes with the people he has called, created, and formed.

But there is another way that the building of the wilderness tabernacle fits into the formation of the people's identity at Sinai. As Timothy Green observes, "If the glory of God goes with his people...then the covenant community functions as the *glory bearer* in the world.... This community *carries* the divine glory of God into the world."[23] Seen in this way, the tabernacle becomes the concrete symbol not only of YHWH's presence with the people but of the people's identity as those called to mediate that presence to the world. "To see the covenant people is to see the covenant God."[24] If that's so, Israel must learn the character of the God who is with them and be formed into those whose ways embody that character for all creation. That instruction and formation is what the wilderness and Sinai experiences are about. In fact, in the middle of the people's experiences at Sinai in the second half of Exodus, YHWH gives Moses one of the clearest descriptions of the divine character: "The LORD! The LORD! a God who is compassionate and merciful, very patient, full of great loyalty and faithfulness, showing great loyalty to a thousand generations, forgiving every kind of sin and rebellion" (34:6-7). Although the second half of this divine proclamation doesn't shy away from divine justice and even punishment, the emphasis is clearly on YHWH's character as that which produces life-giving right-relationships for others. If this is the character of the God who dwells among them, then Israel must be formed into a community that can embody this life-giving compassion, mercy, and faithfulness in the world.

A Holy People with a Holy God

Up to this point, the wilderness-Sinai experience has described the kind of people YHWH is trying to form Israel to be as a priestly kingdom that lives in right-relationships with YHWH and others and carries YHWH's life-giving presence into the world. Immediately after the book of Exodus ends with YHWH's presence filling the newly built tabernacle (40:34), that meeting place becomes the setting for another major part of the people's formation experience at Sinai described in the book of Leviticus: "Then the LORD called to Moses and said to him from the meeting tent, Speak to the Israelites and say to them..." (Lev 1:1-2a). What follows across the book of Leviticus is a series of instructions given to Moses and Aaron at Sinai to govern especially Israel's worship practices and the priests (sons of Aaron) who oversee them. The instructions include rules for making offerings, ordaining priests, maintaining ritual purity in the tabernacle and camp, celebrating annual festivals, and dealing with sexual conduct, criminal acts, and social justice. Scholars are unsure exactly what historical and social settings produced these regulations and how and when they functioned.[25] For contemporary Christian readers in particular, however, all this priestly legislation about animal sacrifices, food rules, ritual practices, and purity ideas isn't a part of their current practice and seems removed from the story of a divine mission to restore creation. So how does this book-length set of priestly instructions in Leviticus add a new element to the formation of the Israelites as YHWH's people in the wilderness?

To the already-given descriptions of Israel's identity as an instrument of blessing, priestly kingdom, community of right-relationships, and a people who carry YHWH's presence into the world, Leviticus adds a new emphasis: *holiness*. The practices and instructions outlined in these priestly texts proclaim YHWH's holiness and call for his covenant people to reflect that holiness. We've already heard the language of holiness in YHWH's original words to the people at Sinai in Exodus 19:1-6, which expressed the divine intention that Israel be a "holy nation" (19:6). But in Leviticus, holiness becomes central, and one divine command in particular is repeated throughout the book: "Be holy because I am holy" (Lev 11:44-45; 19:2; 20:7). For much of the first half of Leviticus in particular (chs. 1–16), the call to holiness concentrates on the Aaronide (Aaron's descendants) priests. They are the ones who need to be holy so that they can serve as priests for the Israelites before YHWH. But Leviticus 17–27 (the so-called Holiness Code), as well as Deuteronomy, broaden the holiness call beyond the Aaronide priests to all Israelites. These Sinai instructions explicitly link holiness with the identity of the covenant people. Israel needs to be holy because YHWH, the God who is in their midst and with whom they stand in a covenant relationship, is holy. And Israel needs to be holy if they are to become the instrument of blessing, priestly kingdom, and presence-bearing community of right-relationships that can participate in the divine redemptive mission in the world.

So what does it mean for Leviticus to say that YHWH is holy? In short, holy means set apart, different, uncommon, and even sovereign. It means that YHWH is a unique covenant God who is completely other than common human beings but also sharply distinct from other powers and principalities, human or otherwise. There is something radically different about the God who dwells in Israel's midst and whose presence Israel is charged to *image* in the world. Leviticus says that the people live in the presence of a holy (wholly other, altogether uncommon) God. So, YHWH's special places, objects, and servants (such as the tabernacle, its instruments, and its priests) must be kept separate and sacred and not be profaned (treated as common or made impure). Priests must safeguard the boundaries of the holy spaces in the tabernacle, ensure that the holy offerings are treated correctly, and keep ritually impure or unclean things away from holy things.[26] YHWH is an *other* who cannot be domesticated or controlled by humans or enlisted to serve their purposes. Treating his places and persons as sacred reminds the people of that fact. But within the context of the larger OT story, to say YHWH is holy (set apart, different, uncommon) also means that this sovereign God has a unique character. And the OT story has already revealed that character. This covenant God is compassionate, faithful, merciful, loyal, and committed to healing creation (see Exod 34:6-7). In other words, in contrast to other death-dealing powers who seek to enslave, YHWH is the set-apart sovereign who enters into life-giving relationships. This God partners with his creatures, empowers them to participate in his work, and allows them to flourish under blessing.

YHWH's holiness in Leviticus raises the question of what it means for Israel to live as a holy people (not just the Aaronide priests, but the whole congregation). The book's instructions call the people to safeguard YHWH's holiness (uniqueness, separateness) in the community and to reflect YHWH's unique character in their systems, institutions, and practices. In other words, holiness for Israel means that they must practice both purity and justice. YHWH's instructions to Moses and the community in Leviticus 19 provide perhaps the most comprehensive illustration of the dual nature of this holiness. In the first place, the people must keep YHWH's sanctuary, offerings, priests, and more from being defiled by following YHWH's instructions. They must correctly practice sacrifices (vv. 5-8) and strictly follow rules for crop-planting, animal breeding, and human sexual relationships (vv. 19-30). For the priestly writers, failure in these regards can defile YHWH's holiness and such defilement risks forcing YHWH to withdraw his holy presence from the community, effectively removing the divine power that allows them to survive as a people.[27]

At the same time, the people must engage in life-giving—not death-dealing—ways of treating others justly that reflect the ethical character of their holy God. So, while Leviticus 19 insists on proper sacrifice and animal breeding, it also requires the people to establish an ethical community that shares their food with the poor and immigrants (vv. 9-10) and prohibits taking advantage of others by stealing, lying, and practicing injustice (vv. 11-16). Leviticus 19 emphatically connects holiness with love in a broad sense. In one of the most famous lines of scripture, YHWH summarizes holiness with this command: "You must love your neighbor as yourself" (v. 18). Yet, true to the broad scope of YHWH's mission in the larger OT story, just a few verses later YHWH clarifies that this love command can't be restricted: "Any immigrant who lives with you must be treated as if they were one of your citizens. You must love them as yourself" (v. 34). A holy people treats outsiders just like insiders. To do so is to take on the identity of a holy God who does the same ("because you were immigrants in the land of Egypt....I am the LORD your God, who brought you out of the land of Egypt" [vv. 34, 36]).

The Love Command

Many Christians have identified the command to "love your neighbor as yourself" as the summary of morals. Leviticus 19 broadened the command to include love for immigrants (vv. 33-34). Jesus extended it further to enemies (Matt 5:43-48). He paired it with the command to love God from Deuteronomy 6:5 (Mark 12:29-31) and explained it using the so-called Golden Rule: "Treat people in the same way that you want people to treat you" (Matt 7:12).

Leaving Sinai and Raising a New Generation

According to the OT plot line, when we turn from Leviticus to Numbers, the Israelites have been in the identity-forming experience at Sinai for nearly a year (Num 1:1). YHWH has begun to shape them toward being a covenant people who carries the divine presence into the world and lives as a priestly kingdom in holiness before a holy God. The first part of Numbers (1:1–10:10) recounts Israel's final nineteen days of instruction at Sinai before they depart to continue their wilderness journey toward the promised land of Canaan. These chapters are devoted to specific preparations for the people's journey (how to make camp, duties of priests, etc.). Almost as if providing a family portrait, however, Numbers opens with a divinely ordered counting of the people (1:2-47). The focus is on males, twenty years old and above, who will be able to fight in the battles to come (1:2-3). But in this listing of persons and families, it's as if we see the faces of the first generation of YHWH's people who came out of Egypt and are now being formed to serve as the instrument of life-giving, restoring blessing in the world. Led by Moses, this generation prepares to live out the identity of being a priestly, presence-bearing, holy community as they continue the journey.

The major transition in the people's story occurs at Numbers 10:11-12. After nearly a year in the narrative's timeline (and a large amount of scripture's space), the Israelites leave Sinai and head back into the wilderness on the way to the promised land. As the Israelites set out from Sinai, YHWH once more provides and protects. Across the stories in Numbers 10:11–25:18, YHWH again provides manna and quail to feed the people (11:1-35), brings sustaining water out of a rock (20:1-13), and defends Israel against enemies (21:1-25; 22:1–24:25).[28] But from the very outset of the post-Sinai journey, the people, who have now seen the identity to which they've been called and the character of the God who has called them, repeatedly yield to the temptation to doubt, complain, and rebel. Even after the intense Torah-giving, formation experience at the holy mountain, the people who set out on this new stage of the wilderness journey immediately struggle with the same fear, mistrust, and rebellion that appeared on the first stage of their journey from Egypt to Sinai (Exod 15:22–18:27). Here again is humanity's ongoing dilemma of struggling to resist self-provision and self-sovereignty in favor of life-giving trust and obedience.

The more the difficulties of the wilderness take their toll, the more the people rebel against who YHWH asks them to be and how YHWH asks them to live. The people's fearful doubting and complaining begin in the very first episode of the journey away from Sinai (11:1-15). As in the earlier part of their wilderness journey, the Israelites fear for their own survival and lack of provisions. But beginning here and throughout the rest of the journey, their fear and doubt take on an increasingly rebellious and disobedient character. In the opening episode, the people don't simply worry about a lack of food, they complain about the provisions YHWH has given. They grumble about having to eat manna when they used to have fish and vegetables in Egypt (11:4-6).

Across the following stories, as YHWH continues to provide and protect, the people increasingly resent and reject the divine gifts as not up to par and not what they desire. Not unlike the temptation faced by the first humans in the garden, YHWH's people in the wilderness grow unsatisfied with the ways that YHWH offers to sustain them. The Israelites (even Aaron and Miriam) challenge Moses's divinely appointed leadership (12:1-16; 16:1-50), quarrel over a temporary lack of water (20:1-13), and even make sacrifices to other gods (25:1-18). The biblical storyteller gives a sad but telling summary: "The people became impatient on the road. The people spoke against God and Moses: 'Why did you bring us up from Egypt to kill us in the desert, where there is no food or water. And we detest this miserable bread!'" (21:4-5). As these instances of the people's rebellion and disobedience mount, they arouse increasing divine anger, and YHWH sends numerous punishments and harsh corrections upon the people in the form of fire, plagues, poisonous snakes, and more.

The rebelliousness of this exodus-generation reaches its climax in Numbers 13–14. After traveling from Sinai, the Israelites reach the wilderness region just outside the southern border of Canaan. In just three chapters of the narrative after Sinai, they are on the doorstep of entering the promised land. In preparation, YHWH instructs Moses to send spies into Canaan. When Caleb, Joshua, and the ten other spies return, they report a good, flourishing land inhabited by powerful people. Caleb urges the people to trust YHWH's promises and enter the land. But the Israelites give in to fear and doubt: "We can't go up against the people because they are stronger than we" (13:31). And mistrust soon turns to outright rebellion: "So they said to each other, 'Let's pick a new leader and let's go back to Egypt'" (14:4). At this crucial moment, YHWH's entire redemptive mission is in jeopardy. The people he has called, created, and formed to be the instrument of blessing and restoration have decided to turn back to Egypt—to retreat symbolically to old powers, masters, and dependencies that lead to death-dealing ways of living with one another in the world. Here, on the border of the promised land, it has become clear that this first generation who came out of Egypt is unwilling to embrace their identity as the covenant people formed to be a priestly kingdom and holy nation.

As we've seen many times throughout the OT story, however, the creating, covenanting God who has determined to restore the life-giving relationships broken by human mistrust and rebellion refuses to allow the divine mission to be thwarted. Symbolically, we may say that "the most common punctuation mark in the narrative of God consists of ellipsis points—dot, dot, dot."[29] And so, here in the wilderness, YHWH alters the whole course of Israel's story and declares that the formation of a priestly, blessing-giving, covenant people will continue through the *next* generation of Israelites. In response to the people's rejection, YHWH proclaims that none of the first generation who came out of Egypt and experienced Sinai—that is, none of those listed in the first counting at the beginning of Numbers (1:1-47)—will enter the promised land (except Caleb and Joshua) (14:29-32). Rather, YHWH announces that he will raise up the generation of Israelite children who were born in the wilderness, form them into the proper identity of the covenant people that he described at Sinai, and bring them into the land.

In order for this transition and transformation to occur, YHWH declares that the Israelites will spend the next forty years (one year for each day of the spies' trip) wandering through the wilderness until the entire first generation (except Caleb and Joshua) has died off and the second generation is ready to enter the promised land (14:33-35). Apparently, YHWH's original intention was for Israel to come out of Egypt, spend a year of formation at Sinai, and then proceed north directly into the promised land. Because of the first generation's mistrust and rebellion, however, they'll take the long road—continuing east for forty years (a common symbol for the length of a generation) around to the opposite side of the Jordan River outside of Canaan.

The OT story virtually fast-forwards through the trials, travails, human rebellions, and divine responses of these next forty years (Num 15–25). By Numbers 26, the first generation has passed away and the second generation has emerged—a fact that the narrative marks with a second counting of the people (males, twenty years old and above) (26:1-62) and a declaration that none of those counted among the first generation (except Caleb and Joshua) now remain (26:63-65). The new generation of YHWH's people has completed the trek through the wilderness and arrived on the "plains of Moab by the Jordan opposite Jericho" (26:3).

Shaping a New Generation

What remains of the wilderness section of the OT story is the identity formation of this new generation and their preparation for entering the promised land. While some of this takes place in the final ten chapters of Numbers, it's Deuteronomy—the last book of the Pentateuch—that provides the most extensive re-articulation of who God is, who God's people are, and how they are called to be in the world.[30]

Deuteronomy is a complex book that likely emerged in different stages throughout Israel's history.[31] It contains a mixture of lengthy stories, detailed law collections, and personal instructions. But most importantly for our purposes, Deuteronomy presents itself as one long sermon—the final sermon delivered by Moses in the plains of Moab just before he died and the new generation of Israelites crossed the Jordan River to enter Canaan (Deut 1:1). The book retells the stories, and even some of the laws, which we've seen along the way of the people's wilderness journey in Exodus and Numbers—although not always in exactly the same manner. Now, however, those stories and laws are presented on the lips of Moses as a grand summary sermon that he addressed to this new generation at the end of forty years in the wilderness (1:3) and on the verge of entering the promised land. Remember, the first generation was gone (except Caleb and Joshua), and the Israelites who stood before Moses were born in the wilderness. They hadn't been in Egypt or experienced Mount Sinai. They needed to hear and respond to the covenant story for themselves. And this is Deuteronomy—Moses's fresh telling of the story of YHWH's deliverance, covenant, and law to shape the identity of the new generation.

Deuteronomy

The English title of the book of Deuteronomy (derived from the Greek translation), which means "second law," points to the nature of the book as a retelling (sometimes in a different manner) of the story of YHWH's deliverance, covenant, and law that appeared in Exodus, Leviticus, and Numbers.

Moses's sermon is full of language that pulls this new generation into God's story as if they'd been there all along. It repeatedly admonishes them to *remember* (or be careful not to forget!) the covenant story and asks them to respond by *hearing, keeping, observing,* and *doing*:

> The LORD didn't make this covenant with our ancestors but with us—all of us who are here and alive right now....Now once the LORD your God has brought you into the land...watch yourself! Don't forget the LORD who brought you out of Egypt....You must carefully perform all of the commandment that I am commanding you right now....Keep the commandments of the LORD your God by walking in his ways and by fearing him. (5:3; 6:10, 12; 8:1, 6)

With words like these, this sermon narrates a particular identity for the new generation of Israelites: they are servants in a treaty-bond with a more powerful ruler (suzerain) who demands loyalty. The language reminds us of the ancient Near Eastern political treaties described above. Deuteronomy's structure, moving from a historical retrospective of past events (chs. 1–11), to laws and demands (chs. 12–26), and then to resulting blessings and curses (chs. 27–30), is especially close to the pattern of some surviving treaties.[32] Both now and later in Israel's story, when kings of great empires such as Assyria and Babylonia will redefine Israel and Judah as vassals who owe loyalty to them, Deuteronomy asserts that the people are indeed subject vassals, but to YHWH as their true sovereign.

The centerpiece of Moses's sermon that aims to shape the identity of this new generation on the brink of the promised land comes in Deuteronomy 6:4-5, the so-called *Shema* (derived from the opening word in Hebrew, "listen!"). Here, Deuteronomy returns to what appeared back in the Ten Commandments at Sinai (Exod 20) as the central aspect of the identity of YHWH's people: "Israel, listen! Our God is the LORD! Only the LORD! Love the LORD your God with all your heart (Heb. *lēb*), all your being (*nepeš*), and all your strength (*mə'ōd*)" (Deut 6:4-5).[33] This new generation, like their ancestors, has been called, created, and formed to a life of undivided loyalty or wholehearted devotion to YHWH. Specifically, they are called to *love*—a term whose biblical meaning goes beyond our culture's common meanings of emotion or affection. The command to love actually appears in some ancient Near Eastern treaties to describe how subject nations should act toward their imperial rulers, and the love command in the OT often appears in covenant contexts describing Israel's relationship with YHWH as their God. To love is to act in faithfulness and loyalty to the commitment that has been made. To love is to act obediently to the demands of the relationship. And Moses calls this new generation to love YHWH in a comprehensive and undivided way—with *all* their *heart, being,* and *strength*. The *heart* (*lēb*), as used by our biblical ancestors, refers not to the seat of emotions but to the source of decision-making—the mind or the will. The notion of one's *being* (*nepeš*) refers not to an immortal, spiritual soul housed in our physical bodies but to the life energy that makes you who you are (in Hebrew thought, you don't have a *nepeš*; you are a *nepeš*). When you combine these notions with the final word *strength*, the message is clear: the identity of YHWH's people is to act faithfully in obedience to YHWH with every aspect of who they are and how they live. As we've already seen, YHWH's people continually struggle to have this undivided, wholehearted devotion, trust, and obedience. As Timothy Green notes, although the Israelites were commanded to remain faithful to the God who called, created, delivered, and provided for them, "new systems that promised life, fertility, abundance, and hope" through other means have already and will continue to emerge as rivals competing for some of the people's dependence and loyalty.[34]

So, why is the formation of this identity for YHWH's people so important? There's no doubt that Deuteronomy is first and foremost focused on Israel's coming occupation of the promised land. So, the people must wholeheartedly obey if they are to possess the land. But Moses's final sermon to the new generation not only calls them to remember, obey, and serve with undivided loyalty so they can inherit the land; it also connects this call to YHWH's larger mission to restore creation. Deuteronomy emphasizes that YHWH asks these things of them because they've been chosen to participate in that mission in a special way. Moses consistently warns the people not to become self-absorbed in the future, thinking that all of their accomplishments are by them or for them alone and forgetting the larger things that YHWH has done and will do (e.g., 8:11-20). Moses repeatedly asserts that Israel has been chosen as the covenant people not because of anything special about them but so that YHWH can fulfill the promises made to Abraham, Isaac, and Jacob:

> It was not because you were greater than all other people that the LORD loved you and chose you.... No, it is because the LORD loved you and because *he kept the solemn pledge he swore to your ancestors.* (7:7-8, emphasis added)

> You aren't entering and taking possession of their land because you are righteous or because your heart is especially virtuous; rather, it is because these nations are wicked . . . and *because he wishes to establish the promise he made to your ancestors: to Abraham, Isaac, and Jacob.* (9:5, emphasis added)

What was the essence of the divine promise to Abraham, Sarah, and their descendants? The promise in Genesis 12:1-3 not only assured Abraham and Sarah of land and descendants. It also flowed out of YHWH's covenant commitment to all flesh to heal and restore creation. The promise to the ancestors was to use the community of Abraham and Sarah's descendants as

The Life of God's People (Part 1): In the Promised Land

(Joshua–2 Kings)

Focus Texts: Joshua 1; 6; 24; Judges 1–2;
1 Samuel 7–8; 2 Samuel 7; 2 Kings 17–25

Location in the Old Testament Story:

1) The Introduction of God's Mission in the World (Genesis 1–11)
2) The Calling of God's People (Genesis 12–50)
3) The Creation of God's People (Exodus 1–15)
4) The Formation of God's People (Exodus 16–Deuteronomy)
5) **The Life of God's People (Joshua–Esther)**
   a) The Voices of Israel's Poets and Sages before, during, and after Exile (Job–Song of Songs)
   b) The Voices of Israel's Prophets before, during, and after Exile (Isaiah–Malachi)

The Pivotal Moment in Israel's Story

"Where the rubber meets the road." "Put your money where your mouth is." "The moment of truth." "It's go time." We often use these catchphrases in our culture to communicate that we've reached a decisive moment of some kind. They mean that the prep time is completed and the time for performance has come. The stage lights are on; the curtain is going up; and the call rings out, "Action!"

When scripture's first five books come to a close, the OT story reaches just such a pivotal moment in the telling of God's mission and Israel's calling to be an instrument within that mission. Up to this point, the larger OT plot line has introduced God's mission to restore creation to life-giving right-relationships, and we've seen God's calling, creation, and formation of Israel to be an instrument of blessing to all families of the earth, a special covenant people who fulfill a priestly role for the world, and a holy nation that carries God's presence into all creation. When we last left the Israelites, they were in transit in the wilderness. Deuteronomy's final sermon had passed on the story of God's deliverance, covenant, and law to a new generation, completing their formation as God's special people. The time has come for Israel to enter the land that God promised to Abraham and Sarah and fulfill the mission for which they've been called, created, and formed. So, a question hangs in the air: will they live out their identity as God's covenant people once they cross the Jordan River and enter the promised land?

The next block of books in the Protestant canon (Joshua–Esther) provides the answer. These books tell the centuries-long story of the covenant people's life from their entrance into the promised land, through their existence as two kingdoms, into the experience of destruction and exile, and into a time of return and restoration to the land after exile. The story runs as follows: The Israelites moved into the land of Canaan from the wilderness, conquered various cities, and established a village society. Within a century, that society developed into a united kingdom ruled from Jerusalem. This united monarchy didn't survive the death of its most successful king, however, and separated into the two kingdoms known as Israel in the north and Judah in the south. These kingdoms existed as related yet independent entities that played prominent roles in the affairs of their region until the northern kingdom met its destruction at the hands of the Assyrians around 720 BCE. Judah survived longer until its fall to the Babylonians in 586 BCE, when Jerusalem was destroyed and many of the people were taken into exile to Babylon. Ultimately, however, the covenant God remained committed to the people he had called, created, and formed, and so he eventually delivered them from exile and restored them to a new community back in the promised land.

This chapter will discuss the first portion of the story of the life of God's people from the entrance into the promised land to destruction and exile (Joshua–2 Kings). The following chapter will discuss the second portion from exile to restoration (1 Chronicles–Esther). The first portion of the story has the feeling of a tragedy. God's people continually struggle with the inclination to fear, mistrust, self-preservation, and self-sovereignty that comprises the basic human dilemma we've seen from the beginning of scripture's narrative. The realities of the world and the fears for their own survival frequently lead them to turn away from the God who drew them into a covenant relationship that promised deliverance and provision. They look to other gods, political alliances, economic structures, and religious systems for safety and security only to be overwhelmed by the violent, death-dealing forces of enemies and empires.

The Life of God's People in the Larger Old Testament Story

The portrayal of Israel's life as a nation that dominates the books of Joshua through Esther makes this section of the OT one of the easiest in which to lose sight of the larger OT story. In these books, scripture's plot line, which has often centered on God's redemptive intentions for all creation, seemingly narrows its focus to Israel's kingdoms, kings, armies, priests, prophets, and people, sometimes to the exclusion—or even at the expense—of others. The story of Israel—called to be an instrument of blessing for the whole world—turns inward on itself, reading like a selective account of political and religious history.

The Christian tradition of labeling this section of the OT canon as the "Historical Books" sometimes strengthens this impression of narrowness.

The Former Prophets

The Christian tradition has labeled the books of Joshua–Kings as part of the "Historical Books" (Joshua–Esther). The Jewish canon labels them as the "Former Prophets" (followed by the "Latter Prophets" in Isaiah–Malachi), a label that shifts attention away from reading these books as historical sources for Israel's past and toward their theological messages. The books do much more than report history; they proclaim and illustrate the importance of God's call for obedience to the Torah.

And biblical scholarship throughout the modern era has often approached these books primarily in order to use them as sources for reconstructing the history of ancient Israel and Judah.[1] One insight from biblical scholarship, however, may help us connect the story of Israel's political, social, and religious life in the land with the larger OT story of God's mission to restore creation and Israel's calling to be an instrument within that mission. For almost a century now, the books of Joshua through 2 Kings have been studied together under the designation coined by modern scholars, "The Deuteronomistic History."[2] The earliest formulations of this idea proposed that these books originated as one large work, composed by one writer, who gathered and revised older materials into a composition for a single purpose—to explain why Israel's history went as it did, especially why the people experienced destruction and exile.[3] Scholars today continue to debate the specifics of this composition (usually proposing more than one major edition coming from different times and places).[4] But the importance of this idea for my purposes here is the notion that the OT books that tell the story of Israel's life as God's people in the promised land were likely written later than the events that they describe—probably reaching their current form after both kingdoms had suffered destruction and exile—in order to retell the story of the people's past for larger theological purposes. This collection wasn't made for the sake of simply recounting history. The finished product took shape in light of the traumatic events of destruction and exile and the serious questions they raised about how the story of God's people had unfolded. These texts tell the story of Israel's life as a story of the people's unfaithfulness to their calling as a covenant community and holy nation, which resulted in destruction and exile. But they also offer a renewed sense of hope and identity to the people on the other side of destruction and exile.

Viewed in this way, we can go through the story of the life of God's people in the land told across Joshua through Esther as the OT canon presents it—not to examine every detail or to offer a reconstruction of Israel's history, but to consider the major elements, key themes, and representative texts within these books in the context of the larger OT story. We can identify places where we see God's larger redemptive mission and Israel's wider role in it as an instrument of blessing, priestly kingdom, and presence-bearing people come through in the realities of their life, successfully or unsuccessfully. We can consider how some of the new elements that enter Israel's story in this section (conquest, monarchy, and exile) might fit into that larger plot line, even if uncomfortably. And we can look for reminders of what Israel's identity was supposed to be in order to participate in God's bigger mission— namely, wholehearted devotion and undivided loyalty.

Obedience, Disobedience, and the Entrance into the Land

The story of Israel's life as God's people begins with their entrance into the promised land of Canaan in Joshua and Judges. These books describe the crossing of the Jordan River, the conquest of Canaan under Joshua, and Israel's initial existence as a tribal society before the establishment of a monarchy. According to Joshua's account in particular, YHWH gave Israel the land of Canaan, often through miraculous events (chs. 1–12), and the people then allotted the land to their various tribes (chs. 13–24). The book depicts a wildly successful invasion in which the Israelites conquered virtually the whole land in three quick sweeps through the center, south, and north.

Even before the people take their first steps out of the wilderness and into the land that YHWH had promised them, the opening of the book of Joshua ties these events into the larger OT plot line. Prior to their first move across the Jordan River, YHWH's opening words to Israel's new leader, Joshua, as he prepares to lead the people into the land, set out a program for the new day into which the people are entering. The program? Success in this new day requires total obedience to YHWH: "Be very brave and strong as you carefully obey all of the Instruction that Moses my servant commanded you. Don't deviate even a bit from it, either to the right or left. Then you will have success wherever you go" (Josh 1:7). This is the message of the stories of Joshua that begin the account of Israel's existence in the land: For those who've been called, created, and formed, *obedience should be the rule that governs how they live as YHWH's people.* YHWH's opening declaration points the people back to the "Instruction" (Heb. *tôrāh*) that they received from Moses in the wilderness to form their identity as YHWH's people.[5] Joshua reports this divine charge to the people, who respond by affirming the rule of obedience at the outset: "We will obey everything you have commanded us and go anywhere you send us. We will obey you in the same way that we obeyed Moses" (1:16-17).

In this opening exchange of YHWH's charge and the people's response, the biblical storytellers once again describe the people's relationship with YHWH in the terms of the ancient Near Eastern political treaties (covenants) I mentioned in the preceding chapter—the treaties between a more powerful sovereign (suzerain) who demands the loyalty of a less powerful ruler or population (vassal), with the expectation that in return for such loyalty YHWH will provide the essentials needed to survive and even flourish.[6] In the pattern of these treaties, the book of Joshua opens the story of the people's life in the land by charging Israel to live as a faithful treaty partner who owes its loyalty and trusts its well-being not to some foreign empire or human conqueror but to YHWH as its sovereign. The people learned in the wilderness that YHWH has established a unique covenant with them and demanded that they embody a higher standard of holiness and fulfill a priestly role in creation. Now, the story of their life in the land opens with the declaration that Israel is to live as YHWH's obedient vassal who shuns rebellion, resists fear, and trusts their existence to their divine ruler.

As the people undertake preparations to enter the land and then engage in various military conflicts to secure it, the remaining stories of Joshua read not like a war history but a theological testimony. YHWH leads them into Canaan; divine power wins battles; and YHWH gives the land to Israel as a gift. The stories illustrate repeatedly the theme that *obedience should be the rule* to govern how the people live in this new day. The people carefully follow YHWH's instructions in carrying out a ritual crossing of the Jordan River, as YHWH miraculously cuts off the waters of the Jordan just as he had those of the sea on the way out of Egypt (Josh 3–4). They unreservedly obey YHWH's commands to circumcise the new generation and celebrate the Passover to mark the end of the wilderness journey (ch. 5). And when they reach Jericho (ch. 6), the first of Canaan's fortified cities that they must capture after their entrance into the land, the people receive precise instructions from YHWH on what to do—instructions that don't resemble the military tactics of an army but the religious rituals of a community in worship. YHWH's very detailed instructions are to march around Jericho in a worship procession once a day for six days and seven times on the seventh day, with the precise formation of seven priests carrying trumpets in front of the ark of the covenant (6:1-4). The story itself contains an overload of repetition, stressing that the people meticulously followed every exact detail in each instance (vv. 6-20). As a result, YHWH miraculously brought down the walls of the city.[7] Here is of Israel's story and declares that the formation of a priestly, blessing-giving, covenant people will continue through the *next* generation of Israelites. In response to the people's rejection, YHWH proclaims that none of the first generation who came out of Egypt and experienced Sinai—that is, none of those listed in the first counting at the beginning of Numbers (1:1-47)—will enter the promised land (except Caleb and Joshua) (14:29-32). Rather, YHWH announces that he will raise up the generation of Israelite children who were born in the wilderness, form them into the proper identity of the covenant people that he described at Sinai, and bring them into the land.

In order for this transition and transformation to occur, YHWH declares that the Israelites will spend the next forty years (one year for each day of the spies' trip) wandering through the wilderness until the entire first generation (except Caleb and Joshua) has died off and the second generation is ready to enter the promised land (14:33-35). Apparently, YHWH's original intention was for Israel to come out of Egypt, spend a year of formation at Sinai, and then proceed north directly into the promised land. Because of the first generation's mistrust and rebellion, however, they'll take the long road—continuing east for forty years (a common symbol for the length of a generation) around to the opposite side of the Jordan River outside of Canaan.

The OT story virtually fast-forwards through the trials, travails, human rebellions, and divine responses of these next forty years (Num 15–25). By Numbers 26, the first generation has passed away and the second generation has emerged—a fact that the narrative marks with a second counting of the people (males, twenty years old and above) (26:1-62) and a declaration that none of those counted among the first generation (except Caleb and Joshua) now remain (26:63-65). The new generation of YHWH's people has completed the trek through the wilderness and arrived on the "plains of Moab by the Jordan opposite Jericho" (26:3).

Shaping a New Generation

What remains of the wilderness section of the OT story is the identity formation of this new generation and their preparation for entering the promised land. While some of this takes place in the final ten chapters of Numbers, it's Deuteronomy—the last book of the Pentateuch—that provides the most extensive re-articulation of who God is, who God's people are, and how they are called to be in the world.[30]

Deuteronomy is a complex book that likely emerged in different stages throughout Israel's history.[31] It contains a mixture of lengthy stories, detailed law collections, and personal instructions. But most importantly for our purposes, Deuteronomy presents itself as one long sermon—the final sermon delivered by Moses in the plains of Moab just before he died and the new generation of Israelites crossed the Jordan River to enter Canaan (Deut 1:1). The book retells the stories, and even some of the laws, which we've seen along the way of the people's wilderness journey in Exodus and Numbers—although not always in exactly the same manner. Now, however, those stories and laws are presented on the lips of Moses as a grand summary sermon that he addressed to this new generation at the end of forty years in the wilderness (1:3) and on the verge of entering the promised land. Remember, the first generation was gone (except Caleb and Joshua), and the Israelites who stood before Moses were born in the wilderness. They hadn't been in Egypt or experienced Mount Sinai. They needed to hear and respond to the covenant story for themselves. And this is Deuteronomy—Moses's fresh telling of the story of YHWH's deliverance, covenant, and law to shape the identity of the new generation.

Deuteronomy

The English title of the book of Deuteronomy (derived from the Greek translation), which means "second law," points to the nature of the book as a retelling (sometimes in a different manner) of the story of YHWH's deliverance, covenant, and law that appeared in Exodus, Leviticus, and Numbers.

Moses's sermon is full of language that pulls this new generation into God's story as if they'd been there all along. It repeatedly admonishes them to *remember* (or be careful not to forget!) the covenant story and asks them to respond by *hearing, keeping, observing,* and *doing*:

The LORD didn't make this covenant with our ancestors but with us—all of us who are here and alive right now.... Now once the LORD your God has brought you into the land...watch yourself! Don't forget the LORD who brought you out of Egypt....You must carefully perform all of the commandment that I am commanding you right now.... Keep the commandments of the LORD your God by walking in his ways and by fearing him. (5:3; 6:10, 12; 8:1, 6) a dramatic illustration of the rule of obedience that is to govern Israel's life as YHWH's people. They obey precisely and extensively, and obedience brings success in this new day. This central message finds expression in the opposite way in the very next story (ch. 7), when one act of disobedience to YHWH's commands by a single person causes the army to be defeated at the city of Ai.

In these narratives of Israel's entrance into the land, glimpses of the larger OT story of YHWH's redemptive mission and Israel's role within it occasionally peek through. As Joshua built a memorial to commemorate the miraculous crossing of the Jordan River that brought the people into the promised land, YHWH declared that his divine acts are not merely for Israel's benefit but are a testimony to the nations—"so that all the earth's people might know that the LORD's power is great" (4:24). Moreover, in the book of Joshua's emphasis on obedience as the life-governing rule for success, we see reminders of the identity required for the people to participate in YHWH's bigger mission—namely, wholehearted devotion and undivided loyalty. The OT story has sounded this note previously. YHWH's first commandment at Sinai (Exod 20:3) asked Israel for the single-minded devotion of having no other gods before YHWH and letting YHWH alone be the fundamental reality that defines the people's identity. In the wilderness just outside the promised land, the *Shema* (Deut 6:4-5) called for absolute devotion to the God who brought the people out of Egypt so that YHWH might fulfill his promise to use them as an instrument of blessing to all the families of the earth (Deut 7:7-8; 9:5). Now, the call to undivided loyalty forms the climax to the stories of the people's entrance into the land in Joshua's final words to the people at the end of the conquest in chapter 24. Just before the people settle into their newly allotted areas, Joshua gathers them at Shechem to renew their pledge of covenant faithfulness to YHWH. True to the ways of this relational God for whom the call to undivided loyalty occurs only in the context of prior, divine gracious activity, Joshua begins by rehearsing the story of what YHWH has done for the people to bring them into the land (24:1-13). In response to YHWH's gracious protection and provision, he then calls the people to be completely devoted to YHWH (vv. 14-28). Joshua insists that they serve YHWH "honestly and faithfully" (v. 14). The Hebrew terms here (*tāmîm* and *'emet*—"completeness" and "truth") express the idea of wholehearted service with integrity. And Joshua goes on to define what this undivided loyalty looks like in the people's lives: "So now put aside the foreign gods that are among you. Focus your hearts on the LORD, the God of Israel" (v. 23).

So the story of Israel's entrance into the land begins in Joshua by showing that *obedience was to be the rule to govern how the people lived as YHWH's called community* (and that life-giving success flows from that obedience). As soon as our biblical ancestors settle into the land of Canaan, however, something changes. In the stories of the book of Judges, the people live together in tribal groups, and YHWH raises up local heroes ("judges") to rescue them from various enemies. YHWH's faithful commitment to his people shines through these stories. But at the same time, the realities of life in a new and vulnerable situation begin to overshadow the call to undivided loyalty. Slowly but surely, the covenant people—and even the judges raised up to lead them—struggle to be faithful to YHWH. Although Joshua established that *obedience was to be the rule* to govern the people's life, Judges shows that *disobedience became the practice.*

Right from the outset, something is amiss. Judges begins by retelling the events of Israel's entrance into the land and the attempts to conquer the people of Canaan (Judg 1), but it suggests that everything didn't transpire in the ideal way we might suppose from the stories of Joshua. From the beginning, the Israelites failed to drive out many of the inhabitants of Canaan (even some of those that Joshua reported they had driven out) and settled for living alongside these groups (e.g., 1:19-21, 27-36). The words of a divine messenger to the people explain these failures as the result of the people's disobedience: "But you didn't obey me. . . . I won't drive them out before you" (2:2-3); "They went after other gods from among the surrounding peoples, they worshipped them, and they angered the LORD" (2:12). Specifically, the narrative reports that the Israelites struggled with the temptation that we'll see again and again in their generations to come—the worship of the god Baal (2:11-13). But why would the covenant community who had experienced YHWH's deliverance in Egypt and provision in the wilderness and heard the call to obedience as the rule for success yield—here and in generations to come—to divide their loyalty with a Canaanite god? Our knowledge of baalism indicates that it was a venerable, centuries-old nature/fertility religion fit for the difficult environment of Canaan. It was a religion concerned with making sure that the rains came, crops grew, and animals reproduced.[8] It was about survival in the real world of needed water, food, and resources. Baal worshippers climbed up to sanctuaries located on elevated hills, surrounded by symbols of fertility such as green trees and wooden poles (Asherah poles), and they engaged in worship practices designed to move gods and goddesses to provide what's needed for life. The worship of Baal might seem strange, but the ideas are familiar even in our day. As Timothy Green notes, still today our society pushes us to trust our survival to institutions that promise financial security, corporate structures that promise advancement, and even "worship centers that proclaim a gospel of prosperity."[9] In the same way, YHWH's people in Canaan struggled with the basic human dilemmas of mistrust and fear over provision and protection.

From this point forward, the stories of Judges depict Israel caught in a repeating cycle of disobedience, oppression by enemies, repentance, divine deliverance, and then disobedience again (e.g., 2:11-23; 3:7-12). The stories also portray Israel in a downward slide featuring increasing unfaithfulness to YHWH and the disintegration of the people's social and moral life.[10] Across the stories in Judges, there is a steady religious and moral decline from obedient and successful leaders like Othniel, to tragic figures like Samson, to complete moral chaos and civil war (chs. 19–21). By the time we reach the end of the account of the people's entrance into the land, *disobedience has become the practice*. And this practice will soon be firmly established under the monarchy that is the next stage to emerge.

War, Violence, and the Mission of God

Before moving to the next part of the story of Israel's life as YHWH's people, let's return to the question raised earlier concerning how some of the new elements that enter the OT story at this point fit into scripture's larger plot line. In the context of Israel's entrance into the land, we encounter one set of those new elements—war, violence, and conquest.

War and Violence throughout Scripture

War and violence commanded and sometimes performed directly by God appear throughout the OT. Matthew Schlimm observes that the OT mentions violence in every book except Ruth.[11] The NT, too, contains images of war and violence connected with God and Jesus, especially in contexts of judgment (e.g., Rev 19:11-16). Christians have long wrestled with the danger that the conquest stories and other violent passages might be used to justify war or the displacement of populations such as Native Americans.[12]

Specifically, in Joshua (introduced in Deut 7 and 20) we see the God-ordained slaughter of the "seven nations" in the land (Hittites, Girgashites, Amorites, Canaanites, Perizzites, Hivites, Jebusites—see Deut 7:1) as a radical act of devotion to YHWH—an act designated by the Hebrew term *ḥerem* ("utterly wiped out as something reserved for the LORD," Josh 6:17). The term itself doesn't have to imply destruction (it simply means something or someone given over to YHWH and placed off-limits for everyone else). Yet, in the stories of Israel's entrance into the land, this action often takes the most violent forms of the total killing of all living things (humans and animals) and the destruction of all property in a conquered Canaanite city.

Holy War?

The war-related actions described in Joshua have sometimes been labeled "holy war." This designation entered biblical scholarship in the early twentieth century, made popular by the 1951 work of Gerhard von Rad (*Holy War in Ancient Israel*). Yet, the label doesn't appropriately recognize the diversity of actions and rationales portrayed in Joshua or elsewhere in the ancient Near East. Similar acts of destruction done in devotion to a god appear in nonbiblical texts (e.g., the ninth-century BCE inscription of King Mesha of Moab). But the OT associates a range of practices with the Hebrew term (*ḥerem*) used in Joshua.[13]

The question of how to interpret divinely commanded violence within scripture has evoked tremendous debate, and many creative, credible, and often helpful suggestions have been given.[14]

Christian Approaches to Divine Violence

Eric Seibert has recently identified seven main approaches among Christian scholars for interpreting biblical texts that portray God acting violently and commanding others to do likewise:[15]

1. Defending God's Violent Behavior (as just or for the greater good)
2. Balancing God's Violent Behavior with God's Other Behavior
3. Critiquing God's Violent Behavior

4. Accepting *and* Rejecting God's Violent Behavior at the Same Time
5. Reinterpreting God's Violent Behavior Symbolically
6. Protesting God's Violent Behavior
7. Celebrating God's Violent Behavior (as necessary to establish justice)

For my telling of the OT story, however, the most pressing question is how this divinely commanded war and extermination of the people in Canaan at Israel's entrance into the land can possibly fit with the larger OT plot line of a God who has undertaken a mission to restore creation to its intended right-relationships and has called Israel to be an instrument of blessing to *all* the people of the world.[16] Suddenly, after YHWH's covenant people have been created and formed to be priests who carry the divine, life-giving presence to the world, those same people become death-dealing agents of war and destruction to the first populations they meet after exiting the wilderness. The OT story has insisted that YHWH's election of Israel didn't necessitate the exclusion of other people but was meant to serve them (see Gen 12:1-3; Exod 19:4-6). Yet here the texts seem to portray exactly the opposite!

So, how, if at all, can we read the stories of the conquest of Canaan within a missional telling of the OT story? Should we read these stories as saying that Israel indeed carried out its role to make YHWH known to the nations, but the Canaanites came to know him as a God of judgment? There are, after all, some texts that portray the Canaanites as especially unrighteous (Deut 18:9, 12)—even as attacking Israel first (Josh 11:1-5)[17]—and their destruction as a form of divine punishment (perhaps illustrating YHWH's promise to Abraham, "those who curse you, I will curse," Gen 12:3). But these claims don't appear consistently, and this explanation seems too far from YHWH's intentions to bestow *life-giving* blessing through Israel. Or, should we conclude that the conquest stories weren't meant to be taken literally but only as a metaphor for the uncompromised obedience that Israel was supposed to have in resisting idolatry? As we've seen, the book of Judges preserves a different tradition of the entrance into the land that doesn't portray such successful slaughter and comprehensive conquest. Additionally, the "seven nations" of Canaan (Deut 7:1) can't be precisely identified as historical entities and were perhaps meant to be symbols of all powers hostile to Israel's existence as YHWH's people.[18]

Perhaps the best option is to see the divinely ordained destruction of the Canaanites as a one-time only stance by YHWH, taken at this point in the OT story in order to preserve the covenant people physically (from destruction) and spiritually (from idolatry) during the critical and risky moment of their initial establishment in the land, but ultimately done for the purpose of using them to bless all peoples in the long run.[19] In other words, the conquest of the Canaanites may represent YHWH's short-term surrender of certain nations for the long-term benefit of all peoples over time.[20] Notice, for example, that YHWH's actions that support Israel in conquest occur at this point in the story when Israel was small, weak, and vulnerable—when the very survival of the group YHWH had chosen to carry his redemptive mission of blessing to the whole world was at stake. These are not divine sanctions for powerful empires. If, at the outset, Israel had lost its very existence or its covenant identity through idolatry, the divine mission would've lost its instrument of implementation. Notice, too, that the command for this kind of war and conquest is never repeated in scripture, nor is it given as a pattern or model for Israel (or any other group) to follow in the future. Even in the next stage of the OT story, when kings such as David and Solomon undertake successful military actions with YHWH's help, they're not given the sanction to carry out the kind of violence depicted here (and are condemned when they do, see 1 Chr 22:7-8). Moreover, the exclusivism reflected in this conquest moment finds extensive counterbalances in the many scriptures we have seen and will see throughout the canon that emphasize the universal scope of YHWH's ultimate concern for humanity and the holistic vision of peace and well-being (*shalom*) that represents YHWH's long-term goal for creation.

Even if we think in these terms, however, there is no fully satisfying (or simple) answer to the question of how to understand the conquest stories at Israel's entrance into the land within a missional telling of the OT story. The actions described in these narratives have been and remain a serious problem for those who sense a larger plot of God's redemptive mission at work in scripture's story. They remind us that the present form of the OT that we read consists of earlier, smaller stories that have been taken up into a new frame of reference in the Protestant canon and made part of a larger story about God's mission and people. And some of those smaller stories, coming as they do from the cultural context of ancient Israel, don't fit easily with the larger narrative that is now visible in this new canonical frame of reference. The conquest stories reflect the common cultural ideas of the ancient Near East, but their exclusivism seems out of touch with what is now the biblical story as a whole.

Perhaps we might use the analogy of a sophisticated piece of music.[21] In its completed form, a musical composition brings all its parts together into a unity created by the ways the various chords and melodies fit with one another. But this unity isn't uniformity. The unity consists of contrasts: chord progressions sometimes run counter to the main melody; a passage in a major key is followed by one in a minor key; a chord full of harmonic tension resolves to a chord with less or no tension. The point is that dissonance and tension are essential elements of music (except for bland, boring music) but dissonance and tension have meaning only within the overall musical composition. So, dissonant chords contribute to the overall harmonic structure of the piece, even as they remain noticeably different from the most prominent sounds. So, too, the conquest stories at the entrance to the land keep the OT from being a bland, one-note work. Yet, they remain dissonant and discordant elements within the whole of Christian scripture that should continue to make us uncomfortable and push us toward ongoing critical reflection.

Life under Monarchy and the Practice of Disobedience

When we left the story of our biblical ancestors during the entrance into the promised land in Joshua and Judges, YHWH had declared that obedience was to be the rule to govern how the people were to live as the divinely chosen instrument of blessing in this new era, but disobedience was gradually becoming the people's practice. The books of Samuel and Kings tell the long story of the next part of Israel's life in the land as YHWH's people.[22] Across five centuries in the story's timeline, the covenant people continue to struggle with their identity as those called, created, and formed to participate in the divine life-giving mission in the world. Here, Israel's story becomes the story of kings and kingdoms in particular. And here, disobedience becomes firmly established as the practice that leads eventually to destruction and exile.

Threats, Fears, and Replacement Kings

The practice of disobedience intensifies almost immediately after the judges' era. The covenant people have the divinely ordained leadership of Samuel, who serves as a prophet, priest, and judge to guide them in living out their identity as YHWH's people (1 Sam 1–7). But soon the threat of the Philistines bears down on them, and they find themselves under attack, at risk of having their very existence swallowed up just when it's getting established. And once more, the Israelites, who have witnessed so much divine deliverance, protection, and provision throughout their story, succumb to the basic human dilemma that has so often plagued them in the past and will continue to plague them throughout their generations ahead—fear for survival and the struggle to trust. As a result, they decide that they need a king of their own who can defend them from threats, fight their battles, and ensure their survival (8:4-5).

The mindset is somewhat understandable. The people's thinking reflects the common discourse of kingdoms and empires in ancient Israel's world. Empires often described the foreign peoples outside the center of their kingdom as uncivilized forces of chaos that threatened the very existence of the homeland and required a powerful human king to subdue and control them.[23] The Israelites also express internal reasons that seem to reflect fear over their own increasing social and moral chaos seen in the downward spiral in the time of the judges and the corrupt leadership of Samuel's sons (8:1-5). They seem to fear that they themselves are in danger of becoming the chaotic force that threatens their own long-term survival.[24] Still, the people's determination to get a king is ironic in the context of their journey with YHWH. Already in the judges' era, for example, when an earlier generation had offered kingship to Gideon after his triumph over Israel's oppressors, he responded by asserting that only YHWH should rule over Israel (Judg 8:22-23)—so any human king would be a poor replacement for YHWH, merely a "substitute king."[25]

The people's insistence that they need a king in 1 Samuel 8:4-6 is even more ironic because it follows another instance of YHWH's miraculous protection recounted in 1 Samuel 7:2-14. As the Philistines pressed their attack, Samuel called the people to the kind of total obedience that Joshua prescribed as the rule for their life (7:2-4; see Josh 24). While Samuel prayed and offered sacrifice, YHWH himself "thundered against the Philistines with a great blast" (7:10), ultimately bringing the Philistine threat to an end and leading Samuel to dedicate a monument called "Ebenezer" ("stone of help") to signify that "The LORD helped us" (7:12). Seemingly in the next breath, however, the covenant people can't resist their survival-oriented inclination to have a king (8:4-5). Even when YHWH has Samuel try to dissuade them with a warning about what they will suffer at the hands of their own king (8:9-18), the Israelites fearfully insist, "There must be a king over us so we can be like all the other nations... [and he can] lead us and fight our battles" (8:19-20).

Even at this moment of Israel's fear-driven turn to human replacement kings, however, the OT story again provides a reminder of what the covenant people's identity is supposed to be in order to participate in YHWH's bigger mission for the sake of all the world—namely, an identity marked by whole-hearted devotion and undivided loyalty. When the covenant people begin to shift farther from the rule of obedience to the practice of disobedience, the same call for wholehearted dedication and unadulterated trust that rang out at Sinai (Exod 20:3), in the wilderness (Deut 6:4-5), and at the entrance into the land (Josh 24) echoes again at the inception of the monarchy. As Samuel introduces Israel's first king, he also proclaims that the people must still fear, worship, and obey YHWH: "Yes, you've done all this evil; just don't turn back from following the LORD. Serve the LORD with all your heart.... Just fear the LORD and serve him faithfully with all your heart" (1 Sam 12:20, 24).

Kingship and the Mission of God

Just as we saw with the elements of war and conquest, the appearance of kings in Israel's life raises the question of how this new element of kingship fits into the larger OT story of YHWH's mission to restore creation and Israel's calling to participate in that mission. The people's decision to insist on having a king is certainly a new development in the covenant relationship and apparently not one that was YHWH's initial idea.[26] It calls into question Israel's identity that we've seen thus far, where the covenant people *as a whole* were called, created, and formed to be an instrument of blessing to all nations. Together, they shared YHWH's special purpose and a special status. But as the story of Israel's kings unfolds across Samuel and Kings, the monarchy often seems to co-opt the notion of Israel's special relationship with YHWH and the world in order to use it to further the wants and needs of the royal establishment.

How does human kingship, which appears as the people's idea at this moment of their life, become part of the larger story of YHWH's mission to restore creation? True to the form we've seen throughout the OT story, the covenant God, who has entered into a genuine, gracious, give-and-take relationship with the peculiar community he has created as his own, seizes the initiative back from his fearful people and incorporates their new reality of kingship into his larger redemptive plot line and Israel's larger identity as YHWH's instrument. Although the stories about Israel's first king, Saul, are honest about the negative side of human kingship (1 Sam 10:17-27a; 12:12-25), YHWH nonetheless grants Saul a prophetic anointing, places the divine spirit upon him, and uses him to rescue the Israelites from oppression (9:1–10:16; 11:1-15). Here, the monarchy's role in the story is similar to the role of the Canaanite conquest and even the judges who protected Israel. At this moment in Israel's life as YHWH's people, the monarchy gives the emerging community some initial strength to gain space and independence in order to establish themselves in the land and begin to form a society that reflects YHWH's social, economic, and religious ways.[27]

The most definitive and surprising instance of YHWH's gracious engagement with the human-generated enterprise of monarchy, however, comes in another moment of divine covenant-making in 2 Samuel 7. Now, once Israel's second and greatest king, David, has become established on the throne—and in spite of the monarchy's origins in the people's fear for survival and lack of trust in divine provision—YHWH announces through the prophet Nathan a covenant promise that stands alongside the earlier promises to Noah, Abraham, and Moses. YHWH unconditionally promises to give David an everlasting dynasty in Israel (vv. 11-13). Not only does YHWH commit to keep David's descendants on the throne forever, he promises to establish a special relationship with these kings: "I will be a father to him, and he will be a son to me.... I will never take my faithful love away from him" (vv. 14-15).

Davidic Royal Theology

YHWH's commitment to David in 2 Samuel 7 (see also 1 Chr 17) gave rise to a tradition in ancient Israel that scholars have labeled "Royal Theology" or "Zion Theology." This was the belief that YHWH had unconditionally committed to the Davidic monarchy and would protect Jerusalem (Mount Zion) as his holy city forever. The tradition appears in numerous places in the psalms and prophets (e.g., Pss 2; 89; 132; Isa 2:1-4). The Babylonian destruction of the temple and the exile raised serious questions for this belief.

With these words, YHWH pledges to become directly and personally involved with the new institution of Israelite monarchy that the people have injected into the divine plot line. Once more, the character of the covenant God in the OT story shines through. YHWH has shown repeatedly that risky cooperation with less-than-perfect partners is his primary mode of redemptive operation in the world, even making the people's ill-conceived and ill-fated actions usable within his restoration purposes.

But we see something even more than that in this covenant-making moment. YHWH doesn't simply pledge to be involved with Israel's kings; he claims the whole enterprise of Davidic kingship for himself, adopting it for his own and pulling it into the experience of his "faithful love." Having already warned the people of the bad things that kings could do (1 Sam 8:7-18), the gracious covenant God isn't willing to stand idly by and let kingship follow whatever course it will. Much like the Creator who works to bring life-giving order out of chaos, or the loving parent who takes a "Let me try to work with that" attitude to the good qualities of a struggling child, YHWH commits to do everything possible to take this potentially disastrous enterprise and make the best of it. In and through the less-than-ideal twists and turns, YHWH remains committed to Israel and the larger purposes he has for them.

The words of David's follow-up prayer to YHWH's promise (7:18-29) express *how* the covenant with David and his house fits within YHWH's broader redemptive purposes. As Christopher Wright observes, the language and themes in this prayer link the new commitment to the Davidic kings with Israel's larger identity and mission for the world.[28] David recalls the exodus, when Israel became "the one nation on earth that God redeemed as his own people" (v. 23). He refers to Israel's priestly calling at Sinai to be those who carry YHWH's "name" into the world so that all people will recognize YHWH as Israel's God (v. 26). And perhaps most importantly, he renews the language of the covenant with Abraham (Gen 12), asking YHWH to "bless" this dynasty with the "blessing" that is meant to be extended to all the families of the earth (v. 29). In David's prayerful expression, the OT story proclaims that YHWH folds the human project of Davidic kingship into the wider redemptive purposes of YHWH's mission and Israel's identity as the instrument within that mission. The king doesn't replace the people as YHWH's instrument, but he represents the community that has experienced YHWH's calling and deliverance. David and his royal successors will represent YHWH's rule over the covenant people and the nations of the world.[29]

They will provide the means to accomplish YHWH's goals for all creation and the task given to Abraham's descendants. Thanks to this gracious enfolding by YHWH, from now on, the agent that leads the covenant people in fulfilling their call to be life-givers and blessing-bringers will be both a descendant of Abraham *and* a son of David.

As we'll see in the next part of the story, Israel's kings will consistently fail to live up to this divine ideal, often yielding to the ongoing dilemmas of pride, fear, mistrust, and disobedience. This reality makes the unconditional character of YHWH's new commitment in 2 Samuel 7 vital. In scripture's story, YHWH remains committed to working through this new human enterprise of the Davidic kingship, even when it so often fails. Eventually, in light of these royal failures, Israel's prophets will project this trust in YHWH's commitment into the future as the hope that YHWH will designate an ideal Davidic leader (*Messiah*, "anointed one") who will live up to the divine intentions and be an agent of life-giving blessing to Israel and, through them, to the world (see Isa 9:1-7; 11:1-9; Mic 5:2-6; Ezek 37:15-28).

Jesus as Messiah

Early Christians interpreted Jesus as fulfilling the hope for a future ideal leader who would usher in God's kingdom. See the opening of the Gospel of Matthew (1:1-17) that describes Jesus as the Messiah (Greek, "Christ") in the line of David.

Kings, Idols, and Alliances: More Practice of Disobedience

In spite of YHWH's efforts to make the best out of the human-initiated kingship and fold it into the divine mission and Israel's identity, readers of the OT story know that all these human sovereigns are replacement kings that the people's fear and mistrust led them to substitute for the true divine ruler, YHWH. In the remaining chapters of Samuel and Kings, these replacement kings repeatedly engage in activities that demonstrate their ongoing struggle with pride, self-sovereignty, mistrust, and fear. In the terms used earlier, we might say that although YHWH established obedience as the rule to govern how Israel should live as the covenant people, disobedience became firmly established as the practice, especially through the activities of Israel's kings.

At times, this disobedience took the form of idolatry and the worship of other gods. At other times, the disobedience was the forging of alliances with other nations to try to provide security and survival, or the social and economic exploitation of the poor and vulnerable to enhance royal power and wealth. And the disobedience began immediately with David, the very one who first received YHWH's covenant promise and is celebrated as the greatest king in Israel's history. At the height of his rule, even David couldn't resist the enticements of royal power and selfish desire (2 Sam 11). After using monarchical authority to take a married woman for himself and to orchestrate the death of her husband (and David's faithful soldier), this human king makes a royal pronouncement to his general that he—like the first humans in the garden—can determine for himself what is right and wrong: "Do not consider this thing to be evil (Heb. *ra'*)" (11:25).[30] Likewise, David's son, Solomon, the builder of the Jerusalem temple and the last king to rule over a unified kingdom of Israel, is remembered for his oppressive social and economic policies and his foreign alliances that led him astray from YHWH (1 Kgs 11).

Even in the ongoing narrative of Israel's kings and their increasing practice of disobedience, however, glimpses of the larger OT story of YHWH's redemptive mission and the covenant people's wider significance within it continue to peek through. We saw these glimpses earlier at the entrance into the land in Joshua (4:24) and at YHWH's covenant with David (2 Sam 7:25-27), both of which emphasized that the divine acts for Israel are meant to be a testimony to the nations that they might all know YHWH. At Solomon's dedication of the newly built Jerusalem temple, Israel's broader calling appears again as Solomon asks YHWH to answer prayer "so that all the people of the earth may know your reputation and revere you, as your people Israel do" (1 Kgs 8:43; see also v. 60).

As the story continues after Solomon's death, the covenant people live for several centuries in the promised land in two side-by-side kingdoms known as Israel and Judah (1 Kgs 12–2 Kgs 17). But the practice of disobedience also continues, especially in the actions of their kings. This part of the biblical story focuses almost entirely on these replacement kings, as the people formed to be YHWH's instrument of blessing and priestly kingdom repeatedly turn to religious, political, and economic systems and loyalties that they think will remove their fears over provision, protection, and survival but that ultimately compromise their identity. For instance, the first story of the newly formed northern kingdom (Israel) under its first king (Jeroboam) shows the people's fear-driven desire to be assured that their God is close at hand and can be accessed at their beckon call, even confined within boundaries that they can control (1 Kgs 12). They build gold calves ("sacred cows"[31]) to make the object of their worship tangible, accessible, and even manageable. Timothy Green poignantly expresses the fearful concern that so often drives this kind of practice among God's people: "When we are threatened by circumstances, when we can't see God at work, when we grow impatient, or when we are simply seeking familiarity, we tend to fashion systems or structures.... We shape plastic, artificial forms in which we can fit God."[32]

The practice of ongoing disobedience to YHWH's instructions becomes even more apparent in the ways that the biblical storytellers introduce each successive king of Israel and Judah. A consistent feature of the story of the two kingdoms in 1–2 Kings is that before narrating selected events from a particular king's reign, the writers give a standard introduction that follows consistent patterns for northern and southern rulers.[33] Along with providing information about the kings such as their age or length of reign, the introductions repeatedly declare that nearly every one of these human replacement kings failed to follow YHWH their God with wholehearted loyalty but instead followed the sinful ways of the rulers who had gone before them. Under Solomon's son Rehoboam, Judah "did evil in the LORD's eyes... built shrines, standing stones, and sacred poles on top of every high hill and under every green tree" (1 Kgs 14:22-23). King Nadab of Israel "did evil in the LORD's eyes by walking in the way of his father Jeroboam and the sin Jeroboam had caused Israel to commit" (1 Kgs 15:26). Israel's King Ahab "made an altar for Baal in the Baal temple he had constructed in Samaria" (1 Kgs 17:32), and although King Jehu overthrew Ahab's ruling house, even he "wasn't careful to keep the LORD God of Israel's Instruction with all his heart" (2 Kgs 10:31). King Azariah (Uzziah) of Judah was more faithful to YHWH, but "the shrines weren't removed" and the people "kept sacrificing and burning incense at them" (2 Kgs 15:4). And the Judean King Ahaz, in panic-stricken fear before approaching armies, "sent messengers to Assyria's King Tiglath-pileser" and sought a political alliance that he thought could rescue his kingdom from its predicament (2 Kgs 16:7).

So the refrain goes, illustrating again and again that disobedience had become the practice of the life of YHWH's people in the land. And, according to the OT story, this disobedience eventually resulted in the fall of the northern kingdom of Israel to the Assyrian empire in the late eighth century BCE instruments by which to bless (give life to) all the families of the earth. Moses concludes the people's wilderness formation by reiterating that YHWH's mission to restore all creation is the reason for which Israel has been called, created, and formed to be the covenant people. At first glance, this element clashes with Deuteronomy's rather hostile view toward the nations who occupy the promised land. It is difficult to see how the book's urging for Israel to destroy or displace these peoples fits with the notion of Israel being a priestly instrument of blessing (we'll consider this question in the next chapter when we read Israel's conquest stories). For now, we may note, however, that Deuteronomy brings the call for Israel to occupy the land of Canaan under the umbrella of the people's participation in YHWH's mission to restore creation.

Conclusion

As readers of the larger OT story, when we arrive at the ending of the Pentateuch—and the ending of the story of the formation of God's people in the wilderness—we find ourselves looking backward and forward at the same time. We look backward to God's missional commitment to restore creation to the right-relationships of blessing with which it began and the formation of Israel as the divinely chosen instrument to participate in that mission. But we also look forward to the rest of the story. For now, once Deuteronomy's final sermon has passed on the story of God's deliverance, covenant, and law to the new generation, we have a people who've been called, created, and formed to live as God's instrument of blessing, special possession, covenant people, priestly kingdom, glory-bearers, and holy nation for the sake of the world.

So, how then will they live as God's people once they cross the Jordan River and enter the promised land?

(2 Kgs 17:1-6). Although this was a historical event that involved factors of military strategy, force sizes, resources, and more, the biblical storytellers give a theological interpretation that explains it as the consequences of Israel having failed to live out its identity as YHWH's particular covenant people: "All this happened because the Israelites sinned against the LORD their God, who brought them up from the land of Egypt" (17:7). They "worshipped other gods," "followed the practices of the nations," "built shrines," "set up sacred poles," and "worshipped images" (vv. 7-10, 12). But above all, the story says that our biblical ancestors fell victim to the human dilemma that has plagued them from the beginning—the struggle to trust and the temptation to fear: "They were stubborn like their ancestors who didn't trust the LORD their God" (v. 14). The replacement kings, shrines, images, and alliances were attempts to survive and thrive driven by fear and selfish ambition. Ironically, however, the very things the Israelites hoped would secure their survival ultimately cost them their identity and then their existence.

As the covenant people's story continued, the southern kingdom of Judah survived for almost two centuries beyond the fall of the Israelite northern kingdom. But the biblical storytellers are explicit that the practice of disobedience also continued: "But Judah didn't keep the commands of the LORD their God either" (2 Kgs 17:19). The remaining stories of the people's life in the land after the fall of the northern kingdom portray the final years and kings of Judah as a rollercoaster of obedience and disobedience (2 Kgs 18–25). King Hezekiah, who was on the throne of Judah at the time of the northern kingdom's fall, "did what was right in the LORD's eyes" by carrying out a reform that removed the nation's shrines, sacred pillars, and other tools of misplaced worship and trust (18:3-4). He resisted the temptation to fear and self-preservation. He "trusted in the LORD" (18:5) and YHWH delivered Judah from an Assyrian invasion (18:9–19:37).[34] But his son, Manasseh, the next king of Judah, swiftly reversed Hezekiah's reforms, lurching the covenant people back to the practice of disobedience through the worship of Baal, building of other sanctuaries, and bloody violence throughout Jerusalem (21:1-18).

Soon after, however, Judah's rollercoaster swung back to obedience. King Josiah "did what was right in the LORD's eyes" (22:2), carrying out an even more sweeping reform than Hezekiah's, removing all the substitute gods, idols, shrines, and altars and calling the people back to wholehearted obedience to YHWH (2 Kgs 22–23). The story portrays Josiah in the mold of

Moses and Joshua, the two figures who established Israel's identity as a covenant people and obedience as the rule that was to govern the community's life. He based his reform on the discovery of an "Instruction scroll" (Heb. *tôrāh* scroll, 22:8) found in the temple whose contents sound similar to the demands for wholehearted obedience that the book of Deuteronomy gave to the people in the wilderness before they entered the land.

Josiah and Deuteronomy

Most scholars think the scroll discovered in the temple that inspired Josiah's reform (2 Kgs 22:8) was some form of the book of Deuteronomy (cf. Deut 30:10; 31:24, 26). Josiah's reforms reflect Deuteronomy's emphases on a single location of worship in the temple (Deut 12) and wholehearted obedience to YHWH (Deut 6:4-5).

And Josiah called the people to renewed covenant obedience in the same terms Joshua used at the beginning of their journey into the promised land: "The king stood beside the pillar and made a covenant with the LORD that he would follow the LORD by keeping his commandments, his laws, and his regulations with all his heart and all his being...All of the people accepted the covenant" (23:3; cf. Josh 1:7; 23:6). In these ways, the OT story once more shows what the identity of the covenant people should've been all along: obedience rooted in trust in YHWH's faithfulness.

Yet even Josiah's renewed obedience failed to stop Judah's rollercoaster plunge back into disobedience. While still describing Josiah's reform, the biblical storytellers already declare that the people's established practice of disobedience under earlier kings like Manasseh had sealed their fate. They haven't followed the rule of obedience that could've given success in this new time of life in the promised land, and now YHWH has determined to enact a judgment that will bring the people's kingdoms to a full end: "The LORD said, 'I will remove Judah from my presence just as I removed Israel. I will reject this city, Jerusalem, which I chose, and this temple where I promised my name would reside'" (2 Kgs 23:27). Across the remaining chapters of 2 Kings, Judah's final kings continue to do evil in YHWH's sight (23:37; 24:9, 19), and soon YHWH's judgment comes. Once more, Judah forged political alliances for survival and tried to rebel against the Babylonian Empire (24:1; 25:1). In response, the Babylonians, under their powerful ruler Nebuchadnezzar, executed two destructive campaigns against Judah and ultimately destroyed YHWH's special city of Jerusalem (25:1-21). They demolished YHWH's temple, broke down the city walls, and left Jerusalem as a burned-out heap of ruins. They carried into forced exile Judah's religious, social, and political leaders, as well as a significant number of the people themselves.

These events began a nearly fifty-year-long period that has come to be called the "Babylonian Exile."[35] Scripture's narrative asserts that these terrible events were not the result of Babylonian military supremacy but YHWH's own actions of judgment brought about by the covenant people's failure to live out obediently their identity as a holy community, life-giving instrument of blessing, and carrier of the divine presence into the world (24:1-4). This era of the OT story that began with such promise—a covenant people called, created, formed, and finally sent to live as YHWH's holy people in the promised land for the sake of the world—ends with an ominous statement from the biblical storytellers: "So Judah was exiled from its land" (25:21b).

An Ending in Exile?

The first part of the story of the life of YHWH's people in the promised land (as told in Joshua–2 Kings) ends in the catastrophe of destruction and exile.[36] By this point, the covenant people have seemingly lost not only their kingdoms but their identity—everything that made them who they were: their promised land, holy city, sacred temple, and the presence of their God in their midst. If we read this ending as part of the larger story told across Joshua through 2 Kings—an account likely written after the events and intended for an audience of exiles and their descendants[37]—we begin to see the significance of the tragic story of Israel's life in the land thus far. As our biblical ancestors told and retold this story, each new generation of YHWH's people (perhaps beginning with the exiles themselves) could hear what they had been called, created, and formed to be and what went wrong. Specifically, they could see that obedience was supposed to be the rule to govern how they lived as the covenant community but disobedience became the practice.

And if we put this story of the people's life as two kingdoms in the promised land into the broader context of scripture's overall narrative, we see how this slide into disobedience happened. As Timothy Green explains, "Beneath the surface of the holy hills, sacred cows, substitute kings, and alliances is the human struggle to trust."[38] The generations of YHWH's people living in the land fell victim to the dilemma that the covenant people have repeatedly faced. They gave in to fear, mistrust, self-protection, and self-sovereignty that led them to replacement kings, false idols, and political allies. Yet, in the end, the religious, economic, and political systems they thought would give prosperity and security cost them their identity and existence.

Even so, within the larger context of the OT story, the covenant people's life doesn't end in exile. There will be another part to the story of Israel's life as YHWH's people. Already within the tragic narrative of Joshua through 2 Kings, there were hints of salvation and restoration to come on the other side of exile. Even before the entrance into the promised land, scripture's narrative asserted YHWH's commitment to the people and the possibility that they could return to YHWH and receive a new future even after judgment and exile (Deut 4:30-31; 31:6-8). And this possibility has appeared in various forms in the people's story thus far, as YHWH promised to stay with them throughout failure and disobedience (2 Sam 7:14-16; 1 Kgs 8:46-51). The story of the covenant people's life in the land up to this point not only allows its readers to see what the people were supposed to be and what went wrong. It also raises the hopeful possibility that by hearing this story, YHWH's people will come to embrace their identity anew. Perhaps, if they ever get the chance to go home from exile, they will finally be what they were called, created, and formed to be as participants within the divine mission in the world.

Chapter 7

The Life of God's People (Part 2): Exile and Return

(1 Chronicles–Esther)

Focus Texts: 2 Kings 25; 2 Chronicles 36; Ezra 9:5-15;
Nehemiah 8:1-12; 9:4-37

Location in the Old Testament Story:

1) The Introduction of God's Mission in the World (Genesis 1–11)
2) The Calling of God's People (Genesis 12–50)
3) The Creation of God's People (Exodus 1–15)
4) The Formation of God's People (Exodus 16–Deuteronomy)
5) The Life of God's People (Joshua–Esther)
    a) The Voices of Israel's Poets and Sages before, during, and after
       Exile (Job–Song of Songs)
    b) The Voices of Israel's Prophets before, during, and after Exile
       (Isaiah–Malachi)

The Life of God's People in the Larger Old Testament Story (Continued)

"Marley was dead: to begin with.... This must be distinctly understood, or nothing wonderful can come of the story I am going to relate."[1] These opening words of Charles Dickens's classic, *A Christmas Carol*, set

– 135 –

an ominous tone for the story that follows—a tale of the greedy life of Ebenezer Scrooge, the difficulties he causes for others, and his transformation after an evening of ghostly encounters. The story of new life and second chances begins at a point of death—a null point, an end. Indeed, as Dickens promises, something wonderful comes of Scrooge's story, but it begins at an end.

As the last chapter explained, the books of Joshua through 2 Kings told the first part of the story of the life of God's people in the promised land. At the beginning of that account, we found ourselves at a pivotal moment in the overall OT story of God's mission and Israel's calling to be an instrument within that mission. The larger OT plot line had introduced God's mission to restore creation to life-giving right-relationships and God's calling, creation, and formation of Israel to be an instrument of blessing to all families of the earth, a special covenant people who fulfill a priestly role for the world, and a holy nation that carries God's presence into all creation. As Israel's story reached the time of their life in the land, they existed as a people called, created, and formed to live as God's instrument. So a question hung in the air: Would they live out this identity once they crossed the Jordan River and entered the land of Canaan?

Thus far the story of the life of God's people in Joshua through 2 Kings has been a tragedy. Israel has continually struggled with the inclination to fear, mistrust, self-provision, and self-sovereignty that comprises the basic human dilemma in scripture's narrative. The realities of the world and the fears for their own survival frequently led them to turn away from the God who drew them into a covenant relationship that promised deliverance and provision. The divine instructions at the entrance into the land established obedience as the rule to govern how Israel would live as God's people, but disobedience increasingly became the practice. They chose human replacement kings and looked to other gods, political alliances, economic structures, and religious systems for safety and security only to be overwhelmed by the violent, death-dealing forces of enemies and empires. The first part of the covenant people's story ended in destruction and exile.

One of the truly remarkable things about the OT story, however, is that the life of God's people didn't end with this catastrophe. As Dickens hinted about Scrooge's tale, unexpected things were still to come. Yet, just as in *A Christmas Carol*, those new things would begin from the point of death.

Remember the words at the conclusion of the last part of the people's story: "So Judah was exiled from its land" (2 Kgs 25:21). This chapter will explore the second portion of the story of the life of God's people (told especially in 1 Chronicles–Esther) that begins at the null point of exile and continues through the people's divinely granted return and restoration back to their land. Here again, we can explore this story not to examine every detail or to offer a reconstruction of Israel's history, but to consider the major elements, key themes, and representative texts within these books in the context of the broader OT story. We can identify places where we see God's larger redemptive mission and Israel's wider role in it as an instrument of blessing, priestly kingdom, and presence-bearing people come through in the new realities of exile and return. And we can look for reminders of what Israel's identity was supposed to be in order to participate in God's bigger mission—the call to a wholehearted devotion and undivided loyalty.

Exile and the Mission of God

Before turning to Israel's restoration that makes up part two of the story of the life of God's people in the land, we need to consider how the catastrophe of the destruction of Jerusalem by the Babylonians and the exile of many of the people to Babylon fits into the larger plot line of the divine mission to restore creation and Israel's calling to be an instrument within that mission. The last chapter explored a similar question for new elements that entered Israel's story such as war, conquest, and kingship. But the elements of destruction and exile that enter the story at this point press that question in an even more forceful way. When part one of the people's story ended in 2 Kings 24–25, Jerusalem was in ruins, a significant number of Judeans found themselves living as displaced refugees or forced exiles in other lands, and those who didn't now lived in a homeland that had become a province of the Babylonian Empire. For readers of scripture's narrative, these events certainly seem to mark the end of Israel's role in God's mission, if not the end of the covenant people themselves and perhaps even of the divine mission itself.

Just imagine the impact of these events on our biblical ancestors and their understanding of themselves as God's people.

The Nature of Exile

For much of the twentieth century, scholars operated with the consensus that the exile didn't entail imprisonment, deprivation, or enslavement but was a reasonably tolerable experience in which the deported Judeans maintained a decent level of freedom and even prosperity, living a relatively benign existence with some sense of communal identity and participating in the social and economic activities of the empire. In recent years, however, interpreters have taken more seriously the traumatic personal, social, and psychological effects of the exile, exploring the ways that this destabilizing experience led the people to recalibrate their social and theological self-understanding.[2]

The very elements of their life on which they thought they could rely were gone, and the feelings of security and identity that they had once known had evaporated. Their world was not what it once was, and there was little hope of ever putting things back the way they were. Readers of the OT story living in today's United States might remember the events and experiences in the late 1990s and early 2000s that removed the long-established feelings of security and safety and led to the new reality of the "Post 9-11 world."[3] Americans had once imagined a secure world of everyday life with dependable institutions—a world where children went safely to school and returned safely home, where the mainland of the United States and its towering symbols of prosperity were thought to be untouchable by warlike acts of violence and killing, and where the economic entities of Wall Street were thought to be reliable sources with which to trust one's future. But in the wake of mass school shootings (even of elementary children), terrorist attacks, and economic collapses, that world disappeared. A sense of safety, security, and identity was gone and in its place were fear, numbness, and paranoia. While some longed for a retro-trip back to an imagined ideal past in a simpler world, most realized that a new world would have to be forged.

So it was for the Israelites and the exile. As long as there was a temple, they had the visible assurance that their God was with them. Now the Jerusalem temple was a burned-out ruin. YHWH himself had promised that there would always be a Davidic king over the people. Now the king sat in exile as a servant of a foreign conqueror. And the land that had been divinely gifted to

Israel was now a province of the Babylonian Empire. The old world of safety, security, and identity was gone. This was truly a null point.

Yet, the biblical storytellers offer a different perspective that folds even this traumatic disaster into the ongoing OT plot line of YHWH's mission and people. This is one of the places where the telling of Israel's story in the Protestant canon's arrangement steers our understanding in a particular way. As we'll see in the next chapter, most of what our biblical ancestors had to say about the experiences and significance of exile appears in the books of the OT prophets. There we'll see extended theological reflections on why exile happened, what it meant for the covenant people, how it somehow contributed to Israel's work on behalf of all nations, and how the people surprisingly found hope in YHWH even in its midst. We'll especially see how prophets such as Jeremiah and Ezekiel viewed the exile as an opportunity for Israel to bring well-being even to the land of their conquerors and for YHWH to make himself known to all nations through the people's experiences (see Jer 29; Ezek 36).[4]

But before we hear any of those deeper reflections, the canonical ordering of the OT story gives a frame of reference that is first provided by the OT Historical Books. In this primary account that stretches from the people's entrance into the land to the resettlement after the exile, surprisingly little is said about the experiences of destruction and exile. The biblical storytellers give only brief, matter-of-fact accounts that almost pass over the approximately fifty years assigned to the exile.[5] Second Kings 25 succinctly reports the destruction of Jerusalem and the essential emptying of the land of Judah (with only the poorest people left behind), mentioning only in passing an episode in Judah just after the destruction (vv. 22-26) and a status change for the exiled Judean king in Babylon thirty-seven years into the exile (vv. 27-30).

The Protestant canon then moves immediately to 1–2 Chronicles, which seem to start the story of Israel's life in the land over again.

1–2 Chronicles

The books of 1–2 Chronicles drew selectively and creatively upon 1–2 Kings (although perhaps an earlier version of Kings than what became the final form) (e.g., compare 1 Chr 13 and 2 Sam 6; 1 Chr 20 and 2 Sam 11). Chronicles reshapes the previous telling of Israel's history for the postexilic community by emphasizing that concerns over temple, worship, and Torah have been central to Israel's life from the beginning and should continue to shape this community's identity in the present and future.[6] So Chronicles begins its narrative account of Israel's history with the monarchy of Saul, David, and Solomon (everything before that time is covered only in genealogies), the primary force behind the establishment of the temple and proper worship. And the rest of the story emphasizes the connections among the kings, priests (Levites), temple, and worship.

The books (originally one composition) begin with a series of family histories tracing the generations from Adam to David (1 Chr 1–9). Then follows another telling of Israel's history under the united monarchy of David and Solomon (1 Chr 10–2 Chr 9) and subsequently the later kings of the southern kingdom of Judah in particular (2 Chr 10–36). Introductory OT textbooks often point out that specific concerns and characteristics in this account suggest that it was written during the later period of the return to the land and the rebuilding of the Jerusalem temple described more fully in Ezra and Nehemiah.[7]

Chronicles, Ezra, Nehemiah

In the Protestant canon's arrangement, the books of 1–2 Chronicles, Ezra, and Nehemiah form a type of second history of Israel alongside the first history in Joshua–2 Kings. While the first history tells a tragic story that begins with creation and ends with exile, the second begins with creation ("Adam" is the first word in 1 Chr 1:1) and moves beyond the exile to the return, rebuilding of the temple, and a new commitment to live under YHWH's Torah.

For our purposes, notice that like the ending of 2 Kings, the narrative of 2 Chronicles 36 quickly passes over the events of the exile with even less detail (vv. 9-21). It simply narrates the Babylonians' destruction of the temple and city and their deportation of survivors. It then moves immediately to events some fifty years later and describes King Cyrus's royal Persian decree that the Judean exiles could return home and rebuild the Jerusalem temple (vv. 22-23).

All in all, the life of YHWH's people narrated in the OT Historical Books passes over the exile almost as a small parenthesis in Israel's story. Unlike the prophetic books to come, scripture's main storyline gives virtually no attention to the details of the communities that lived in Babylon or the ones who remained in Judah. In and among these brief treatments, however, the first canonical descriptions of the exile in Kings and Chronicles provide the defining frame of reference for understanding the larger treatments that appear later. That frame of reference is to interpret the exile not as the result of Babylonian military supremacy or even Judah's corresponding weakness but as YHWH's own judgment on his people. Even before this climactic moment, for example, as scripture's storytellers recounted the disobedient practices of Judah's kings, they had relayed YHWH's announcement: "The Lord said, 'I will remove Judah from my presence just as I removed Israel. I will reject this city, Jerusalem, which I chose, and this temple where I promised my name would reside'" (2 Kgs 23:27). And now at the end of the Kings account they declare, "It was precisely because the LORD was angry with Jerusalem and Judah that he thrust them out of his presence" (2 Kgs 24:20). Second Chronicles makes the depiction of exile as YHWH's judgment more explicit by saying that Jeremiah had prophesied that the people would go into exile for seventy years (Jer 25:11-12; 29:10-14) and asserting that YHWH brought this exilic period so that the "land finally enjoyed its sabbath rest" (36:21).

Some OT books in the next section of the canon will suggest that this explanation—that complex historical happenings were caused solely by religious unfaithfulness—is too simple (e.g., Job, Lamentations). Even so, by identifying the destruction and exile as YHWH's own purposeful judgment on the covenant people, the narrative of the people's life in the land folds even this catastrophe into the OT's larger plot line. Exile was YHWH's response to the actions of the covenant partner that he had called, created, and formed, so it was done at his initiative, under his power, and within the context of his ongoing relationship with the people. Additionally, by referring to Jeremiah and the need for the land to have a Sabbath (2 Chr 36:21), the story of the people's life in the land says the exile was not only carried out by YHWH but served a particular larger purpose.[8]

Perhaps most important, the brief, almost passing treatment given to the exile in Kings and Chronicles suggests that the story of YHWH and

Israel will not get stuck in this moment. The exile will not be the null point but only a dot in the larger plot line—a tragic, deathly moment to be sure, but one from which wonderful new things will come. So 2 Kings 25 moves slightly beyond Jerusalem's destruction and narrates the later release of the Judean King Jehoiachin from prison in Babylon (vv. 27-30). The reference to Jeremiah's prophecy of seventy years in 2 Chronicles 36:21 likewise suggests that the exile will have an ending point. Chronicles then takes readers of the OT to that next point beyond exile when YHWH moved King Cyrus of Persia to "carry out the LORD's promise spoken through Jeremiah" (v. 22) and declare the beginning of the exiles' return home. And this is where the next book of Ezra, the first of two books that tell the story of the people's return and rebuilding, begins, with the same royal decree that marks the start of a new moment in the OT plot line.

The first presentation of the exile in the OT Historical Books—albeit brief—affirms, as Christopher Wright says, *"God's people, even under judgment, remain God's people for God's mission."*[9] The narrative merely suggests at this point what will become explicit in the reflections of the prophets to come—namely, that YHWH somehow used the experience of exile to further shape the covenant people as an instrument for divine purposes and that Israel's mission to all nations remained intact throughout the exile.

Return and Restoration

After this implicit acknowledgment that Israel's identity and mission didn't die out in the exile, the telling of the OT story in the Protestant canon's Historical Books completes the narrative of the people's life in the land by describing the return from exile and rebuilding of the community in the books of Ezra and Nehemiah. These books (originally a single composition in the Hebrew scriptures) begin precisely where Chronicles ended, relating King Cyrus's Persian decree that allowed the Judean exiles to return home and reconstruct the Jerusalem temple as the fulfillment of Jeremiah's prophecy about exile (Ezra 1:1-4). From that point, they tell the story of the long and difficult process of the return of various groups from Babylon at different times and the rebuilding not only of the temple but of the Jewish community itself, a process that stretches nearly one hundred years in the story's chronology.

Jews

The use of the terms *Jew* and *Jewish* (an English translation of the Greek *Ioudaios* and Hebrew *Yehudi*) to refer to those that the story has previously called "Judeans" is most appropriate for the period after the exile. In this context, the term denotes a more specific ethnic and religious identity initially related to the particular community around Jerusalem in the Persian period.

A Long Return

Just as with the earlier portrayal of Israel's life before the exile in Joshua through Kings, scholars have long attempted to sort out the chronological details, historical events, and literary sources in Ezra and Nehemiah, comparing them to archaeological and sociological data in order to reconstruct Israelite history in the Persian period.[10] For my purposes, however, I note that these books tell their story in ways that are different from a simple historical report. While describing the return and rebuilding, the presentation in Ezra and Nehemiah often takes the form of personal memoirs delivered in first-person, claiming to present the thoughts and perspectives of Ezra and Nehemiah as leaders (e.g., Ezra 7:27–9:15; Neh 1:1–7:73; 11:1–13:31), and both these memoirs, as well as the various narratives in the books, focus on theological matters, especially the concern to establish proper worship for the postexilic community. If we explore this part of the story of YHWH's people within the larger OT plot line, we can once again consider the major elements, key themes, and representative texts where we see YHWH's larger redemptive mission and the covenant people's wider role in it. We can look for reminders of the identity of wholehearted devotion and undivided love that the people were supposed to have in order to participate in the bigger divine mission of being a blessing to the nations.

The exiles didn't simply return all at once en masse and immediately restart their existence as a distinct community in Jerusalem. Nor was the land devoid of other people during the exile or return. The nearly century-long process unfolded through several stages. It began with an initial return that culminated in laying the foundation of the new temple in Jerusalem (ca. 537 BCE; Ezra 1–5). Along the way, however, the returning exiles encountered numerous challenges from inside and outside of Judah, including opposition from local political leaders, conflicts within their own community, and questions of authorization by the Persian imperial authorities. But even in the midst of letters back and forth to the Persian kings and hostile interactions with neighbors, leaders such as Zerubbabel and Jeshua succeeded in completing the rebuilding of the Jerusalem temple about two decades after the first group of returning exiles arrived in the land (ca. 515 BCE; Ezra 6:13-22). Over the next seventy years, leaders such as Ezra and Nehemiah came to the postexilic Jerusalem community and instructed them in the Torah, offered resolutions to community problems, and rebuilt the city's walls.

The successful rebuilding of YHWH's temple within about twenty years after the beginning of the return would seem to be the joyous climax. But things were still amiss for this postexilic people. Even as late as the time of Nehemiah's leadership in Jerusalem nearly a century after the beginning of the return, the people were still struggling to rebuild the city and re-constitute the covenant community in Jerusalem within the new political and social realities of the Persian Empire.

Identity, Mission, and a New Era

In the midst of the ongoing struggles of this postexilic community told in the books of Ezra and Nehemiah, scripture's narrative once again sounds the themes of Israel's wider significance in the divine mission. But this postexilic part of the story focuses mostly internally on the identity required for the covenant people to fulfill that significance. Thus, the portrayal of the people's reestablishment in the land after exile is similar to the way that the book of Joshua focused on Israel's particularity and protection at the first moments of Israel's entrance into the land. And just as we've seen throughout the overarching OT story, the call for Israel to live out its identity as an obedient covenant people originates in YHWH's own faithfulness and provision that took the initiative. Right from the opening of the postexilic story, the biblical writers again proclaim that YHWH has shown his faithfulness by fulfilling Jeremiah's prophecy and bringing the exiles back to the land (Ezra 1:1-4) and then helping them finally to rebuild the temple (Ezra 6:13-22). According to the canonical story, however, before much more can happen in a positive way there must be an act of repentance by the covenant people. When viewed within the larger OT plot line, this act becomes a way that the postexilic community can begin to recapture its identity as those wholeheartedly devoted to

YHWH and thus be able once again to participate in the divine redemptive mission for the world as it continues into the future.

So, just after Ezra's arrival in Jerusalem to instruct the returned exiles in YHWH's ways, he offered a repentance prayer for his people that acknowledged their long history of mistrust and disobedience, identified exile as a consequence of their past, and confessed that the people had yet to return to the undivided commitment required by YHWH (Ezra 9:5-15). Instead, they had continued to break the same prohibitions in YHWH's Torah as their ancestors who first entered the land of Canaan, intermarrying with other peoples of the land in unions that could lead them away from the fully devoted worship of YHWH alone (vv. 10-14). Later, in the midst of Nehemiah's efforts to rebuild the city, Ezra climbed a wooden platform before an assembly of the whole postexilic community and led them in a covenant renewal ceremony (Neh 8:1-12). He read aloud the "Instruction (*tôrāh*) scroll from Moses...explaining and interpreting it so the people could understand what they heard" (v. 1, 8).

Ezra Reads the Torah

The exact contents of the Instruction scroll that Ezra reads to the people in Nehemiah 8:1-12 remain uncertain. Based on his description of the words, scholars have suggested that perhaps the scroll contained portions of the legal commands in Deuteronomy or even a copy of the Pentateuch that Ezra carried with him from Babylon.

Ezra led the people back to YHWH's Torah in order to rededicate themselves in allegiance to YHWH, reject idolatry, and recover the identity that YHWH expects. They respond by turning to YHWH in a community celebration festival (8:13-18).

In the midst of these calls for renewed identity and commitment, Ezra's condemnation of intermarriage with the non-Jewish people who lived alongside the postexilic Jerusalem community creates a difficult wrinkle in this part of the larger OT plot line. At various places, Ezra's and Nehemiah's efforts to reestablish the identity of an uncompromised, fully devoted people set apart for YHWH took the form of a strangely and harshly literal separation of the Jewish people from their non-Jewish neighbors. It's true that the exiles had returned to a land that wasn't empty but was occupied not only by Judean families who had not experienced exile but also by foreigners who had settled (voluntarily or otherwise) into the conquered land in the years after the destruction and exile. The question of how to maintain a holy "differentness" for YHWH's people in a context so full of other religious, social, and political influences was real. But in the practices of Ezra and Nehemiah, this effort at identity definition and preservation took the sharp-edged form of boundaries and divisions, even to the point of forcibly destroying families within their own community. At the urging of the community's leaders, Ezra ordered that the people must divorce any non-Jewish wives and expel from the community any children they have had with them (Ezra 10:1-15). Likewise, Nehemiah, in some of the harshest language in scripture, asserted that allowing non-Jewish wives and half-Jewish children in the reestablished community hopelessly compromised its ability to be faithful to YHWH. He even reported that he cursed and physically assaulted some of those he considered guilty (Neh 13:23-25).

How can this ethnic exclusivism and harsh boundary drawing possibly fit with the larger OT story in which Israel remains called to be YHWH's instrument of blessing to all nations? The elements that appear at this moment in scripture's story raise the same kinds of questions as the people's war and conquest in Joshua and the emergence of the monarchy in 1–2 Samuel. There is no easy solution, and certainly not one that removes the discrimination, violence, and ethical problems created by having these actions portrayed in Christian scripture. All readers of the OT story should continually wrestle with how to read these passages in a way that doesn't perpetuate their harmful treatment of women and children on an ethnic or any other basis.

But perhaps we might view the exclusionary practices urged by Ezra and Nehemiah within the postexilic community as we viewed the acts of war and conquest at the entrance into the land. Ezra and Nehemiah's actions reflect a particular approach to reestablishing the identity of the returned community in the midst of a diverse religious and social situation—an approach that relies on drawing boundaries. This approach insists that YHWH's true people are only those of the ethnically pure line of returned exiles and no others may participate with them. And it seems to be motivated by some degree of commitment to the YHWH-alone religion that the prophets had proclaimed and by a fear that the land's inhabitants who weren't part of the exiles didn't share that commitment (see Ezra 9:10-15).

However, this is a short-term approach only. It won't work long-term if this re-formed community is to fulfill its mission to be an instrument of YHWH's life-giving blessing to the nations. Still, perhaps for this moment, when the fledging community of returning exiles was in its first century and most vulnerable to losing its identity in the midst of the Persian Empire, the harsh exclusionary approach was a necessary survival mechanism. Perhaps they thought that the rigid separation of the postexilic Jewish people from their non-Jewish neighbors was the way that YHWH could initially reestablish them back in the land, protect them during that risky process, and solidify a distinctive religious and cultural identity that could eventually allow them to return to their broader purpose within the larger divine vision for the world.

Boundaries, Identity, and the New Testament Letters

For a comparison with the boundary-making, internal emphasis of Ezra and Nehemiah, consider the ways that many of the letters written by Paul and others to the early Christian communities have very little outward focus but devote most of their concern to maintaining the integrity of the community in a hostile situation.

As we'll see, the prophets who come from this postexilic community and appear in the next part of the canon envision a different way of reconstituting the people's identity in this vulnerable time—an inclusive vision that doesn't rely on boundary-making but sees the Judean community as a means to draw foreigners into YHWH's people (e.g., Isa 60:1-3; Jonah). Yet, in Ezra and Nehemiah, we may feel the sense of risk that accompanied the long process of return.

Esther

The book of Esther presents a mixed example of inclusiveness and exclusiveness. This book doesn't extend the basic OT plot line but tells the story of the Jewish community living in exile in the Persian kingdom. On the one hand, the Jews there operate and even advance within the foreign kingdom (as Esther becomes queen). But they are also forced into an exclusivistic identity (that results in violence against non-Jews) as a defense mechanism for their survival.

In and among these difficult elements, perhaps the most revealing moment in this new era is the lengthy prayer of a group of Levites in Nehemiah 9:4-37, which I described in chapter 2 as one of the places where scripture's narrative rehearses Israel's past as a series of dots that connect within a larger plot line. The prayer makes confession to YHWH by moving through the major parts of Israel's life before, into, and out of exile (vv. 7-31), and finally to the present hardships of the postexilic community living under the dominance of the Persian Empire (vv. 32-37). The Levites look back over the different episodes of Israel's past and see a story whose plot line reveals the character of both YHWH and the people: "You have been just in all that has happened to us; you have acted faithfully, and we have done wrong" (v. 33). And in light of their long journey with their God, the postexilic community responds with a renewed commitment ("a firm agreement in writing" [v. 38]) to the identity to which they've been called as participants in YHWH's life-giving work in the world: "[We] make a solemn pledge to live by God's Instruction, which was given by Moses, God's servant, and to observe faithfully all the commandments, judgments, and statutes of our Lord God" (Neh 10:29).

Into the Future

When we reach the end of the second part of the narrative of the life of God's people in the land, the covenant people's story has come full circle. The people who were called, created, and formed to be the instrument within the divine mission of restoration had gotten sidetracked into exile by their own fear, mistrust, and rebellion. But now they're home. At the end of the OT's main narrative plot line, they have a chance for a new future. They have a chance to get the mission to be God's instrument for the sake of the world going again. The final words of Nehemiah proclaim that everything is purified, provided, and prepared to go forward (Neh 13:30-31). There is a postexilic group back in Jerusalem working to rebuild their city, renew their community, and reinvigorate their identity as God's covenant people, even as others of Abraham and Sarah's descendants work to maintain their identity and calling in foreign lands (see Esther). And so we're left leaning into the future, wondering how this second-chance community of returned exiles will live in this new day.

This question is not answered in the canonical OT. The prophets in the final section of the canon will have more to say about how the reconstituted people should live into their future and what YHWH intends to do with them as his covenant partner. But as our biblical ancestors told their story, they left its ending open for us who have followed them and who see ourselves as part of the broader community called to participate in God's redemptive mission in the world.

C h a p t e r   8

The Voices of Israel's Poets, Sages, and Prophets

(Job–Song of Songs; Isaiah–Malachi)

Focus Texts: Job 4–5; 31; 38–41; Psalm 22; 47; 67; 105;
117; Isaiah 1; 49; 52–53; 66; Jeremiah 2–3; 4; 29; 31;
Ezekiel 36; Haggai 1; Zechariah 8

Location in the Old Testament Story:

1) The Introduction of God's Mission in the World (Genesis 1–11)
2) The Calling of God's People (Genesis 12–50)
3) The Creation of God's People (Exodus 1–15)
4) The Formation of God's People (Exodus 16–Deuteronomy)
5) The Life of God's People (Joshua–Esther)
   a) **The Voices of Israel's Poets and Sages before, during, and after Exile (Job–Song of Songs)**
   b) **The Voices of Israel's Prophets before, during, and after Exile (Isaiah–Malachi)**

New Voices within the Life of God's People

There is something meaningful about taking time to reflect on significant periods in our lives. By thinking back over our high school years, for instance, we might perceive things we missed in the moment or understand things in new ways. I'm reminded of the devotional poem "Footprints in the Sand" (at-tributed to Mary Stevenson during the Great Depression in the 1930s) where the speaker tells of a dream in which she looked back over the various scenes of her life as a walk with God on the beach. She saw two sets of footprints during most scenes but only one set in the most difficult moments of her life. Thinking that perhaps she'd been abandoned during those moments, she received a new perspective in hindsight, as her divine companion explained that she saw only one set of footprints in the toughest times because that's when the Lord carried her.

The Protestant canon's arrangement of the OT creates this kind of reflec-tion experience for anyone trying to see a larger narrative plot line across the whole. As we've seen, the canon first presents the entire story of Israel's calling, creation, formation, and life as God's people within God's mission in Genesis through Esther—from emergence to exile to restoration. In the next two sections of the OT (Job–Song of Songs; Isaiah–Malachi), however, the Protestant canon presents a series of books whose content effectively takes readers back to the beginning of Israel's life as God's people and moves for-ward again. The individual books in these two sections contain Israel's poetry, worship compositions, wisdom writings, and the traditions and proclama-tions associated with Israel's prophets.

Many of the writings in these sections fit into and could be plotted at various points along the storyline of Israel's life already given. For instance, we could've stopped halfway through 2 Kings and read Hosea and Amos, or we could've paused after Ezra and Nehemiah and read Haggai and Zechariah.[1] But the Protestant canonical arrangement groups them together after the tell-ing of the main narrative plot in the OT Historical Books.

The Jewish Canon

The Jewish canon's arrangement gives a different reading expe-rience. It breaks the main storyline at the point of the destruction of Jerusalem and the exile (at the end of 1–2 Kings) and moves to the books of the prophets, poetry, and wisdom at that point before pro-ceeding to the experiences of the return and restoration at the end of the canon in Ezra, Nehemiah, and 1–2 Chronicles.

In one sense, the writings in these two sections, especially the prophetic books, are another telling of Israel's story from different perspectives and with different emphases. However, because we encounter these voices of Israel's poets, sages, and prophets only after we've witnessed the main storyline of God's people, we hear them in a different way than if we encountered them as isolated writings or even at their appropriate plot points along the way of the main narrative. Their canonical placement gives them the feel of being reflections on God and God's people offered at the weary end of the long, up-and-down journey told across the OT thus far. In their canonical spot, these books point to a moment when God's people arrived at the end of their story into and out of exile, looked back over the many experiences of their journey with God, and gathered the writings, traditions, prayers, worship songs, and prophetic words that reflected all the good and bad, successes and struggles, answers and questions, beliefs and uncertainties that were part of their call to live as God's people in the realities of their world.

Since my effort in this book is primarily to offer a narrative telling of the OT, I devote less space to these last two sections of the canon. They are often left completely out of overviews of the OT because they don't fit readily into the larger plot line. Sarah Koenig compares their usual treatment to the ways that the many songs in the literary version of J. R. R. Tolkien's *Lord of the Rings* were left out of the recent movie adaptations (or sung only in the background) because they didn't advance the main storyline.[2] For my purposes, I suggest we include these books by thinking of them within their canonical location as theological voices giving different viewpoints on the main storyline of the life of God's people that has already been told. The wisdom, poetry, and prophetic writings delve deeply into the covenant people's experiences that have occurred throughout their story and offer additional perspectives on who God is, who God's people are, and how God's people should live in a world filled with the difficult realities of obedience and disobedience, judgment and salvation, suffering and restoration, exile and return.

The perspectives and reflections found in these books articulate once more God's larger redemptive mission and Israel's identity as God's missional instrument. But the sages, poets, and prophets see new dimensions of this mission and identity in the various moments of Israel's story. Here again, then, we can explore these parts of the OT not to examine every detail but to consider especially the places where we see God's larger redemptive mission and Israel's wider role in it as an instrument of blessing, priestly kingdom, and presence-bearing people come through, even if in new and sometimes unexpected ways. We can also look for those places where these poetic and prophetic voices remind Israel what their identity was supposed to be in order to participate in God's bigger mission of blessing to the nations—namely, a people with wholehearted devotion and undivided loyalty.

The Voices of Israel's Poets and Sages (Job–Song of Songs)

In the first of the OT's final canonical sections, we find two things: a group of writings that seek wisdom in the complex issues of life in the world (Job, Proverbs, Ecclesiastes, Song of Songs) and a large collection of Israel's prayers and worship texts that reflect the whole gamut of the people's history and experience (Psalms).[3] These wisdom and worship books preserve the words of Israel's poets and sages who offered theological reflections on the realities of the people's life together and with God. And some of these writings, perhaps written during the crisis experiences of defeat and exile, give voice to a wide range of honest, human reactions to suffering and struggle, reactions that include abrasive expressions of grief and anger, questions about God's justice, despair over injustice, and hope for finding meaning in life's complexities. In some ways, these writings allow us to hear what has often been missing from the telling of scripture's story thus far—the human voices and personal experiences of the ones who have lived the journey of those called to be God's people in the world.

Wisdom, Experience, and the Life of Faith

Job, Proverbs, and Ecclesiastes in particular explore the complexities of the life of faith by examining human experiences (both good and bad) and seeking meaning in the realities of the world.

Song of Songs

The book known as "Song of Songs" or "Song of Solomon" is sometimes also considered part of the OT wisdom literature. Like the other wisdom books, it focuses on human experiences (although there is a long tradition of reading the book as an allegory for the love of God and Israel or Christ and the church). But Song of Songs has unique content that consists of a series of poems between two lovers that explore the joys and tensions of human love and sexuality.

Biblical scholars identify these books as part of a larger type of literature found in the Bible and the ancient world that has come to be known as "wisdom literature."[4] There seems to have been a movement or tradition within ancient Israel (and elsewhere) that involved sages and teachers trying to comprehend and communicate specific ways to understand the workings of the world and to achieve the good life of well-being day in and day out. Compared with the other parts of Christian scripture, the wisdom literature is noticeably less focused on the worship of YHWH or YHWH's deeds and more centered on the daily realities of human life. It shares many elements with the common wisdom tradition of the ancient Near East and takes the form of instructional literature that looks for patterns in everyday human experience and the natural world and draws observations about life.

Ancient Near Eastern Wisdom Literature

Numerous surviving ancient Near Eastern texts show that wisdom literature was a widespread phenomenon in cultures such as Mesopotamia, Egypt, and Canaan. The texts include collections of instructional sayings meant for children, proverbs covering many topics, and Job-like compositions wrestling with suffering and divine justice.[5]

Still, the wisdom literature acknowledges the reverence of YHWH as the starting point of this quest (Prov 1:7) and sees life's patterns as an order that YHWH has established in creation for humans to discover.

The wisdom books of Job, Proverbs, and Ecclesiastes are uniquely suited to appear in these final sections of the OT canon. They reflect upon and try to find meaning in all the complex twists and turns that have occurred in the life of God's people. These books offer a wide range of diverse perspectives on faithful living, suffering, justice, and the meaning of life. Our biblical ancestors didn't provide a simple resolution or a single, authoritative answer to the complexities of life with God in the world. Rather, they entered into a complicated conversation full of different ideas generated by the experiences of God's people throughout their story. It is not incidental that many of these wisdom books are poetry rather than narrative. Poetic language has more give to it; it's less buttoned-up and allows for ever new levels of meaning. Israel's sages have left us just such a dialogue about who God is, who God's people are, and how God's people experience life in the world.

A World That Makes Sense?

As the wise teachers among YHWH's people settled into life after the exile, they found the space to look back over their whole story and try to understand more fully what had happened, why, and what it all meant. And the more they looked, the less straightforward it seemed. Their traditions had told them that suffering, loss, and exile were simply the divinely guaranteed outcomes of disobedience, unfaithfulness, and human imperfection (see Deut 4:25-27; 1 Kgs 8:46-51; 2 Kgs 17:7-23). But the realities of suffering and questions about YHWH's justice seemed more complicated. Had everyone who suffered in Israel been equally guilty? Is what happens in life simply the result of some math equation of disobedience and punishment? What can human beings really expect to receive from YHWH and why? Why do innocent people sometimes seem to suffer while the wicked prosper? Weren't other nations just as guilty as Israel yet didn't suffer destruction and exile?

In the order of the Protestant canon, the main storyline of YHWH's people told from Genesis to Esther gives way next to the book of Job. On the surface, it's a story of a righteous person whose motives and lifestyle come under scrutiny when he experiences personal tragedies. Three friends (and eventually a fourth) meet Job and dispute the cause of his sufferings and the justice of YHWH. The sages of YHWH's people preserved a supersized section of arguments back and forth among Job and his friends in the center of the book (4:1–42:6) that contests virtually every traditionally held belief about God, justice, suffering, and how the world works, leaving unanswered questions about every one.

Job doesn't explicitly sound the themes of the divine mission or Israel's role as an instrument, and in this telling of the OT story I won't explore the many nuances of its contents and interpretation.[6] Yet, Israel's sages have given to us in Job a masterpiece of reflection on the complex question of why their people's story went as it did and what that might say about human suffering, divine justice, the problem of evil, and the stability of life in the world. By telling the story of Job and his friends, the sages explore the reasons for suffering and evil in life and the motivations that lead people to worship YHWH. But they do so by putting several different voices into an unresolved conversation. So Job's friends argue that a secure moral order of sin and punishment explains human suffering: the world works according to an order in which good actions are ultimately rewarded and evil actions are ultimately punished (chs. 4–5). If there is suffering, it's because of intentional disobedience or general human imperfection.

But Job himself objects that it's not so simple! Not only is it possible for the wicked to prosper but, he insists, imperfect human beings don't really have a fair shot at being righteous before a holy, sovereign God (9:15-20). The divine governance of the world just seems random (12:13-25). "Doesn't he see my ways, count all my steps?" Job asks; "let him weigh me on accurate scales" (31:4, 6). Even YHWH's response to Job (chs. 38–41) doesn't provide any resolution to the debate. Instead, YHWH seems to assert that not everything in life can be reduced to just versus unjust (or to any categories that humans might easily understand) and that suffering and unpredictability will always be a part of the human experience. Still, the book's portrayal of YHWH's relationship to a creation full of many complex elements suggests that it's possible for the covenant people to sense YHWH's care-taking, life-giving presence even in the midst of suffering and unpredictability.

The book of Job is long on questions and short on answers. Coming as it does after the main storyline of the covenant people within YHWH's mission, it invites a deep reflection on what has transpired in that story. But it insists that such reflection not be simplistic. Israel's sages suggest that in order to think about the experiences we've seen in the story of YHWH's people, we must learn to listen to Job, his friends, his God, and somehow all of them together.

Proverbs and Ecclesiastes continue the reflections of Israel's poets and sages on the realities of life with YHWH in the world and what the covenant people's experiences say about how life works, what is significant, and what one can expect from YHWH. These two books stand side by side (after Psalms) and form another conversation that, like Job, brings together different perspectives without a simple resolution. The many wisdom poems, sayings, and instructions preserved in Proverbs share the confident view of Job's friends—namely, that what happens in life ultimately makes sense because there is a moral order to the world in which good actions are rewarded and evil actions are punished. So the sages in Proverbs aim to transmit the insights by which young people in particular can learn to have a good life before YHWH (Prov 1:8-19). They encourage people to seek wisdom in both good and bad experiences in order to perceive this divinely ordained order and live in accordance with it.

By contrast, the voice of the sage preserved in Ecclesiastes takes the more skeptical perspective of Job himself to a new level. He has a sense that everything is not quite so reliable and humans may not actually be able to know how YHWH and the world work. So there is a pointlessness to all our efforts to find meaning and success in life (Eccl 1:2). The ways of YHWH and the experiences of human life remain baffling and unpredictable and trying to pin them down is just like "chasing after wind" (2:11). "People don't know anything that's ahead of them," the sage says (9:1). "I also observed under the sun that the race doesn't always go to the swift . . . nor wealth to the intelligent, nor favor to the knowledgeable, because accidents can happen to anyone" (9:11). Standing after the main telling of Israel's story, Ecclesiastes says that one couldn't have predicted how the covenant people's life would go in the past, nor can one predict how it will go in the future.

In the end, then, the voices of Israel's poets and sages leave us with a complex dialogue about wisdom, experience, and faith that befits the complexity of Israel's life as YHWH's people. The writings are a multi-voiced conversation that doesn't resolve into a single viewpoint on issues such as divine justice, righteous rewards, and human suffering.

Worship, Prayer, and the Life of Faith

Israel, the Worshipping Community

As the covenant people stepped into their new reality on the other side of exile and return, their poets and sages also found space to look back over their life as a worshipping community. They had been a community centered on the worship of YHWH—worship that found expression in the temple with its ceremonies, priests, and practices, but also in the prayers and songs of worshippers as they expeireced all the ups and downs that make up the life of faith. All along their journey told across scripture's narrative, the community of YHWH worshippers went into YHWH's sanctuary, played music, sang songs, lifted their hands in prayer, made offerings and sacrifices, and recited liturgies that brought their personal and communal lives into YHWH's holy presence. This worship was done by individuals, the community, and even the king in both scheduled and unscheduled times. And the occasions for worship could be times of celebration or distress due to a wide variety of reasons.[7]

Throughout all the different occasions, Israel's priests and other worship leaders wrote, preserved, and collected the songs, prayers, and liturgies of the people, some of which were associated with well-known figures such as David, who were remembered for their involvement in music and worship.

The Psalms in Israel's Worship

Most if not all of the psalms were originally composed to be used in worship in ancient Israel rather than for personal meditation. They were likely written by members of priestly guilds (see those associated with Korah in Pss 42–43 and Asaph in Ps 50). Although seventy-three psalms mention David in their title, the Hebrew phrase translated "of David" more accurately means "dedicated to," "in honor of," or even "about" David and was likely an after-the-fact insight into how these prayers illuminate the stories of David's life.

In the postexilic moment of Israel's story—as the people faced a new and open future—their poets and sages gathered many of these prayers, songs, and liturgies into the collection of 150 poems found in the book of Psalms.[8] Although these worship poems originated in different historical eras (and individually went through various phases of editing and collection), the anthology of prayers, songs, and liturgies allowed new generations to face their open and uncertain future by hearing once again—and even taking up for themselves—the voices and experiences of those who had gone before, who had struggled to remain faithful, and who had offered their words and feelings to YHWH about all the good and bad experiences they endured as individuals and a community. Not surprisingly, then, there are many different types of psalms that reflect a wide variety of circumstances, although most are either songs of praise (hymns) or pleas for help in times of distress (laments/complaints).[9] And they allow us to hear the covenant people's honest responses to YHWH and his actions—responses that were sometimes expressions of gratitude or pleas made out of trust and hope, but other times sharp criticisms of YHWH by his very own people.[10]

Worship, Prayer, and the Mission of God

In and among all the expressions of praise, thanksgiving, plea, and even honest lament, despair, and sometimes anger, the prayers and worship songs of the covenant people return over and over to YHWH's larger mission to restore creation to divinely intended right-relationships and Israel's role as the instrument to help bring that bigger mission to the nations.

First, Israel's words of worship and prayer consistently proclaim the larger idea that YHWH wants to bring the knowledge of his name, character, and saving work to the nations so that *all the people—all the earth*—will join with the original covenant people in hearing, knowing, and worshipping YHWH. Israel's psalmists repeatedly assert that YHWH is the Lord of all the earth and call on all the peoples of all lands to turn to YHWH: "Sing praises to *our* king! Sing praises because God is king *of the whole world*!...God is king over the *nations*" (Ps 47:6b-8). The Israelite worshipper says, "*All the earth* worships you....All you nations, bless *our* God!" (Ps 66:4, 8), and the praise leader commands, "Give to the LORD, *all families of the nations*—give to the LORD glory and power!...Tell the nations, 'The LORD rules!'" (Ps 96:7, 10). Israel's psalmists even declare that YHWH's good and gracious treatment of Israel provides the motivation for all other nations to turn to YHWH: "Praise the LORD, all you nations! Worship him, all you peoples! *Because* God's faithful love toward *us* is strong, the LORD's faithfulness lasts forever! Praise the LORD!" (Ps 117). One worshipper even turns the ancient priests' blessing from Num 6:22-27 into a prayer for Israel but for the sake of fulfilling Abraham's calling to be an instrument of blessing to the nations: "Let God grant us grace and bless us; let God make his face shine on us, *so that* your way becomes known on earth, *so that* your salvation becomes known among *all the nations*" (Ps 67:1-2). Israel's psalmists pray for the time when the "leaders of *all* people are gathered *with* the people of Abraham's God" (Ps 47:9).

These prayerful expressions of YHWH's mission to bring his name and praise to all the earth sometimes also include the proclamation that YHWH will defeat and subdue the nations beneath an exalted Israel: "He subdues the nations under us, subdues all people beneath our feet" (Ps 47:3). Some of these prayers are directed specifically at "enemies" who've acted in violent, destructive, and deadly ways toward YHWH's worshipper (see Pss 3; 4; 10), asking YHWH to defeat and even destroy those threats. But others are more general, referring broadly to nations and their rulers being made subject not only to YHWH but to Israel and its king. The prayers of the "royal psalms," which focus on Israel's earthly king, provide the most noticeable examples: "Just ask me and I will make the nations your possession," YHWH offers the Israelite king; "You will smash them with an iron rod; you will shatter them like a pottery jar" (Ps 2:8-9; see also 149:6-9). Although these requests are violent and vengeful-sounding—seemingly a contrast with YHWH's mission to bring his life-giving blessing to all nations—it's important to remember that they are prayers, not actions the covenant people intend to carry out themselves. And they are the honest prayers of those who've been severely hurt and abused. Even more important, the nations identified in these prayers are those who reject YHWH and oppose YHWH's work in the world: "The earth's rulers take their stand; the leaders scheme together against the LORD" (Ps 2:2). So, these aren't selfish pleas for personal revenge but hopeful cries that YHWH would establish justice, protect his people, and remove the roadblocks to the spread of his knowledge and worship throughout the world.

Second, Israel's prayers and worship songs explicitly call upon the covenant people themselves to make YHWH known to the nations in active ways, proclaiming YHWH's deeds as a witness to all people, attracting others to YHWH by how they live as YHWH's worshippers, and serving as an instrument to nourish devotion to YHWH in all the earth.[11] Over and over the psalmists urge their fellow Israelites not only to call upon YHWH for themselves but to "make his deeds known to all people!" (Ps 105:1). "Proclaim his mighty acts among all people," the music leader tells the congregation; "Declare God's glory among the nations; declare his wondrous works among all people" (Ps 9:11; 96:3). And other worshippers declare their own intention to witness, even among the rulers of the nations: "I will talk about your laws before rulers with no shame whatsoever" (Ps 119:46); "I will give thanks to you, my Lord, among all the peoples" (Ps 57:9).

Perhaps the most interesting observation about the voices of Israel's poets and worship leaders in Psalms is that their re-articulations of YHWH's mission and Israel's role as the witness-bearing instrument within it appear across all the different types (genres) of prayers and songs that represent all kinds of situations in the lives of individual worshippers and the covenant community. The psalmists remember and proclaim the larger divine story not just in good times but even in the midst of personal difficulties, national humiliation, and communal suffering. Predictably, it's easiest during the good times of stability, normalcy, and victory reflected in the psalms of praise and thanksgiving. So, as quoted above, the hymn-singer of Psalm 117 praises YHWH for the "faithful love" his people have received and calls on "all you nations" and "all you peoples" to do the same (vv. 1-2). Likewise, the worshipper of Psalm 98 gives thanks to YHWH for the "wonderful things" (v. 1) that he has done and proclaims that YHWH has "revealed his righteousness in the eyes of all the nations" (v. 2; see also Pss 47; 66; 67; 100). By incorporating the bigger vision of YHWH's work in and for the whole world into celebrations of success and prosperity, our biblical ancestors fought the temptation to take the credit for themselves or lose sight of the fact that these times are gracious gifts from their God.

Even among the prayers for help (laments), Israel's worship poets give voice to YHWH's larger mission and Israel's identity within it. The intense and lengthy plea for deliverance in Psalm 22 culminates with a broad vision that the sufferer's deliverance will result in all peoples being drawn to YHWH: "Let all those who are suffering eat and be full!...Every part of the earth will remember and come back to the LORD; every family among all the nations will worship you" (vv. 26-27) (see also Pss 57; 126). The psalms that reflect the earlier reality of the monarchy and offer prayers for the king or describe liturgies related to the king—psalms that we might expect to be the most narrow in their vision—also articulate the bigger missional activity of YHWH and Israel (represented by its human king) for the world. In the earlier discussion of the monarchy within the larger OT story (see ch. 6), I noted that the Davidic kings were enfolded into YHWH's call to Abraham's descendants and became the representatives and means by which Israel would bring YHWH's life-giving blessing to the world (2 Sam 7). So, the royal psalmist in Psalm 72 prays for the king to have God's wisdom, justice, and protection, but alludes to the language of Abraham's calling by praying, "Let all the nations be blessed through him" (v. 17) (see also Pss 2; 18).

Perhaps most surprisingly of all, even some of the prayers, pleas, and laments that reflect the catastrophe of exile still express the larger missional vision. In the midst of the utter loss and destabilization of everything that made their life understandable, Israel's worshippers didn't let go of the conviction that YHWH's actions and their experiences have a bigger significance. As a suffering worshipper looked back on the divine anger that brought forth judgment, he prayed for YHWH's compassion and Jerusalem's rebuilding for a specific reason: "The nations will honor the LORD's name; all the earth's rulers will honor your glory because the LORD will rebuild Zion; he will be seen there in his glory" (Ps 102:15-16). And in Psalm 126, the community reflected on earlier times when YHWH "changed Zion's circumstances for the better" (v. 1), remembering that these "great things" were a witness "among the nations" (v. 2) and praying that YHWH would do them once more (v. 4).

The Voices of Israel's Prophets (Isaiah–Malachi)

After the writings of Israel's poets and sages, the Protestant canon ends with a collection of the books of Israel's prophets (Isaiah–Malachi). In light of this canonical arrangement, we can think of the prophets as theological witnesses who offered testimonies that could be plotted at different points along the storyline. As Bo Lim explains, "The prophetic collection doesn't tell a story but provides an inspired commentary on how God's people should understand the story narrated in the Pentateuch and Historical Books."[12] These writings represent the voices and traditions of a long line of Israel's prophets who confronted the people with YHWH's messages at various moments along their journey into and out of exile, often challenging them concerning their growing unfaithfulness to their calling and offering hope that their calling remained through YHWH's mercy in the face of seeming evidence to the contrary. Within scripture's story, the prophets are the foremost figures who beckon Israel to faithfulness to YHWH and to its mission as YHWH's instrument.

YHWH's Spokespersons and Their Messages

Some have called these prophets the "covenant police" among our biblical ancestors—those who sought a solution to the ongoing dilemma of their people's struggle with mistrust, fear, and self-sovereignty and the disastrous effects that dilemma continually brought.[13] They were YHWH's spokespersons and go-betweens, who brought YHWH's message to the covenant community through diverse ways and means. Although popular culture today often thinks of prophets as predictors of the future—crystal-ball-gazing prognosticators who foretold events thousands of years beyond their time—the main Hebrew term for prophet (*nābî'*) means one who "calls" or "is called." Close reading of the books shows that Israel's prophets were much more *forth*tellers than *fore*tellers. They were those called by YHWH to speak forth the divine messages to their day, their time, and their people. If YHWH was Israel's king, the prophets were the king's royal messengers to his subjects. Much like the royal heralds who worked for ancient human kings, the prophets were those who received a message from the divine king (sometimes portrayed as a visit in a vision to YHWH's heavenly throne room) and went out under commission to proclaim that message to the people (see Isa 6).

Prophets in the Ancient Near East

Prophets existed in other cultures outside of Israel and Judah, and prophecy was a widespread religious phenomenon in the ancient world. Texts describing the words and actions of prophets from various places have survived, with two major collections coming from the city of Mari in the eighteenth century BCE and Assyria in the seventh century BCE. Like Israel's prophets, the prophets from other places functioned as messengers who presented divine words in first-person and helped their kings and communities understand the actions and requirements of their gods.

The books themselves don't preserve simple transcripts of the prophets' preaching. They are collections that brought together over time the words of the prophets, as well as traditions about the prophets and the words of other prophetic figures who carried on the traditions of the original prophets.[14] Even so, within these collections we can hear the voices of YHWH's commissioned spokespersons cut through the people's moments of obedience and disobedience, prosperity and suffering, deliverance and destruction.

The Protestant canon has grouped the prophetic books into two sections, each of which contains books that relate to all three eras of Israel's story before, during, and after the exile. The first section (called "Major Prophets" due to the longer length of these books) consists of the three largest prophetic books (Isaiah, Jeremiah, and Ezekiel).[15] The second section consists of the twelve smaller prophetic books from Hosea through Malachi ("Minor Prophets"— books of shorter length). This grouping includes prophetic voices that go back to the time of the monarchies under the Assyrian Empire (Hosea–Micah), move through Judah's experiences of destruction and exile during the days of the Babylonians (Nahum–Zephaniah), and then proceed into the postexilic restoration of Jerusalem under the Persian Empire (Haggai–Malachi).[16]

In the face of the covenant people's ongoing struggle with mistrust, self-preservation, and self-sovereignty, the prophets challenged their community with YHWH's messages that centered around a few major themes.[17] First, they proclaimed the *sovereignty of YHWH*, not only over Israel but over all nations. And this sovereignty should govern every realm of life—not just religion, but politics, ethics, agriculture, economics, and more. Second, the prophets boldly *identified the people's sins*. They criticized Israel for worshipping other gods besides YHWH but also for hypocritically offering sacrifices and prayers to YHWH while at the same time violating his laws and not following his ways. They also criticized their people for political and social sins. Kings led Israel into rebellions and alliances without YHWH's approval. And the poor and vulnerable in society suffered not only at the hands of individuals who treated them unjustly but also as a result of economic structures and institutions that systematically disadvantaged them. Third, the prophets *announced both judgment and hope*. They explained tragic events such as destruction and exile as moments of divine punishment. Yet they also proclaimed the possibility of a new future beyond judgment grounded in YHWH's own faithful commitment to the people.

As the different prophets challenged the covenant people along these themes in various moments across all three eras of their journey into and out of exile, the prophets' words once again declared YHWH's mission to restore creation and Israel's calling to participate as the instrument of that mission to bring life-giving blessing to all nations. Even in the midst of sin, judgment, and exile, the prophets proclaimed YHWH's grace-filled, unaltered commitment to this mission and calling. Additionally, the prophets offered a renewed and intense emphasis on the kind of identity Israel must have in order to be YHWH's missional instrument. They condemned the religious, political, and social actions that were out of line with this identity. They declared what YHWH's sovereignty, judgment, and mercy implied for how Israel should live in its politics, economics, and worship. And they called the people to change their ways and live in holiness, justice, and righteousness. Even more, they became convinced that YHWH himself would have to change the people's character and enable them to live with the wholehearted obedience that would allow them to participate fully in the divine redemptive mission

Prophetic Voices before Exile

Prophets such as Isaiah, Jeremiah, Hosea, Amos, and Micah spoke to YHWH's people during the days of their life in the land especially about the path of mistrust, unfaithfulness, and disobedience they saw as leading toward destruction and exile.[18] Some spoke to the northern kingdom (Hosea, Amos), some to the southern kingdom (Isaiah, Micah, Jeremiah). These preexilic prophetic voices expressed YHWH's larger redemptive mission to the nations and Israel's wider role in it as an instrument. However, they gave most of their attention to proclaiming the kind of character YHWH's people must have in order to fulfill their calling as YHWH's missional instrument. They criticized the people's present character and actions and called for change. They confronted head-on the covenant people's perennial dilemma of turning away from YHWH in fear for self-preservation or in the desire for self-sovereignty. And they condemned the religious, political, and social actions that those fears and desires produced. Isaiah, Hosea, and others saw the people's worship of other gods, exploitation of the poor, greedy accumulations of land and wealth, and misguided political alliances as symptoms of the perpetual problem of turning away from YHWH but also as indicators of a character that would prevent the people from fulfilling their calling as the covenant community of life-givers and blessing-bringers.

Identity Crisis and Character Transformation

The preexilic prophets identified the root of the covenant people's perennial dilemma and flawed identity as the problem of divided loyalties. Although Israel was called to wholehearted love for YHWH (Deut 6:4-5), the people lived with compromised allegiances. So the prophet Isaiah, nearly two centuries before the destruction of Jerusalem, used the powerful metaphor of a parent and child (1:1-4), and communicated YHWH's words that the people of Israel are like children he has raised but who now refuse to acknowledge his ways and instead have become rebellious, corrupt, and "weighed down with crimes": "They have abandoned the LORD, despised the holy one of Israel; they turned their backs on God" (1:4). Instead of acknowledging YHWH as their Lord, they've looked to other political, social, and religious systems and sources to provide for their well-being. Isaiah declared, "They are full of sorcerers... they hold hands with foreigners' children. Their land is full of silver and gold... they have countless chariots. Their land is filled with idols; they worship their handiwork" (2:6-8).

In the preexilic prophets' view, this root sickness of divided loyalties produced symptoms that affected every area of the covenant community's political, social, economic, and religious life. Not only have the people and their leaders looked to political alliances outside of YHWH's will (e.g., Isa 30:1-2; 31:1-4; Jer 27:1-7; Hos 7:11-16), they've engaged in social and economic practices, institutions, and systems that marginalize, exclude, and even oppress the most vulnerable members of society—the poor, immigrants, widows, and more. The social and political elites among the people have leveraged access to resources to their own benefit and scarfed up land and houses, pushing the needy out of their way: "How dare you crush my people and grind the faces of the poor?... God expected justice, but there was bloodshed; righteousness, but there was a cry of distress! Doom to those who acquire house after house, who annex field to field until there is no more space left and only you live alone in the land" (Isa 3:15; 5:7-8). And YHWH's judgment message through Isaiah even declared that Israel's worship had been corrupted by their sinful actions. "Stop bringing worthless offerings," YHWH said, "Your incense repulses me. New moon, sabbath, and the calling of an assembly—I can't stand wickedness with celebration!... Your hands are stained with blood. Wash! Be clean! Remove your ugly deeds from my sight" (1:13, 15-16).

In the same preexilic context, the prophet Hosea spoke to the northern kingdom of Israel and vividly depicted the covenant community's same sickness of divided loyalties and its symptoms. He used the symbol of his marriage to an unfaithful spouse to depict YHWH as a metaphorical husband joined to a people who simply can't be loyal (Hos 1–3).[19] Their loyalty, YHWH proclaimed, is as fleeting as a "morning cloud" or "dew that vanishes quickly," but YHWH desired "faithful love (Heb. *ḥesed*, 'loyalty')" and the "knowledge of God" (6:4, 6). Likewise, Jeremiah, speaking a century or so later to the southern kingdom and perhaps during the time of a major religious reform undertaken by King Josiah in an attempt to correct the people's divided loyalties (see 2 Kgs 22–24; Jer 1:2), used another image to depict the covenant community's perennial dilemma of turning from YHWH to look to other sources of life. He accused the people of forsaking the "spring of living water"—an ever-flowing and consistent source of provision—in favor of digging their own wells, not realizing that they were "broken wells that can't hold water" (2:13). In other words, the people's mistrust and rebellion have made them hesitant to depend on YHWH and led them to seek their own self-made means of security and support, but without realizing these self-made wells just won't hold up. Jeremiah saw the same flawed identity of divided loyalties and compromised allegiances as Isaiah and Hosea: "Have you noticed what unfaithful Israel has done? She's gone about looking for lovers on top of every high hill and under every lush tree.... Yet even after all this, disloyal sister Judah didn't return to me with all her heart but only insincerely, declares the LORD" (3:6, 10).

Together, these prophetic voices before the exile warned the covenant people that the sickness of divided loyalties and its symptoms have prevented them from having the kind of identity they need in order to participate in YHWH's larger mission. Still, while these prophets announced divine judgment, they held out hope for something different and called the people to change in response to YHWH's words and actions. So Isaiah, after describing a divine punishment that has come upon the people (1:5-9) proclaimed that the proper response was not more worship (1:10-15) but changed behavior and righteous actions: "Learn to do good. Seek justice: help the oppressed; defend the orphan; plead for the widow" (1:17). Amos challenged the citizens of the northern kingdom, "But let justice roll down like waters, and righteousness like an ever-flowing stream" (5:24). And Micah famously reminded his Judean community, "He has told you, human one, what is good and what the LORD requires from you: to do justice, embrace faithful love, and walk humbly with your God" (6:8).

However, as time passed and the OT plot line moved toward the experiences of destruction and exile, the prophets increasingly sensed a futility to their calls for change. They seemed to conclude that YHWH's people simply can't break free from their habit of turning to other sources of provision, protection, and worship and their addiction to self-made wells, replacement kings, and substitute gods. There was a deeper character problem that made them unable simply to change their actions. As Timothy Green says, the prophets realized something about their people—namely, that the "inability to trust the Lord wholeheartedly seems to be engrained in the very nature of who they are."[20]

In response, the preexilic prophetic voices began to sound a theme of hope that will become prominent among the later prophets in the exile. They looked beyond their immediate horizon—to the "time [that] is coming" (Jer 31:31)—and proclaimed that somehow, someday YHWH will accomplish his intentions for the people by doing for them what they can't do for themselves. YHWH will deal with the human dilemma of divided loyalties by transforming the people's character so that they can live out their identity as the instrument of the divine redemptive mission.[21] Using the very word that so often described the people's habit of forsaking YHWH to seek other sources of provision and protection ("turn/turning," Heb. *šûb*), Hosea gave YHWH's promise of a new character and identity (14:4): "I will heal their faithlessness [literally, 'their turning [*šûb*]']". With the same terminology, Jeremiah announced YHWH's intentions to his audience: "Turn [*šûb*], O turning [*šûb*] children, and I will heal your turning [*šûb*]" (3:22, author's translation). And later, in perhaps the most dramatic image of transformation, Jeremiah proclaimed that YHWH will transform the people's "heart"—the very seat of will and decision-making with which Israel was initially called to love YHWH undividedly (see the discussion of Deut 6:4-5 in ch. 5): "I will put my instructions within them and engrave them on their hearts [*lēb*]" (31:33). As we've seen, the Torah in the OT refers not just to particular laws that express YHWH's will but to the whole story of YHWH's character and intentions. In the face of the people's dilemma of ingrained disloyalty, Jeremiah promised a divine transformation that would reshape their will ("heart") around YHWH's will (Torah) and enable them to live out the covenant identity to which they had been called: "I will be their God, and they will be my people" (v. 33).

Israel, the Nations, and the Mission of God

Alongside the preexilic prophets' challenges to Israel and Judah, they also sounded the theme of YHWH's mission to restore creation and the covenant people's calling to be the instrument of life-giving blessing to all nations. But living through the experiences of conflict, war, and oppression at the hands of hostile neighbors (like Damascus and Philistia) and powerful empires (like Assyria and Babylonia), prophets such as Isaiah, Jeremiah, Amos, and Micah developed complicated views concerning the surrounding nations within the story of YHWH and his people.[22]

On one hand, the predominant message from the preexilic prophets is that YHWH will eventually deliver Israel from hostile nations, bringing divine judgment on them for their acts of injustice and oppression. Perhaps the most striking examples of these judgment proclamations appear in the so-called Oracles against the Nations (e.g., Isa 13–27; Jer 46–51; Amos 1–2).[23] Here, the prophets announce divine judgment on surrounding nations for various crimes they've committed against Israel, Judah, and other communities, and the judgments often take the form of military disaster.

Oracles against the Nations

Collections of the prophets' announcements of divine judgment against surrounding nations appear in several books (e.g., Isa 13–27; Jer 46–51; Ezek 25–32; Amos 1–2) and make up the entirety of some smaller books (Obadiah; Nahum). This type of prophetic speech may have originated in connection with ancient warfare. In the OT prophets, the oracles proclaim YHWH's sovereignty over all nations, since even foreign nations are held accountable by Israel's God for their abuses and injustices.

During the turbulent years of Israel's conflicts with Damascus in the mid-eighth century BCE, Amos declared the hope that YHWH would one day act in judgment against those who hurt his people: "For three crimes of Damascus, and for four, I won't hold back the punishment, because they have harvested Gilead with sharp iron tools. I will send down fire on the house of Hazael; it will devour the palaces of Ben-hadad" (1:3-4). Likewise, Isaiah, probably in a later context, announced judgment on the mighty kingdom of Egypt: "Look! The LORD is riding upon a swift cloud, and is coming to Egypt. Egypt's idols will tremble before God; the Egyptians' hearts will melt within them" (19:1).

How can these prophetic proclamations of judgment and disaster possibly fit into the larger OT plot line of a God who has undertaken a mission to restore creation to its intended right-relationships and has called Israel to be an instrument of blessing to *all* the people of the world? This is a similar issue to what we encountered with the stories of conquest and war in the book of Joshua (although these prophetic oracles don't usually envision complete annihilation of peoples and cultures but focus on political dynasties and rulers). Some of the perspectives discussed with those stories might also be relevant here (see ch. 6). For instance, perhaps we should conclude that these descriptions weren't meant to be taken literally but only as symbols for divine judgment on oppression and injustice (and it's much clearer here than in Joshua that the recipients of destruction had engaged in sinful behaviors). As we saw at the beginning of Israel's calling, the role of blessing-bringer to the nations was never without the possibility that some could suffer judgment (especially those who "curse" YHWH's people; see Gen 12:3).

Perhaps most important here, however, the Oracles against the Nations, unlike the conquest stories in Joshua, are presented as something that *YHWH* does without Israel's participation. Israel is passive in the actions envisioned by the prophets. So perhaps these divine actions are meant to bring the knowledge and experience of YHWH's sovereignty to all nations directly, without using Israel as an instrument of either blessing or curse.[24] And YHWH's aim is not simply to defend his own covenant people but to have the faithful defense of the suffering and oppressed become a sign that draws all peoples to him. For example, as John Oswalt observes, Isaiah concludes that YHWH's acts of judgment against the nations (Isa 13–24) will show his faithfulness to the poor and distressed, and this will lead even "tyrant nations" (25:3) to worship YHWH and to come to the feast he will prepare for "all peoples" on his holy mountain (25:6).[25]

On the other hand, the prophets' view on the mission to the nations includes the belief that YHWH will use Israel to show his glory (name, ways, and character) to the nations in a way that will draw all peoples to YHWH's presence.[26] Depictions of Israel's actions in this regard will appear most fully among the prophetic voices in exile. Yet, already among the preexilic voices, Jeremiah explicitly links his calls for Israel to change its unfaithful ways to the belief that YHWH can then use them as a blessing-bringing instrument: "If you return ['turn,' *šûb*], Israel . . . if you get rid of your disgusting idols . . . if you swear by the living God in truth, justice, and righteousness, *then the nations will enjoy God's blessings*" (4:1-2, emphasis added).[27] Likewise, both Isaiah and Micah proclaim that YHWH's intention is to raise up the holy mountain in Jerusalem and draw all nations to it so that they can learn YHWH's "ways," "paths," and "Instruction" (*tôrāh*) (Isa 2:1-3; Mic 4:1-2). And both prophets declare that the result of this divine missional work will be the reestablishment of the kind of right-relationships that YHWH intends for the world: "Then they will beat their swords into iron plows and their spears into pruning tools. Nation will not take up sword against nation; they will no longer learn how to make war" (Isa 2:4; Mic 4:3).

Prophetic Voices in Exile

In the next era of the story of YHWH's people—the time of destruction and exile—the voices of Israel's prophets continued to denounce the ways that the people's identity and actions were out of keeping with what was required to participate in the divine mission of restoration. Prophets such as Ezekiel, living among a community of exiles in Babylon, used the people's long history of rebellion and failure as the divine explanation of why the exile had occurred: "They will know that I am the LORD when I disperse them among the nations and scatter them throughout the lands. . . . The land will be emptied of everything in it because of the violence of all who live there" (12:15, 19). However, when we place the prophetic voices of exile found in parts of Isaiah, Jeremiah, Ezekiel, and elsewhere into the overall plot line of the OT story, an amazing new perspective emerges. These spokespersons give a daring and surprising word from YHWH that proclaims that the exile will not just be the means of divine punishment for Israel but also the vehicle whereby the covenant people's identity will be truly transformed, making them able to fulfill their mission of being an instrument of blessing to the nations.[28]

A New Hope and a New Heart

The first part of this new prophetic vision is a seemingly nonsensical hope that YHWH will turn the lowest point of exile into a grace-filled means of transformation for the covenant people. In the ancient world's common ways of thinking, the destruction of a people's capital city and the exile of its citizens signaled an end point, maybe even the defeat of their God and the permanent loss of their identity as a people. However, not only do the exilic prophets interpret Jerusalem's destruction and exile as the actions of Israel's own God, who remains sovereign and uses these events to discipline his rebellious children, but they also call YHWH's people to adopt an ethic (guiding lifestyle principle) of hope and waiting, never losing the expectation that YHWH will make a new move and restore them for a new future. In the earliest stages of the exile, for example, Jeremiah sent a letter to the exiles in Babylon urging them to maintain hope in YHWH's assurance of a future beyond this experience: "When Babylon's seventy years are up, I will come and fulfill my gracious promise to bring you back to this place. I know the plans I have in mind for you, declares the LORD, they are plans for peace, not disaster, to give you a future filled with hope" (Jer 29:10-11). Likewise, nearly half a century later, as the years of exile droned on, another prophet urged the same ethic of hope: "Youths will become tired and weary, young men will certainly stumble; but those who hope in the LORD will renew their strength; they will fly up on wings like eagles; they will run and not be tired; they will walk and not be weary" (Isa 40:30-31).[29]

But what is the source of such a radical hope for a future beyond exile? As we've heard from the prophetic voices before the exile, Israel's prophets knew all too well that YHWH's people were plagued by the perennial dilemma of half-hearted devotion and divided loyalty and that this dilemma produced effects ranging from idolatry to economic injustice to violent oppression to ill-advised political policies. The preexilic prophets called for change. And the OT Historical Books preserve the stories of the people's repeated attempts to reform their ways (e.g., 2 Kgs 22–24). But these reforms never lasted. And the earlier prophetic voices seemed to acknowledge that there was a deeper issue—a more fundamental problem of the "heart/mind/will" (Heb. *lēb*) that desperately needed resolution if there was to be a future at all.

Now, into the middle of what appeared to be the end point of a story marked by repeated failure, the prophets of exile return to the hints of resolution given elsewhere and proclaim that YHWH has promised to do for the people what they can't do for themselves—that is, to transform their very character (heart/mind/will) so that they can receive the hoped-for new future and faithfully live out their calling to participate in the divine mission. Already Jeremiah had hinted that a "time is coming" when YHWH will "engrave" his Torah on the people's "hearts" (Jer 31:31, 33). And now, deep into the exile, the prophet Ezekiel announces that YHWH will use this very experience to transform his people for a new future. Because Ezekiel was formerly a priest in Jerusalem before his exile to Babylon, he uses priestly language and ideas (similar to the book of Leviticus) to portray Israel's dilemma, its effects, and its promised divine resolution. In the most vivid portrayal, Ezekiel first depicts the people's idolatry and death-dealing wrong relationships as polluting acts that have made Israel's land impure and necessitated the exile as a form of cleansing (Ezek 36:16-38).

But Ezekiel then proclaims YHWH's promise to do a "grand transforming act" for his people that will constitute the "divine resolution to the human dilemma."[30] He announces that YHWH will give the people a brand new "heart/mind/will" (*lēb*; 36:26). YHWH will completely transform their very character so that new actions can flow into a new future. This will no longer be a "stony heart" (or mind/will) that resists YHWH's calls to undivided trust and fails to be a means of life-giving nutrients to others out of fear for its own survival. It will be a "living" heart (lit., "heart of flesh") that that can grow into its intended shape and be a source of life. It's almost as if YHWH promises to change the people's "default settings" from self-centeredness and self-sovereignty to a first inclination toward YHWH's calling and character. And Ezekiel goes even further to announce that YHWH will give his own divine "spirit" (breath/wind; Heb. *rûaḥ*) to the people to enable them to live out obediently the identity for which they were called, created, and formed as the covenant people (36:27-28).

Yet even in the midst of this powerful promise of transformation for Israel, YHWH's words through Ezekiel keep the focus on the larger story of the divine mission to all people. Ezekiel makes the surprising assertion that the partnering, relational, covenant God has become so linked to the chosen covenant people that their disobedience and destruction have ruined YHWH's reputation among all the nations (36:20-22). And now YHWH declares that even Israel's dramatic transformation and restoration will occur so that all peoples may recognize YHWH's holy character: "Then the nations will know that I am the LORD.... When I make myself holy among you in their sight" (36:23).

YHWH's Servant to the Nations

As Ezekiel's words about YHWH's larger purposes suggest, the exilic prophets did something even more amazing than re-envisioning exile as a means of the people's transformation. They insisted that the exile didn't cancel or even delay the covenant people's task of being the instrument to bring the life-giving blessing and knowledge of YHWH to the nations. No, in a most unexpected way, they proclaimed that the job of carrying YHWH's presence to the nations remained to be done even in the midst of exile. In fact, these prophets announced the surprising divine word that the exile would actually become the vehicle by which Israel could carry out its task of being YHWH's instrument.[31]

A series of poems now found in Isaiah 40–55, a collection that scholars often date to the time of the Babylonian Exile, provides the most explicit expressions of this radical reconfiguration of identity and mission.[32] These so-called Servant Poems in Isaiah 42, 49, 50, and 52–53 describe a figure called "the Servant" whom YHWH has appointed to administer justice (good judgment and just treatment) in the midst of the experience of exile not only to Israel but to all nations. In contrast to some of Israel's unjust kings of the past, the Servant won't further damage those who are weak and vulnerable ("He won't break a bruised reed; he won't extinguish a faint wick" [42:3]) but will establish just and life-giving practices that allow for well-being among all peoples (42:4). The only text that gives an identity for the Servant identifies him as "Israel" (the collective people; see 49:3). Even if more precise identities were intended, the Servant figure symbolizes the role the prophets called Israel to fulfill within the bigger story of YHWH's work to redeem all nations and restore creation—and it's a role to be performed right in the midst of exile.

The Servant in Christian Interpretation

Later Christian interpreters identified Jesus with the servant figure in Isaiah's poems. New Testament texts make several references to the suffering servant from Isaiah 52–53 in particular (e.g., Matt 8:17; Acts 8:32-33). The context of Isaiah shows that these poems had an original meaning for the covenant people in exile and that they shouldn't be understood as simple predictions of Jesus. Rather, Jesus's followers found in the servant poems a significant way to understand and articulate the meaning of God's actions in Christ's life, death, and resurrection.

As I noted earlier, some of the Psalms proclaimed YHWH's desire to bring the knowledge of his name, character, and saving work to the nations so that all the people (indeed, all the earth!) will join with the original covenant people in hearing, knowing, and worshipping YHWH (e.g., Pss 46; 67). Likewise, in Isaiah 49, right in the middle of a promise to bring home Israel's survivors (vv. 5-6), YHWH declares a broader purpose for the Servant: "I will also appoint you as light to the nations so that my salvation may reach to the end of the earth" (v. 6). And the Servant poem in Isa 52:13–53:12 boldly asserts that even the sufferings of YHWH's servant served the larger purpose of causing "many nations" to "see" and "ponder" new things (52:15). Even though the Servant was "pierced" and "crushed" because of the people's sins (53:5), YHWH's "plans will come to fruition through him" and the Servant will be the instrument to "make many righteous" (53:10-11).

Prophetic Voices after Exile

The main storyline of YHWH's people told in the OT Historical Books described the long and difficult process of the return from exile and the rebuilding not only of the temple but of the Jewish community itself, a process that stretched nearly one hundred years in the story's chronology. This narrative showed us a fledging restoration community in Jerusalem trying to reestablish its identity in the midst of a vulnerable religious and political situation. Into this new circumstance on the other side of destruction and exile, prophets such as Haggai, Zechariah, and Malachi gave fresh articulations of YHWH's mission and Israel's identity.

First, these postexilic prophets challenged their people concerning the proper identity they must have in order to live out their calling as YHWH's covenant community in this restoration moment (compare Ezra and Nehemiah). While urging the postexilic community to rebuild YHWH's temple in Jerusalem, they scolded the people to engage in proper religious and ethical behavior, prioritizing the rebuilding of YHWH's house over their own immediate needs (Hag 1:3-11), resisting the temptation to offer half-hearted devotion and improper sacrifices (Mal 1:6-14), and turning away from unjust and violent actions that cheat and harm one another (Mal 2:10-16). These prophets didn't just condemn the religious, political, and social actions that were out of line with the identity required of YHWH's covenant community. They called the people to renew their undivided trust and wholehearted obedience to YHWH in order to allow for a new future marked by just and life-giving relationships. So Zechariah proclaimed to this rebuilding community, "People from far away will come and build the LORD's temple. . . . It will happen if you truly obey the voice of the LORD your God" (6:15). And again, "These are the things you should do: Speak the truth to each other; make truthful, just, and peaceable decisions within your gates" (8:16).

Second, and perhaps most remarkable, in the middle of the prolonged and difficult realities of community rebuilding on the other side of destruction and exile, the postexilic prophets once more proclaimed the hope-filled belief that YHWH's larger mission to restore creation and his intention to use Israel as the instrument in that mission were still in effect. Even through the reconfigurations and recalculations brought on by judgment, exile, and return, the Creator and covenant God remained committed in grace to bringing life-giving blessing to all nations. Nothing could be a more daring statement of hope for a community struggling to rebuild not simply buildings but their own religious and social identity! In so many ways, postexile life for the covenant people was life on the backside of divine glory. Long in the past were the times of YHWH's mighty deeds of the exodus and the triumphant accomplishments of David and Solomon. Although prophets such as Jeremiah and Ezekiel had proclaimed a glorious restoration after exile, with righteous leaders and a safe and flourishing kingdom basking in the divine presence, the postexilic community found itself embroiled in economic hardships, communal conflict, and grief-ridden disappointment.

Into this context, the postexilic prophets told the people to shift their focus to the bigger perspective of YHWH's purposes—sacrifice the concern over their own provision and prosperity to prioritize the things of YHWH (Hag 1:3-11); believe in YHWH's intentions to bring divine favor to all peoples through Jerusalem (Zech 8:20-23); and don't neglect the practices of obedience, righteousness, and justice that make you who you are as YHWH's people (Mal 1–3).

In so doing, the newly returned-home people could reactivate their participation as YHWH's instrument of blessing within the divine mission to restore creation. Here, after all of the covenant people's missteps, wrong turns, and failed navigation, this fledgling postexilic community, which was vulnerable to losing its religious and cultural identity, might be tempted to turn inward, allowing the fears of survival to lead to exclusivism and boundary-making. But just at this moment, the prophets return to the earlier message (see Isa 2:2-4; Mic 4:1-4) that YHWH's purpose is to draw all nations to the restored Jerusalem so that they can know his character, ways, and life-giving blessing through his covenant people.

Zechariah announces this instrumental, missional role for the restored Jerusalem:

> Rejoice and be glad, Daughter Zion,
>> because I am about to come and dwell among you, says the LORD.
> Many nations will be joined to the LORD on that day.
>> *They* will become my people,
>>> and I will dwell among *you*. (Zech 2:10-11, emphasis added)

> Just as you were a curse among the nations, house of Judah and house of Israel,
>> so now I will deliver you; you will be a blessing.
> . . . .
> Many peoples and mighty nations will come to seek the LORD of heavenly forces in Jerusalem and to seek the favor of the LORD. (Zech 8:13, 22)

Likewise, the last portion of the book of Isaiah, which scholars often date to the postexilic period,[33] gives YHWH's restoration of Jerusalem a missional purpose: "Arise! Shine! Your light has come.... Nations will come to your light and kings to your dawning radiance" (Isa 60:1, 3). Some of these prophecies include the idea that YHWH will defeat threatening enemies and even use nations to serve and protect vulnerable Israel in order to ensure its survival for YHWH's purposes (e.g., Isa 63:1-6; 66:24; Zech 14:1-5).

The Nations Come to Jerusalem

The theological vision of YHWH drawing the nations to Jerusalem isn't completely free of nationalistic themes that reflect Israel's own political and economic interests. The texts sometimes portray foreign nations being eliminated or made to serve Israel, although usually threatening enemies only. While we should acknowledge these elements, they don't prevent the theological vision from transcending its cultural and ideological contexts in light of the larger canonical story.

But a broader perspective on YHWH's mission and Israel's identity remains operative. So, Isaiah 66 provides the culminating promise of the missional, covenant God who works through Israel on behalf of the world:

I'm coming to gather all nations and cultures. They will come to see my glory... by sending out some of the survivors to the nations... that haven't heard of my fame or seen my glory. They will declare my glory among the nations. They will bring your family members from all nations as an offering to the LORD.... From month to month and from Sabbath to Sabbath, all humanity will come to worship me, says the LORD. (Isa 66:18-20, 23)

Chapter 9

The End Is the Beginning

The Ending of the Old Testament and the Ongoing Story of God

Focus Texts: Nehemiah 10:28-39; Malachi 4

"All good things must come to an end." Tradition attributes this quote to Geoffrey Chaucer, an English poet from the Middle Ages (1300s). Although Chaucer had other things in mind, the OT, when read as the story of God's mission and God's people, eventually comes—like one of Chaucer's "good things"—to an end. In the Protestant canon, Israel's prophets got the final word. But, as I noted in the last chapter, rather than ending with a narrow focus on mere survival after exile or on nationalistic political revival for the Jerusalem community, these prophetic voices proclaimed a bigger message that challenged their people to recapture the vision of their role within God's mission to all nations and recommit to the identity of wholehearted obedience to which they had been called. In other words, the ending of the OT in the prophetic books returned to the larger plot line about God's mission to restore creation and reminded us that the story of Israel as God's people is a smaller story that fits into and finds meaning within that larger plot line. Through all the various episodes in the covenant community's story—from the first moments of calling to the weary end of the long road home from exile—scripture's narrative has maintained a larger, missional focus: God's people have been called to be partners with God in the divine redemptive mission for the world.

– 179 –

At the same time, the last chapter also noted that the concluding voices of the Protestant canon make the ending of the OT a non-ending—in fact, they make it a new beginning. After the main storyline of Israel's life, exile, and return (Genesis–Esther), the final two canonical sections presented the voices of Israel's poets, sages, and prophets that offered new perspectives on the calling, identity, and experiences of God's people. But these concluding voices also extended the same plot of God's mission and Israel's calling into an open-ended future beyond the immediate moment. They looked forward to a time when God would bring the work of restoration and renewal to completion. This non-ending testifies to what Timothy Green calls the "underlying conviction" of scripture's narrative that "God is actively at work doing something in his world" and the divine redemptive mission remains ongoing, even beyond "the covers of a book called the Bible."[1]

In light of the broad perspective and unfinished quality of the OT's plot line highlighted by the final portion of the Protestant canon, I conclude my telling of the OT story in this chapter by looking briefly at three elements: (1) the specific ending of the OT in the final verses of the book of Malachi; (2) the possibility of seeing the OT story as continuing into the NT (and reading the NT writings within the frame of reference provided by the OT); and (3) the ongoing power of the OT story that reaches beyond the bounds of scripture into the pressing realities of life in today's church and world.

The Ending of the Old Testament Story

Stories told through books, movies, and more have become known in our culture for memorable concluding lines and final words. These are the last offerings of a story to its audience. They can provide closure, leave us hanging, or wreck our previous conceptions. But they ultimately place the story into the minds of the readers and hearers in a certain way that will last. From great literature, we might think of endings found in works such as *The Great Gatsby* (by F. Scott Fitzgerald), "So we beat on, boats against the current, borne back ceaselessly into the past," or *Gone with the Wind* (by Margaret Mitchell), "After all, tomorrow is another day." From modern movies, we might think of *The Matrix*, "Where we go from there is a choice I leave to you," or *Toy Story 3*, "So long…partner," or even the classic *King Kong*, "It wasn't the airplanes. It was Beauty killed the Beast."

Likewise, there is an ending to the OT story, consisting of six final verses that proclaim one last message from YHWH to his people through the words of the prophet Malachi (4:1-6). The identification of this specific ending for the OT depends on the use of the Protestant canon. As the introductory discussion in chapter 1 noted, different canonical listings of the scriptures (Jewish, Roman Catholic, Orthodox) preserve different arrangements of the books.

The Hebrew/Jewish Canon

Present-day Jewish Bibles reflect the order of books found in Hebrew manuscripts. Since the Jewish canon moves from the Pentateuch to the Prophets and finally to the Writings (featuring poetic and wisdom texts), it has a different ending than the Protestant canon. It ends with the decree of King Cyrus of Persia in 2 Chronicles 36:22-23 that the Jewish exiles could return to Jerusalem and rebuild the temple. The final words are an invitation to participate: "Whoever among you belong to God's people, let them go up, and may the LORD their God be with them!" (v. 23).

So there is more than one ending to the OT story, depending on the canonical frame of reference. In the Protestant canon, the ending appears in the final verses of Malachi. Just as in a classic novel or popular movie, YHWH's final words through the prophet deposit the whole OT story into the minds of its readers in a lasting way. But they also reinforce the broader and ongoing quality of the story of YHWH and his covenant community that has been on display throughout the entire narrative of scripture. After a renewed promise of judgment on the wicked and transformation of the righteous, here are the final words of the OT story:

> Remember the Instruction [Heb. *tôrāh*] from Moses, my servant,
>   to whom I gave Instruction and rules for all Israel at Horeb.
> Look, I am sending Elijah the prophet to you,
>   before the great and terrifying day of the LORD arrives.
> Turn the hearts [*lēb*] of the parents to the children
>   and the hearts [*lēb*] of the children to their parents.
>   Otherwise, I will come and strike the land with a curse. (Mal 4:4-6)

To put this ending into context, let's step back and recap the overall OT story as I have told it in this book. Taken as a whole, the OT is the story of how God's good creation of right-relationships and life-giving blessing became distorted because of human fear, mistrust, and self-sovereignty, and how God has undertaken a mission to restore creation to the life-giving relationships that were divinely intended. Genesis first provided the *introduction of God's mission* by depicting the divinely intended creation of life-giving right-relationships (Gen 1–2), humanity's distortion of that good creation (Gen 4–9), and God's commitment to enter into a covenant relationship with all living beings that would somehow turn out to be restorative for creation as a whole (Gen 9).

God's mission began to take shape with the *calling of God's people* (the descendants of Abraham and Sarah) to be the instrument of blessing to all peoples (Gen 12–50) and then the *creation of God's people* in the exodus event as a distinctive community (Abraham's descendants joined by different races and ethnicities) that has YHWH as the fundamental, life-defining reality (Exod 1–15). Through the people's subsequent wilderness journey and the giving of the Torah to the community, the remainder of the Pentateuch portrayed the *formation of God's people*, as God attempted to shape the people he had called and created into a holy (specially designated) nation—that is, God's covenant people marked by obedience to God and right-relationships with one another, a kingdom serving as priests for the world, and glory bearers carrying God's holy and transforming presence into the world (Exod 16–Deuteronomy). What followed was the account of the *life of God's people* (Joshua–Esther) as they moved into the land, lived as kingdoms, repeatedly lost their way into disobedience, mistrust, self-provision, and self-sovereignty, went into exile, and eventually returned to try to reconstruct their city, temple, and identity as God's called-out instrument.

Throughout this story, one plot element stands out. In order for God's covenant people to fulfill the missional role for which they had been called, created, and formed, they were to love/obey their God with all their heart/mind/will (*lēb*)—an undivided trust and wholehearted obedience. Yet consistently scripture's narrative showed that God's people struggled with the fundamental problem of divided loyalties and fears of self-preservation that caused them to turn to other gods, replacement kings, and survival-oriented political alliances. Even so, throughout the people's journey into and out of exile, God promised to give them a new *lēb* (heart/mind/will)—a transformed character that would be able to abandon divided loyalties and offer complete devotion to God. This grace-filled transformation, the OT story said, would enable God's people to fulfill their ongoing calling to be partners in God's redemptive mission and instruments of life-giving right-relationships to the world.

In light of this larger plot line, when we arrive at the final words of the OT—coming as they do at the end of the postexilic prophetic voices who spoke to the struggling community of returnees in Jerusalem during the years after the exile—a long, rich history stands behind those words. We remember that Israel was called to be the instrument that God could use in the mission to restore creation. We remember that they got sidetracked into sin and exile and have returned home to the struggles of rebuilding and renewal. And so, at this moment, when we might be tempted to think that perhaps the grand story of scripture has fizzled out in a pitiful end and God's creation-wide redemptive mission of restoration has reached a null point, the final words of the OT proclaim just the opposite! The OT story ends by looking forward to the ongoing work of God still to come. The final words proclaim that God's mission with his people and for his creation isn't finished but remains underway with an open-ended quality that includes further work to be done by God and further action needed by God's people.

So, the conclusion of the OT story in Malachi 4:1-6 starts with a divine announcement of the coming "day of the LORD" that will bring about judgment on the wicked and healing for the righteous. But note especially what's here in light of the larger OT story. Just like the other prophetic voices throughout the exile and postexile, these final words envision a full transformation of God's people—a "sun rise" on those "revering my name" that will bring "healing" (v. 2). As we've seen throughout scripture's narrative, these final words once more link that promise with the call to wholehearted obedience—a call for God's people to "remember the Instruction from Moses" (v. 4), the very Torah given during their formation in the wilderness that initially called them to love/obey God with all of their heart/mind/will (Deut 6:4-5).

Likewise, the final two verses (4:5-6) combine promised divine action with further action required from God's people. First, verse 5 promises that God will continue to speak to the people by sending them a prophet in the mold of the great Elijah.

Elijah the Prophet

The reference to Elijah in Malachi 4:5 recalls one of Israel's earliest and most significant prophets from the early monarchy (ninth century BCE). Second Kings 2:10-12 says that Elijah didn't die but was taken into heaven on chariots. The NT Gospels identify the coming of John the Baptist with the fulfillment of this divine promise to send Elijah (Matt 11:12-15; 17:10-13; Luke 1:13-17).

Then, the last words of the OT story give a final missional command to God's people.[2] Using the language of parent-child relationships, the final words charge the covenant community to "turn the hearts [lēb]" of people to one another so that creation itself (lit. "the land") will not know "curse" (ḥerem, "destruction") but blessing and life (v. 6). There couldn't be a more appropriate final line for the larger OT story! Through God's promised transformation and their renewed obedience to God's commands through the Torah and prophets, the covenant people are to be about the mission of changing people's lēb (heart/mind/will) and restoring right-relationships (like healthy families) to the life-giving benefit of all creation.

With these last words, the OT story ends with the "dot, dot, dot" of a divine ellipsis.[3] The work of God's mission to restore creation to life-giving right-relationships is not ended. The calling of God's people to participate as partners in the divine mission goes on. God will continue to work. God's people will continue to be called, created, formed, transformed, and enabled. The OT story has reached its conclusion. But the ending is a non-ending. It's a "to be continued." It's an open-ended invitation to become actors in the divine missional story. It's a dot, dot, dot. It's a new beginning.

The Ongoing Story of God

With this ellipsis-like non-ending of the divine missional story, readers of the OT are left leaning into the future for more. For those working from a Christian frame of reference and reading the OT within the larger canon of Christian scripture, this ending naturally leads to thinking about the NT writings. Is it possible to see the OT story—particularly, the story of God's mission to restore creation—as continuing into the NT, and what might it be like to read the NT writings as a whole within that frame of reference?

Certainly, there are other ways to approach the NT. For instance, although the canonical arrangement of the NT books generally moves from Jesus (the Gospels) to the apostles (Acts and then particular apostles in the letters) and to the consummation of God's kingdom (Revelation), it doesn't read like a sequential, unfolding story where each subsequent book advances the plot line.[4] The NT is more like an anthology that explores the same topic from a variety of perspectives and within many different contexts. Even so, the OT story, especially when engaged with a narrative, missional perspective, yields the creative possibility of thinking of the NT as part of a larger plot line that spans the whole of Christian scripture and centers around the grand mission of God in the world.[5]

First, some words of caution are in order. Christian interpreters often read backward from the NT to the OT. This frequently results in interpreting the OT in NT terms and losing sight of the integrity, content, and contexts of the OT itself. At times, this is what the NT writers themselves did, as the Gospel of Matthew, for example, picks out various OT texts from differing contexts and identifies them as prophecies of Jesus's life and ministry (e.g., Matt 1:22-23; 2:5-6; 4:14-16). But today's Christian readers, who need to take seriously the whole of Christian scripture, should acknowledge the differences between the OT and NT (and between Judaism and Christianity), and be careful not to contribute to the legacy of some modern interpreters who've viewed the OT as a story of failure or the community of Israel (or Judaism) as only a placeholder that became irrelevant with the emergence of the NT and Christianity.[6] The OT doesn't inevitably or naturally lead to the NT, nor does it depend on the NT for meaning or significance. However, if one operates from a Christian frame of reference, then one can explore possible connections between Israel's calling and mission and the church's self-understanding and identity as they are described in the NT.

The content of the NT centers on Jesus and the generations of his followers (the church), yet the earliest believers—who were and remained Jews—understood their faith and practice as an extension of God's promises to Israel (see Rom 11:17). So, as Christopher Wright says, telling the OT story invites us to ask how the NT proclamations about Jesus and the church are connected "not just to the identity and functions of the God of Israel but also to his mission."[7] Viewed in this way, the NT writings—like the OT texts before them—have the divine redemptive mission as a common thread that unites their different contexts and perspectives: "From Matthew to Revelation, they bear witness to God's purpose to redeem and restore all things in Christ. Mission is woven into the very fabric of the New Testament."[8] How might we identify the ways that the NT texts tell the story of God's mission and form their readers into participation in that mission? In other words, how might we read both the OT and NT in terms of a larger plot line across the whole canon of Christian scripture from creation (Genesis) to renewed creation (Revelation)?

What follows below is only a sketch (for further thought) meant to be suggestive (not comprehensive). It begins by recalling the essence of the OT's larger plot line: God's good creation of right-relationships became distorted because of human mistrust and self-sovereignty and, in response, God called into being a people (who would turn out to be the manifold descendants of Abraham and Sarai) and then created, formed, taught, and shaped them, so that they could be the instrument of the divine mission to restore creation to the right-relationships with which it began. But when the OT ended on the other side of exile and return, that story of God's mission and God's people hadn't yet been completed. It was open-ended, with a divine ellipsis, as God promised to continue to call and form a covenant people to share in the mission to restore creation.

Within the frame of reference given by the whole canon of Christian scripture, we could say that the OT makes up the first part of a larger plot line that began with all humanity created to be God's image-bearers who mediate life-giving blessing to creation (Gen 1–2). When humanity failed to live out its created identity, God called the covenant people of Israel into the story as a specific agent (part of the whole but set aside for a special purpose) who would embody the calling of all humanity and thus be a channel through which all creation could be restored to its divine purposes. Israel's story became the smaller subplot within the bigger scriptural plot line.

Jesus and the Mission of God

When we move forward in Christian scripture from the end of the OT, Jesus is the next decisive figure to enter the larger story of God's redemptive mission.[9] The first words of the NT give an immediate introduction and make a direct connection to the OT: "A record of the ancestors of Jesus Christ, son of David, son of Abraham" (Matt 1:1). From the perspective of the larger canonical story, just as Israel was called out from humankind for a special purpose, Jesus is one of the covenant people of Israel ("son of Abraham") who has been assigned a special divine purpose as Messiah ("Christ").[10] Put simply, the NT perspective is that "God's mission through Israel climaxes when God the Father sends the Son into the world, in the power of the Holy Spirit, to bring about God's salvation at every level."[11]

This perspective is, as Michael Lodahl says, a "new twist" in scripture's plot line, as the NT declares that God has established a "new and decisive covenant" through Christ.[12] Even so, the NT writings see Israel's long experience with God as the context for understanding Jesus's life, death, and resurrection. They explain God's work in Christ as a "faithful continuation of God's labor in the history of the people of Israel."[13] Jesus is not only the Son of God but also the long-awaited Jewish Messiah—the member of Abraham's own descendants especially empowered and sent to bring to fruition God's promises to Israel and through them to the world. Jesus embodies what humanity was called to be as the image of God. He also embodies what Israel was called to be when God chose Israel to be a special, specific agent called out from the whole of humankind to work on its behalf.

Seen in the context of scripture's larger story, the NT's confession that Jesus is the incarnate Son of God (God come as a human being—Mark 1:1; John 1:1, 14) parallels God's initial commitment to a redemptive mission for all creation given after the flood in Genesis 9. As we saw there, God responded to his distorted creation by committing to engage with all living beings in a way that would turn out to be redemptive. Scripture's vital testimony from the very beginning is that salvation requires God and not just an assigned creaturely representative. God first engaged personally and directly with creation as a covenant partner to meet them in their condition of need in order to bring about the needed restoration. Only after that, did God call Israel to be the human instrument of that divine redemption. Seen from this perspective, Jesus—as the incarnate Son of God—culminates God's missional commitment to enter directly into a covenant relationship with all creation. Jesus is God made human because salvation requires God to meet humankind in its need and not just send a human agent. And as the NT Gospels portray Jesus's works of the kingdom of God—healing the sick and the lame and restoring broken human lives to their divinely intended wholeness and blessing—they identify Jesus with the covenant God's character and actions that had been on display throughout the OT story.

As we noted, however, the NT texts identify Jesus not only with God's mission but also with Israel's role as instrument within that mission. They identify Jesus as both the incarnate Son of God and the Jewish Messiah—the ideal representative and leader of Israel, descended from Abraham, standing in the line of David, and fulfilling the prophets' promises of God's saving agent to come for Israel and the world (Matt 1:1). Jesus fulfils God's mission from the OT but also embodies Israel's calling to be an instrument of blessing to all nations. On one level, in his own life, death, and resurrection, Jesus lives what Israel as a whole was called to be. He shows anew what it is to be a "covenantally faithful child of God" and makes God known to all people through his life and teachings.[14] On another level, as Israel's Messiah, Jesus is also the king and savior who gathers a renewed Israel in order to purify, (re)form, and empower the faithful community for the missional role to which God's people were originally called.

Jesus's embodiment of Israel's mission is perhaps most noticeable in the ways that various strands of the NT identify Jesus with Abraham, his calling, and his mission of blessing to all the families of the earth. In the very first NT book, for instance, the writer of Matthew begins by identifying Jesus as the son of Abraham (Matt 1:1) and ends by commissioning Jesus's followers to carry his message through his power into all the world (Matt 28:16-20).[15] Jesus steps into the role given to Abraham and his descendants and becomes the decisive means through which God's people will be reconstituted and empowered so that God will be universally made known. The OT prophets' vision of YHWH using Israel to draw all nations to himself (e.g., Isa 2:2-5) also stands near the heart of the NT's understanding of the work of Jesus and his followers. Just as YHWH set his "servant" Israel to be a "light to the nations" (Isa 49:6), so Jesus reconstitutes Israel—now all those who would believe in him as God's son and Israel's Messiah—to be a "light" that shines to the world and leads all people to praise the "Father who is in heaven" (Matt 5:14-16).

The Church and the Mission of God

So Jesus embodies and fulfills what Israel was called to be within God's mission—the faithful covenant "Son" who could be the instrument of God's life-giving blessing and restoration to the world. But Jesus exits the drama of scripture's narrative after only a short time. When we move forward in the Bible's larger plot line, the next actor to enter the story is the church—the community of Jesus's followers that grew from his earliest disciples within Judaism to believers from different cultures, ethnicities, and polities who received the spreading witness of Christian congregations and converts. Numerous perspectives on the church appear across the NT writings. But what if we look at the church as it enters the story after the life, death, and resurrection of Jesus within the frame of reference of the broader plot line of God's mission to restore creation that began in the OT? Seen in this way, just as humanity was originally called to be the image of God and Israel was later called to represent the covenant God and participate in his saving actions for the world, so the church in the NT becomes the "body of Christ" that is to represent Jesus, who was the new image of the Creator and has fulfilled God's saving purposes with God's covenant people (1 Cor 12:27).

In other words, when read in the context of the larger canonical story, the church—the wider community of Christ's followers—is called through the invitation of Israel's own Messiah to join in the mission that was given to Israel. Just as God through Abraham brought Israel into being as his covenant people, the NT announces that God through Christ has brought into being a broader people who've been called to covenant faithfulness and to a role in bringing God's life-giving right-relationships to all nations. The Gospels in particular proclaim that God's redemptive mission began with Israel, reached its culmination in Jesus as Israel's Messiah, and continues unfinished through believers empowered by the Spirit. The church is an extension of Israel and shares in the same mission. Perhaps the most powerful image of this conviction appears in Paul's metaphor that followers of Christ have become like branches that have been "grafted in" and "shared the root" of the olive tree, a symbol for God's original covenant with Israel (Rom 11:17). Other places make the church's link with Israel's mission more explicit. As Christopher Wright observes, Jesus's statement that his followers will serve as witnesses to all the earth in Acts 1:8 parallels YHWH's words to Israel in Isaiah 43:10-12. Even more directly, Paul in Acts 13:47 identifies the church's mission with the mission of Israel as YHWH's servant in Isaiah 49:6, applying the singular "you" spoken to the servant ("I will also appoint *you* as light to the nations" [Isa 49:6]) to the "us" commanded of Paul and his fellow believers ("This is what the Lord commanded *us*: I have made you a light for the Gentiles" [Acts 13:47]).[16]

Two elements are especially noteworthy when we view the NT portrayal of the church as part of the larger plot line of God's mission that began in the OT. First, even as Jesus called those who believed in him to join in Israel's original mission, he redefined Israel by expanding the covenant community to include people from every race, ethnicity, and nationality. As the Gospel of Luke emphasizes, the work of Jesus was a "boundary-breaking mission" that sought to bring God's redemptive promises to Gentiles as well as Jews and to draw the poor, marginal, immigrant, and others into the covenant community and its mission.[17] And throughout the various NT letters, Jesus's disciples express the conviction that through God's work in Christ, the missionally called-out people of God include not just Abraham's ethnic descendants but also his spiritual descendants—those who've come to share Abraham's faith in God now made manifest through Christ (Rom 9:6-9). Christ's life, death, and resurrection have created a multiethnic community that can through faith inherit the missional promises and calling of the OT covenant people.

The Church and Israel

Christian interpreters have sometimes viewed the church in the NT as a replacement for Israel, usually assuming that Christ's followers have displaced a failed Israel as the new recipients of God's salvation and promise. This "replacement theology" should be avoided in light of the larger missional plot line of Christian scripture. From the canonical viewpoint, Jesus, as God's Son and Israel's Messiah, re-formed, reconstituted, and even expanded Israel so that the covenant people could fulfill their original calling and mission in new ways through him.

Second, the NT portrayal of the church defines how God's people should perform their missional calling for the world in light of Jesus's own way of carrying out God's redemptive work. Just as Jesus became the means of God's salvation by giving his own life for the world, so the church, in his image and as his body, must be the instrument of blessing to the nations through the practice of self-sacrificial love. Repeatedly, the various strands of the NT emphasize that God's people can only fulfill their calling as instruments within God's mission if they imitate Christ's own instrumental way and share in Christ's sufferings (Rom 8:16-17; 2 Cor 4:10-12). Jesus admonished his followers that all who want to participate in his mission must "say no to themselves, take up their cross, and follow me . . . all who lose their lives because of me and because of the good news will save them" (Mark 8:34-35). But no more powerful portrayal of this self-giving missional activity appears than in Paul's letter to the Philippians. There, the cruciform mission of self-sacrificial love on behalf of all creation becomes the defining mark of Christ's character and the lifestyle that Christ's followers are to embody in their world (Phil 2:5-11).

In the end, then, for those thinking about Christian scripture as a whole, perhaps the story of Jesus, the church, and even the entire NT is the continuation of the larger canonical plot line of God's mission to restore creation and the calling of God's people to be the instrument of that mission in the world. The story of a crucified and raised Messiah and the faithful acts of his followers certainly introduces new and even unexpected elements into the larger plot line. Yet their story seems to find its beginning and ending in the same comprehensive vision of God's redemptive purposes. That vision began in Genesis with God's covenant commitment to a restorative, life-giving engagement with all living beings (Gen 9:8-11) and the promise to use his own chosen people to bless all the families of the earth (Gen 12:1-3). Fittingly, that vision ends in the NT book of Revelation with an image of the fulfillment of God's comprehensive restoration mission of blessing for all. The NT's conclusion offers a final vision of the time when Christ's self-emptying love will gather people from every nation, language, and ethnicity to live together in a renewed creation sustained by God's life-giving presence (Rev 7:9-17; 21:1–22:5).

God's Story and Our Story

We've reached the end of this particular telling of the OT as the story of God's mission to restore creation and the calling of God's people to be the instrument of that mission. I want to conclude by returning to the significance of this kind of narrative and missional telling of the OT. At the outset of this book, I mentioned that stories have power; they can transform lives, communities, and worlds. Telling a story can give us creative, powerful, and new understandings that have the potential to change the way we see the realities of our existence. The introductory discussion in chapter 1 also noted that missional interpretation not only seeks to explore how the Bible tells the story of God's mission in the world but also how the biblical texts draw contemporary readers into the missional community described in that story in order to equip them to engage in God's mission in new and changing contexts. In short, there is something powerfully meaningful and potentially transformative about stories, especially missional ones.

So now, at the end of our exploration, I conclude by lifting up two things that might happen if we read the OT in this narrative and missional way as the story of God's mission and God's people.

A Story That Shapes Us

First, when we tell the OT story in this way, the distinct and diverse OT texts come together into a story that shapes us. The narrative, canonical, and missional frames of reference invite us to find in the OT a formative narrative—a story that offers a particular way of understanding who God is, who we are, and how we should live our lives in the world. Here is a story that calls us to find our identity in something bigger than our own experiences, fears, wants, and interests. This story says we're part of a community of people brought into being by God's gracious acts, meant to live in covenant love and faithfulness with God and others, and asked to be the image (representative) and instrument of the covenant God's holy, life-giving presence and blessing for all people through right-relationships marked by justice, righteousness, self-sacrifice, hospitality, and love.

For readers of scripture's narrative today, especially those in the modern western world, this story comes to us in the midst of a culture marked by competing stories that are trying to shape our understandings of God, ourselves, and our lives in conflicting ways. We live—as ancient Israel did—in a social context that Walter Brueggemann has described as one of "conflict and competition between deeply held metanarratives [overarching, defining stories], which are seldom enunciated and only evidenced in bits and pieces."[18] For ancient Israel, there were, for instance, the old and powerful myths of Babylon (such as the *Enuma Elish*), which portrayed the gods as competing deities working to outmaneuver one another in the search for praise and described human beings as afterthought creations made to relieve the gods of the burden of work and left to imitate the gods in often violent competitiveness over resources and blessing. These stories communicate particular understandings of the nature of divinity and humanity and how to live in the world. For readers of the OT living in our social context, we hear a dominant cultural narrative that says the individual is the primary unit of importance and each of us should pursue her or his happiness by consuming as many goods as possible, mostly by competing to outspend, outmaneuver, and outgain our neighbors.

Into the midst of these competing narratives, the OT story offers its alternative truths about who God is, who we are, and how we are called to live in the world. It invites us to imagine our God, our world, and our lives according to the larger plot line of God's restorative mission for all creation and the calling of God's people to participate in that mission. It has the power to shape us away from a reality defined by individualism, consumerism, competitiveness, fear, and self-preservation and into an identity marked by covenant, faithfulness, holiness, love, and self-giving right-relationships.[19] In this way, the OT story doesn't just recount God's mission through God's people; it becomes a means to bring that mission to reality through the formation of a missional people.

A Story That Prompts a Response

The second thing that happens when we tell the OT as the story of God's mission and God's people is that it becomes a story that prompts a response. I began the exploration of the OT (ch. 2) with a portion of the Levite priests' prayer in Nehemiah 9:1-31, one of several OT passages that pauses the dramatic action and rehearses Israel's past in the form of a story that has unfolded across time (see also Deut 26:5-9; Josh 24:1-13; 2 Kgs 17:7-23). Now, at the end of this exploration, I return to that prayerful rehearsal of the story, especially to note the people's response that follows in Nehemiah 10:28-39.

As I described in chapter 2, the setting of this priestly prayer in Nehemiah 9–10 is a national assembly of fasting and repentance during the days of the return from exile and the efforts to rebuild Jerusalem and re-form the missional community of God's people. There the priests offered a prayer seeking forgiveness and reconciliation that rehearsed Israel's story (9:1-31). It begins even before Israel's emergence with YHWH's actions as creator (v. 6), moves to the call of Abraham (vv. 7-8), and then recounts the exodus from Egypt (vv. 9-11), the giving of the law at Mount Sinai (vv. 13-14), YHWH's provision and the people's rebellion during forty years in the wilderness (vv. 15-22), the entrance into the promised land and the period of the judges (vv. 23-28), disobedience and rebellion during the time of the kingdoms of Israel and Judah (vv. 29-30), destruction and exile as divine judgment (vv. 30-31), and finally the present hardships of the postexilic community living under the dominance of the Persian Empire (vv. 32-37).

What interests me at the end of our exploration of the OT is the response prompted by the priests' prayerful telling of Israel's story. Hearing the story moves the Jerusalem community to make a covenant ("a firm agreement in writing" [9:38]) with some very specific actions included. Not only do the people commit to keep God's "Instruction" (*tôrâh*) in general (10:29), they also pledge to implement or restore some very specific social and economic practices—everything from not intermarrying with the neighboring peoples (10:30) to not buying or selling on the Sabbath (10:31) to paying a yearly offering to provide for the temple (10:32-34) to bringing a sacrificial offering of the first of their crops and firstborn of their livestock (10:35-39). In other words, the effect of this community hearing the story of their life as God's people prompts them to respond with very concrete actions by which they rearrange specific elements of how they live in the world, even leading them to new economic practices.

This story-telling example from Nehemiah 9–10 suggests that telling the OT story of God and God's people may likewise prompt those of us who hear it today to respond by realigning our lives, even in ways that change how we conduct aspects of our social relationships and money practices. Put more generally, the larger OT plot line of God's mission and God's people prompts us to respond by asking how these texts draw us into the divine redemptive mission in the world and invite us to reimagine and realign our identity and actions as if we are living as active participants in that mission.

By reading the OT as a missional story that shapes us and prompts us to respond, we come to see that scripture's narrative expresses a conviction and a call. At the heart of the larger plot line of God's mission and God's people is the conviction that those who truly engage in scripture's story will not operate as self-centered individuals or remain on the sidelines as spectators too fearful to risk joining the game. Instead, they will hear the call of the OT story away from individualism to community, away from mistrust and self-centeredness to faith and obedience, away from divided loyalties to undivided love, and away from survival to mission. They will hear the call to come out of the spectator stands and enter the playing field. They will hear the call to participate as part of God's people in what God is doing to restore creation to the life-giving right-relationships, wholeness, and blessing for which it was intended. They will find in the OT the beginning of a new story for their lives and their world.

Bibliography

Achtemeier, Paul J., and Elizabeth Achtemeier. *The Old Testament Roots of Our Faith*. Rev. ed. Peabody, MA: Hendrickson, 1994.

Alter, Robert. *The Art of Biblical Narrative*. New York: Basic Books, 1981.

Anderson, Gary A., and Joel S. Kaminsky, eds. *The Call of Abraham: Essays on the Election of Israel in Honor of Jon D. Levenson*. Christianity and Judaism in Antiquity 19. Notre Dame, IN: University of Notre Dame Press, 2013.

Auwer, J.-M., and H. J. de Jonge. *The Biblical Canons*. BETL 163. Leuven: Leuven University Press, 2003.

Bartholomew, Craig G., and Michael W. Goheen. *The Drama of Scripture*. Grand Rapids, MI: Baker Academic, 2000.

Bauckham, Richard. *Bible and Mission: Christian Witness in a Postmodern World*. Grand Rapids, MI: Baker Academic, 2003.

Beach, Bradley, and Matthew Powell, eds. *Interpreting Abraham: Journeys to Moriah*. Minneapolis: Fortress, 2014.

Blenkinsopp, Joseph. *Creation, Un-Creation, Re-Creation: A Discursive Commentary on Genesis 1–11*. London: T and T Clark, 2011.

Bosch, David J. *Transforming Mission: Paradigm Shifts in Theology of Mission*. Maryknoll, NY: Orbis Books, 1991.

Brettler, Marc Zvi. *The Creation of History in Ancient Israel.* London: Routledge, 1995.

Brooks, Roger, and John J. Collins, eds. *Hebrew Bible or Old Testament? Studying the Bible in Judaism and Christianity.* Notre Dame, IN: University of Notre Dame Press, 1990.

Brueggemann, Walter. *Theology of the Old Testament: Testimony, Dispute, Advocacy.* Minneapolis: Fortress, 1997.

Carr, David M. *The Formation of the Hebrew Bible: A New Reconstruction.* Oxford: Oxford University Press, 2011.

Childs, Brevard S. *Introduction to the Old Testament as Scripture.* Philadelphia: Fortress, 1979.

Clifford, Richard J. *The Wisdom Literature.* Interpreting Biblical Texts. Nashville: Abingdon Press, 1998.

Clines, David J. A. "Humanity as the Image of God." In *On the Way to the Postmodern, 1967–1998,* by David J. A. Clines, 480–95. 2 vols. JSOTSup 292–94. Sheffield: Sheffield Academic Press, 1998.

Collins, John J. *Does the Bible Justify Violence?* Facets. Minneapolis: Fortress, 2004.

Dickens, Charles. *A Christmas Carol: The Original Manuscript.* Oxford: Benediction Classics, 2012.

Dozeman, Thomas B. *Exodus.* Eerdmans Critical Commentary. Grand Rapids, MI: Eerdmans, 2009.

Flemming, Dean. *Why Mission?* Reframing New Testament Theology. Nashville: Abingdon Press, 2015.

Fredrickson, Dale C. *Help Me Be: Praying in Poems.* Create Space Independent Publishing Platform, 2013.

Frei, Hans W. *The Eclipse of Biblical Narrative: A Study in Eighteenth and Nineteenth Century Hermeneutics*. New Haven, CT: Yale University Press, 1974.

Frick, Frank S. *A Journey through the Hebrew Scriptures*. 2nd ed. Belmont, CA: Wadsworth/Thomson Learning, 2003.

Glasser, Arthur F., with Charles E. Van Engen, Dean S. Gilliland, and Shawn B. Redford. *Announcing the Kingdom: The Story of God's Mission in the Bible*. Grand Rapids, MI: Baker Academic, 2003.

Goheen, Michael W. *A Light to the Nations: The Missional Church and the Biblical Story*. Grand Rapids, MI: Baker Academic, 2011.

Green, Joel, ed. *The CEB Study Bible*. Nashville: Common English Bible, 2013.

Green, Timothy M. *The God Plot: Living with Holy Imagination*. Kansas City, MO: Beacon Hill, 2014.

Greenway, William. *For the Love of All Creatures: The Story of Grace in Genesis*. Grand Rapids, MI: Eerdmans, 2015.

Guder, Darrell L., ed. *Missional Church: A Vision for the Sending of the Church in North America*. The Gospel and Our Culture. Grand Rapids, MI: Eerdmans, 1998.

Hauerwas, Stanley, and L. Gregory Jones, eds. *Why Narrative? Readings in Narrative Theology*. Grand Rapids, MI: Eerdmans, 1989.

Hays, Christopher B. *Hidden Riches: A Sourcebook for the Study of the Hebrew Bible and the Ancient Near East*. Louisville: Westminster John Knox, 2014.

Hunsberger, George R. "Proposals for a Missional Hermeneutic: Mapping the Conversation." *Missiology* 39 (2011): 309–21.

Janzen, David. *The Necessary King: A Postcolonial Reading of the Deuteronomistic Portrait of the Monarchy*. Hebrew Bible Monographs 57. Sheffield: Sheffield Phoenix, 2013.

Kaiser, Walter C., Jr. *Mission in the Old Testament: Israel as a Light to the Nations.* 2nd ed. Grand Rapids, MI: Baker Academic, 2001.

Kelle, Brad E. "An Interdisciplinary Approach to the Exile." In *Interpreting Exile: Displacement and Deportation in Biblical and Modern Contexts,* edited by Brad E. Kelle, Frank Ritchel Ames, and Jacob L. Wright, 5–38. SBLAIL 10. Atlanta: Society of Biblical Literature, 2011.

Koenig, Sara. "The Beginning of the Story: Genesis–Deuteronomy." In *A Compact Guide to the Whole Bible: Learning to Read Scripture's Story,* edited by Robert W. Wall and David R. Nienhuis, 39–50. Grand Rapids, MI: Eerdmans, 2015.

———. "The Witness of Israel's Poets and Sages: Job–Song of Songs." In *A Compact Guide to the Whole Bible: Learning to Read Scripture's Story,* edited by Robert W. Wall and David R. Nienhuis, 65–78. Grand Rapids, MI: Eerdmans, 2015.

Kratz, Steven. *The Holocaust in Historical Context: Ancient and Medieval Cases 1.* Oxford: Oxford University Press, 1994.

Lim, Bo. "The Witness of Israel's Prophets: Isaiah–Malachi." In *A Compact Guide to the Whole Bible: Learning to Read Scripture's Story,* edited by Robert W. Wall and David R. Nienhuis, 79–91. Grand Rapids, MI: Eerdmans, 2015.

Lodahl, Michael. *The Story of God: A Narrative Theology.* 2nd ed. Kansas City, MO: Beacon Hill, 2008.

McDonald, Lee Martin. *The Origin of the Bible: A Guide for the Perplexed.* T and T Clark Guides for the Perplexed. New York: T and T Clark, 2011.

Milgrom, Jacob. *Leviticus 1–16: A New Translation with Introduction and Commentary.* Anchor Bible 3. New York: Doubleday, 1991.

Miller, Patrick D. *The Ten Commandments.* Interpretation: Resources for the Use of Scripture in the Church. Louisville: Westminster John Knox, 2009.

Miller, Patrick D., Jr. "Syntax and Theology in Genesis Xii 3a." *Vestus Testamentum* 34 (1984): 472–76.

Moberly, R. W. L. *Old Testament Theology: Reading the Hebrew Bible as Christian Scripture*. Grand Rapids, MI: Baker Academic, 2013.

Moore, Megan Bishop, and Brad E. Kelle. *Biblical History and Israel's Past: The Changing Study of the Bible and History*. Grand Rapids, MI: Eerdmans, 2011.

Nelson, Richard D. *Deuteronomy*. Old Testament Library. Louisville: Westminster John Knox, 2002.

Newbigin, Lesslie. *The Gospel in a Pluralist Society*. Grand Rapids, MI: Eerdmans, 1989.

Newsom, Carol A. *The Book of Job: A Contest of Moral Imaginations*. Oxford: Oxford University Press, 2009.

Niditch, Susan. *War in the Hebrew Bible: A Study in the Ethics of Violence*. New York: Oxford, 1993.

Olson, Dennis T. "The Book of Judges." In volume 2 of *The New Interpreter's Bible*, edited by Leander E. Keck, 721–888. 12 vols. Nashville: Abingdon Press, 1998.

Oswalt, John N. *The Holy One of Israel: Studies in the Book of Isaiah*. Eugene, OR: Cascade Books, 2014.

Propp, William H. C. *Exodus 1–18*. Anchor Bible 2. New York: Doubleday, 1998.

Römer, Thomas. *The So-Called Deuteronomistic History: A Sociological, Historical and Literary Introduction*. London: T and T Clark, 2007.

Rowley, H. H. *Israel's Mission to the World*. London: SCM, 1939.

———. *The Missionary Message of the Old Testament*. London: Carey Kingsgate, 1944.

Sanders, James A. *Canon and Community: A Guide to Canonical Criticism*. Guides to Biblical Scholarship. Philadelphia: Fortress, 1984.

Schlimm, Matthew Richard. *This Strange and Sacred Scripture: Wrestling with the Old Testament and Its Oddities*. Grand Rapids, MI: Baker Academic, 2015.

Schmid, Konrad. *The Old Testament: A Literary History*. Translated by Linda M. Maloney. Minneapolis: Fortress, 2012.

Schniedewind, William M. *How the Bible Became a Book: The Textualization of Ancient Israel*. Cambridge: Cambridge University Press, 2004.

Seibert, Eric A. "Recent Research on Divine Violence in the Old Testament (with Special Attention to Christian Theological Perspectives)." *Currents in Biblical Research* 15 (2016): 8-40.

Seitz, Christopher R. *The Character of Christian Scripture: The Significance of a Two-Testament Bible*. Studies in Theological Interpretation. Grand Rapids, MI: Baker Academic, 2011.

Smith, Mark S. *The Early History of God: Yahweh and the Other Deities in Ancient Israel*. 2nd ed. Biblical Resource Series. Grand Rapids, MI: Eerdmans, 2002.

———. *The Priestly Vision of Genesis 1*. Minneapolis: Fortress, 2009.

Sneed, Mark R. *The Social World of the Sages: An Introduction to Israelite and Jewish Wisdom Literature*. Minneapolis: Fortress, 2015.

Spellman, Ched. *Toward a Canon-Conscious Reading of the Bible: Exploring the History and Hermeneutics of the Canon*. New Testament Monographs 34. Sheffield: Sheffield Phoenix, 2014.

Steck, Odil H. *The Prophetic Books and Their Theological Witness*. St. Louis: Chalice, 2000.

Sternberg, Meir. *The Poetics of Biblical Narrative*. Indiana Literary Biblical Series. Bloomington, IN: Indiana University Press, 1985.

Strawn, Brent A. "Slaves and Rebels: Inscription, Identity, and Time in the Rhetoric of Deuteronomy." In *Sepher Torath Mosheh: Studies in the Composition and Interpretation of Deuteronomy*, edited by Daniel I. Block and Richard L. Schultz. Peabody, MA: Hendrickson, forthcoming.

Sweeney, Marvin A. *Reading the Hebrew Bible after the Shoah: Engaging Holocaust Theology*. Minneapolis: Fortress, 2008.

Tullock, John H. *The Old Testament Story*. 6th ed. Upper Saddle River, NJ: Prentice Hall, 2002.

Vaughan, Roberts. *God's Big Picture: Tracing the Storyline of the Bible*. Downers Grove, IL: InterVarsity, 2002.

von Rad, Gerhard. *Holy War in Ancient Israel*. Translated by Marva J. Dawn. Eugene, OR: Wipf and Stock, 2000; orig. 1951.

Wall, Robert W., and David R. Nienhuis, eds. *A Compact Guide to the Whole Bible: Learning to Read Scripture's Story*. Grand Rapids, MI: Eerdmans, 2015.

Warrior, Robert Allen. "Canaanites, Cowboys, and Indians: Deliverance, Conquest, and Liberation Theology Today." In *The Postmodern Bible Reader*, edited by D. Jobling, T. Pippin, and R. Schleifer, 188–94. Oxford: Blackwell, 2001.

Wright, Christopher J. H. *Deuteronomy*. New International Biblical Commentary Old Testament Series 4. Peabody, MA: Hendrickson, 1996.

———. *The Mission of God: Unlocking the Bible's Grand Narrative*. Downers Grove, IL: IVP Academic, 2006.

———. *The Mission of God's People: A Biblical Theology of the Church's Mission*. Biblical Theology for Life. Grand Rapids, MI: Zondervan, 2010.

Notes

Preface

1. See the comprehensive examination of the relationship of major parts of the OT to history in Megan Bishop Moore and Brad E. Kelle, *Biblical History and Israel's Past: The Changing Study of the Bible and History* (Grand Rapids, MI: Eerdmans, 2011).

1. Introduction

1. The term *YHWH* (pronounced with vowel sounds like those of *hallway*) designates the Hebrew personal name of Israel's God in the OT. It is often translated as "Lord" in modern English translations.

2. See Brent A. Strawn, "Slaves and Rebels: Inscription, Identity, and Time in the Rhetoric of Deuteronomy," in *Sepher Torath Mosheh: Studies in the Composition and Interpretation of Deuteronomy*, ed. Daniel I. Block and Richard L. Schultz (Peabody, MA: Hendrickson, forthcoming).

3. Walter Brueggemann, *Theology of the Old Testament: Testimony, Dispute, Advocacy* (Minneapolis: Fortress, 1997), 67.

4. Notice, for example, how many of the OT prophetic books that preserve poetic speeches by various prophets begin with a superscription that places the prophet into a specific time period (e.g., "The Lord's word that came to Hosea, Beeri's son, in the days of Judah's Kings Uzziah, Jotham, Ahaz, and Hezekiah, and in the days of Israel's King Jeroboam Joash's son" [Hos 1:1]).

5. R. W. L. Moberly, *Old Testament Theology: Reading the Hebrew Bible as Christian Scripture* (Grand Rapids, MI: Baker Academic, 2013), 287.

6. For accessible treatments of many of these issues, see David M. Carr, *The Formation of the Hebrew Bible: A New Reconstruction* (Oxford: Oxford University Press, 2011); Konrad Schmid, *The Old Testament: A Literary History*, trans. Linda M. Maloney (Minneapolis: Fortress, 2012); Lee Martin McDonald, *The Origin of*

the Bible: A Guide for the Perplexed, T and T Clark Guides for the Perplexed (New York: T and T Clark, 2011).

7. See Christopher B. Hays, *Hidden Riches: A Sourcebook for the Comparative Study of the Hebrew Bible and Ancient Near East* (Louisville: Westminster John Knox, 2014).

8. For a comprehensive resource on this topic, see Moore and Kelle, *Biblical History and Israel's Past*.

9. Brueggemann, *Theology of the Old Testament*, 67, 70.

10. For example, the poems in Psalms, which can rarely be assigned to specific historical circumstances, nonetheless communicate profound truths about the experiences of human life and the divine-human relationship.

11. H. H. Rowley, *Israel's Mission to the World* (London: SCM, 1939); H. H. Rowley, *The Missionary Message of the Old Testament* (London: Carey Kingsgate, 1944).

12. See, for example, Walter C. Kaiser Jr., *Mission in the Old Testament: Israel as a Light to the Nations*, 2nd ed. (Grand Rapids, MI: Baker Academic, 2001 [orig. 2000]); Vaughan Roberts, *God's Big Picture: Tracing the Storyline of the Bible* (Downers Grove, IL: InterVarsity, 2002); Arthur F. Glassner, with Charles E. Van Engen, Dean S. Gilliland, and Shawn B. Redford, *Announcing the Kingdom: The Story of God's Mission in the Bible* (Grand Rapids, MI: Baker Academic, 2003). At the time of the writing of this book, work is underway on a commentary series (The Story of God Commentary) from Zondervan that aims to interpret the biblical text in the context of the Bible's overarching narrative and canonical setting.

13. For example, both Roberts (*God's Big Picture*) and Glassner et al. (*Announcing the Kingdom*) propose that the "kingdom of God" is the unifying motif across the biblical writings.

14. Paul J. Achtemeier and Elizabeth Achtemeier, *The Old Testament Roots of Our Faith*, rev. ed. (Peabody, MA: Hendrickson, 1994 [orig. 1962]).

15. Robert W. Wall and David R. Nienhuis, eds., *A Compact Guide to the Whole Bible: Learning to Read Scripture's Story* (Grand Rapids, MI: Eerdmans, 2015).

16. Christopher J. H. Wright, *The Mission of God: Unlocking the Bible's Grand Narrative* (Downers Grove, IL: IVP Academic, 2006). See also Christopher J. H. Wright, *The Mission of God's People: A Biblical Theology of the Church's Mission*, Biblical Theology for Life (Grand Rapids, MI: Zondervan, 2010). For a

similar recent approach, see Timothy M. Green, *The God Plot: Living with Holy Imagination* (Kansas City, MO: Beacon Hill, 2014).

17. See Roger Brooks and John J. Collins, eds., *Hebrew Bible or Old Testament? Studying the Bible in Judaism and Christianity* (Notre Dame, IN: University of Notre Dame Press, 1990).

18. I will also follow the conventions of the Hebrew texts, in which YHWH is designated by masculine grammatical terms, and use masculine pronouns to refer to YHWH when discussing individual OT passages.

19. See the analysis in Steven Kratz, *The Holocaust in Historical Context: Ancient and Medieval Cases 1* (Oxford: Oxford University Press, 1994).

20. Post-Holocaust theology is playing an increasingly important role in biblical studies, especially within Jewish interpretation. See, e.g., Marvin A. Sweeney, *Reading the Hebrew Bible after the Shoah: Engaging Holocaust Theology* (Minneapolis: Fortress, 2008).

21. For two of the classic, yet different, formulations of canonical interpretation, see Brevard S. Childs, *Introduction to the Old Testament as Scripture* (Philadelphia: Fortress, 1979) and James A. Sanders, *Canon and Community: A Guide to Canonical Criticism*, GBS (Philadelphia: Fortress, 1984). More recently, see Christopher R. Seitz, *The Character of Christian Scripture: The Significance of a Two-Testament Bible*, Studies in Theological Interpretation (Grand Rapids, MI: Baker Academic, 2011) and Ched Spellman, *Toward a Canon-Conscious Reading of the Bible: Exploring the History and Hermeneutics of the Canon*, New Testament Monographs 34 (Sheffield: Sheffield Phoenix, 2014).

22. Biblical readers can observe this kind of reframing of older materials into particular arrangements to produce new meanings even at the level of individual biblical books. Note, for instance, the way the NT Gospels adapt and arrange older traditions about the life and teachings of Jesus in different ways in order to present four different literary portraits of Jesus designed for four particular audiences and circumstances (see the explicit reference to such reframing in Luke 1:1-4). For example, Matthew gathers the traditions into a portrayal of Jesus as the long-awaited Jewish Messiah, while Mark gathers the traditions into a portrayal of Jesus as the suffering servant who redeems the world through his own self-sacrifice.

23. I use the Protestant canon in this book not out of a sense that it is superior to all others, but in light of my own context and intended audience (see preface).

24. Fixed, authoritative collections of the OT and NT did not emerge before the second century CE at the earliest and generally in the third and fourth centuries CE. Detailed studies of the different canons of the OT and the debates over their historical development are available in various works. See, for example, McDonald, *Origin of the Bible;* J.-M. Auwer and H. J. de Jonge, eds., *The Biblical Canons*, BETL 163 (Leuven: Leuven University Press, 2003); William M. Schniedewind, *How the Bible Became a Book: The Textualization of Ancient Israel* (Cambridge: Cambridge University Press, 2004).

25. The question of whether to adopt the shorter Hebrew list of books or the larger Greek list was a major issue for Protestants in the sixteenth century. Beyond the canonical books, both the Jewish and Christian traditions later developed other writings designed to expound their belief and practice. These include Jewish collections such as the Mishnah and the Talmuds (see discussion in McDonald, *Origin of the Bible*, 239).

26. Narrative interpretation emerged in earnest within biblical studies in the 1970s and 1980s, perhaps marked most clearly by Hans Frei's *The Eclipse of Biblical Narrative*, which attempted to recover the importance of narrative for biblical interpretation (Hans W. Frei, *The Eclipse of Biblical Narrative: A Study in Eighteenth and Nineteenth Century Hermeneutics* [New Haven, CT: Yale University Press], 1974). Even before this time, however, an emphasis on narrative and story had long occupied a special place in the study of OT theology, especially in the first half of the twentieth century. For some important later works that shaped the study of narrative within biblical interpretation, see Robert Alter, *The Art of Biblical Narrative* (New York: Basic Books, 1981) and Meir Sternberg, *The Poetics of Biblical Narrative*, Indiana Literary Biblical Series (Bloomington: Indiana University Press, 1985).

27. See Craig G. Bartholomew and Michael W. Goheen, *The Drama of Scripture* (Grand Rapids, MI: Baker Academic, 2000).

28. For early discussion of the possibilities and problems of this conception of narrative, see the essays in Stanley Hauerwas and L. Gregory Jones, eds., *Why Narrative? Readings in Narrative Theology* (Grand Rapids, MI: Eerdmans, 1989).

29. Wright, *The Mission of God*, 64.

30. Brueggemann, *Theology of the Old Testament*, xv. See also pp. 71–78.

31. I thank my colleague Samuel M. Powell for this metaphor.

32. Some of the earliest, full-scale formulations of these perspectives in contemporary study appeared in works from the 1980s and 1990s. See especially Lesslie Newbigin, *The Gospel in a Pluralist Society* (Grand Rapids, MI: Eerdmans,

1989) and David J. Bosch, *Transforming Mission: Paradigm Shifts in Theology of Mission* (Maryknoll, NY: Orbis Books, 1991). Many of the early formulations of a missional ecclesiology for the church were then consolidated and made widely available in Darrell L. Guder, ed., *Missional Church: A Vision for the Sending of the Church in North America*, Gospel and Our Culture (Grand Rapids, MI: Eerdmans, 1998).

33. Bosch, *Transforming Mission*, 1.

34. See ibid., 390.

35. Three recent attempts to read the Bible in this way are Wright, *The Mission of God* (see also Wright, *The Mission of God's People*); Michael W. Goheen, *A Light to the Nations: The Missional Church and the Biblical Story* (Grand Rapids, MI: Baker Academic, 2011); and Richard Bauckham, *The Bible and Mission: Christian Witness in a Postmodern World* (Grand Rapids, MI: Baker Academic, 2003). For a recent, comprehensive treatment of the NT in particular, see Dean Flemming, *Why Mission?*, Reframing New Testament Theology (Nashville: Abingdon Press, 2015).

36. George R. Hunsberger, "Proposals for a Missional Hermeneutic: Mapping the Conversation," *Missiology* 39 (2011): 309–21.

2. The Old Testament as Story

1. Brueggemann, *Theology of the Old Testament*, 67.

2. Compare Wright's (*The Mission of God*, 27) categories for the OT story that loosely parallel mine used here: election (calling), redemption (creation), covenant (formation), and ethics (formation).

3. Michael Lodahl, *The Story of God: A Narrative Theology*, 2nd ed. (Kansas City, MO: Beacon Hill, 2008), 23.

4. Green, *The God Plot*, 20.

3. The Introduction of God's Mission

1. Modern scholarship adopted the label "Yahwist" for this source because its texts consistently refer to God by using the Hebrew personal name YHWH.

2. For a helpful exploration, see Hays, *Hidden Riches*, 41–74.

3. For example, the Babylonian story *Enuma Elish* is actually a story about how Marduk, the patron god of Babylon, became the supreme god and established Babylon as the center of his worship and rule.

4. Technically, verse 1 opens with what is called a temporal or genitival clause in Hebrew, a similar construction to what is found at the beginning of other creation stories from the ancient Near East (e.g., the Babylonian *Enuma Elish*).

5. Illustration from Sara Koenig, "The Beginning of the Story: Genesis–Deuteronomy," in *A Compact Guide to the Whole Bible: Learning to Read Scripture's Story*, ed. Robert W. Wall and David R. Nienhuis (Grand Rapids, MI: Eerdmans, 2015), 43.

6. Various hymns of praise in the Psalms explicitly use the imagery of YHWH splitting the sea and shattering the heads of sea monsters in his role as creator (see Ps 74:12-15).

7. The word *dome* translates the Hebrew term referring to "something pounded out," like a bowl or lid that could be placed into a volume of water.

8. *The CEB Study Bible*, 6 OT.

9. Green, *The God Plot*, 223.

10. For some explorations of this topic, see David J. A. Clines, "Humanity as the Image of God," in *On the Way to the Postmodern: Old Testament Essays, 1967–1998*, by David J. A. Clines, 2 vols., JSOTSup 292–93 (Sheffield: Sheffield Academic Press, 1998), 480–95; Mark S. Smith, *The Priestly Vision of Genesis 1* (Minneapolis: Fortress, 2009); Joseph Blenkinsopp, *Creation, Un-Creation, Re-Creation: A Discursive Commentary on Genesis 1–11* (London: T and T Clark, 2011), 26–28.

11. As I indicated in the introduction, the term *YHWH* (pronounced with vowel sounds like those of *hallway*) designates the Hebrew personal name of Israel's God in the OT. In Genesis 2, the English name, "Lord God" represents a combination of the Hebrew words *YHWH* and *'elôhîm*, with the second term being the more generic designation, "God."

12. The term (*'ādām*) appears throughout Genesis 2 accompanied by the definite article in Hebrew, yielding the category designation, "*the* human," rather than a personal name.

13. The testimony of the OT writers is that the animals also possess this divine breath and share an intimate connection with God, just as humans do (see Ps 104:30). The Genesis 2 story expresses this idea when it describes the animals being formed by God in the same way that humans were (v. 19), also illustrating that humans and animals share an intimate connection as those created in the same way by the same Creator.

14. Green, *The God Plot*, 231.

15. For example, see the Israelites' reference to YHWH as their "Eben*ezer*" ("Stone of Help") in 1 Samuel 7:12.

16. Green, *The God Plot*, 232; Wright, *The Mission of God*, 195.

17. The Hebrew pronouns and grammatical forms in the first few verses of chapter 3 make it clear that although the woman is the snake's primary conversation partner, both the man and woman are present together throughout the scene.

18. Blenkinsopp, *Creation, Un-Creation, Re-Creation*, 75.

19. Green, *The God Plot*, 234.

20. Wright, *The Mission of God*, 433.

21. For a sample discussion of approaches, see Blenkinsopp, *Creation, Un-Creation, Re-Creation*, 121–26.

22. See *ANET* 265.

23. See Blenkinsopp, *Creation, Un-Creation, Re-Creation*, 2.

24. For discussion and examples, see Hays, *Hidden Riches*, 75–96. Textbooks also often helpfully point out that the flood story in Genesis 6–9 seems to be a combination of two different sources, a feature that explains some of the apparent contradictions in the text (e.g., compare 6:19 and 7:2).

25. For a book-length study of this theme of God's love for and commitment to all creation that emerges from the early stories in Genesis and inspires care for animals and nature, see William Greenway, *For the Love of All Creatures: The Story of Grace in Genesis* (Grand Rapids, MI: Eerdmans, 2015).

26. For a survey of interpretations, see Blenkinsopp, *Creation, Un-Creation, Re-Creation*, 152.

27. Wright (*The Mission of God*, 196) discusses how Christian and Jewish interpretations of Genesis 11 have often differed over emphasizing the themes of pride or fear.

28. As Wright (*The Mission of God's People*, 78) summarizes the force of Genesis 11, "In this way, even the great Mesopotamian empires are relativized and negated. The greatest human civilizations cannot solve the deepest human problems. God's mission of blessing the nations has to be a radical new start."

4. The Calling and Creation of God's People

1. The designation *Fertile Crescent* refers to the relatively fertile, crescent-shaped region that stretches from Mesopotamia, along the coast of the Mediterranean Sea, and to the Nile River in Egypt.

2. Wright, *The Mission of God*, 212; Wright, *The Mission of God's People*, 66; Achtemeier and Achtemeier, *The Old Testament Roots*, 11.

3. For more on this contextual meaning of the term *bless/blessing*, see Goheen, *A Light to the Nations*, 31.

4. Patrick D. Miller Jr., "Syntax and Theology in Genesis Xii 3a," *Vestus Testamentum* 34 (1984): 474. For this interpretation within a narrative and missional reading of the OT, see Wright, *The Mission of God*, 200n16. The interpretations of this phrase as an exception often note that the second Hebrew participle ("those who curse you") is actually singular whereas the first ("those who bless you") is plural, as is the other reference to blessing "all the families of the earth" in the final phrase of verse 3.

5. Wright, *The Mission of God*, 254.

6. Ibid., 253; Rowley, *Missionary Message*, 32.

7. See the discussion of the interpretation of Genesis 12:1-3 in Moberly, *Old Testament Theology*, 46–51. For a collection of wide-ranging discussions on the issue of election within Christianity and Judaism, see Gary A. Anderson and Joel S. Kaminsky, eds., *The Call of Abraham: Essays on the Election of Israel in Honor of Jon D. Levenson*, Christianity and Judaism in Antiquity 19 (Notre Dame, IN: University of Notre Dame Press, 2013).

8. Robert Allen Warrior, "Canaanites, Cowboys, and Indians: Deliverance, Conquest, and Liberation Theology Today," in *Voices from the Margin: Interpreting the Bible in the Third World*, ed. R. S. Sugirtharajah (Maryknoll, New York/London: Orbis/SPCK), 277–85.

9. Moberly (*Old Testament Theology*, 46) notes that this understanding has become the typical Christian interpretation (see also Wright, *The Mission of God*, 263).

10. For a recent collection exploring this history of interpretation, see Bradley Beach and Matthew Powell, eds., *Interpreting Abraham: Journeys to Moriah* (Minneapolis: Fortress, 2014).

11. As with the two stories of God's covenant with Abraham in Genesis 15 and 17, the stories of Abraham's giving away his wife as his sister in chapters 12

and 20 may have originated as different versions of the same story from different sources (see also Gen 26:1-11 in which Isaac gives away his wife, Rebekah, as his sister). Even so, the present appearance of these stories within the canonical arrangement further illustrates Abraham's ongoing struggle to trust in God to fulfill the promise of descendants.

12. Frank S. Frick, *A Journey through the Hebrew Scriptures*, 2nd ed. (Belmont, CA: Wadsworth/Thomson Learning, 2003), 145 (emphasis original).

13. See commentaries such as William H. C. Propp, *Exodus 1–18: A New Translation with Introduction and Commentary*, AB 2 (New York: Doubleday, 1998) and Thomas B. Dozeman, *Exodus*, Eerdmans Critical Commentary (Grand Rapids, MI: Eerdmans, 2009).

14. The different names (Horeb, Sinai) for the holy mountain seem to reflect traditions that emerged in different geographical areas in ancient Israel and Judah. It's often thought that Horeb was the name used by northern traditions, such as those that might underlie the book of Deuteronomy (see Deut 1:6, 19; 5:2).

15. The lack of a personal name for Pharaoh in these biblical stories suggests that the emphasis is not on a particular ruler but on what the pharaoh represented as a symbol in the ancient cultural world.

16. For an identification of specific Egyptian deities that may correspond to some of the plagues, see the chart in John H. Tullock, *The Old Testament Story*, 6th ed. (Upper Saddle River, NJ: Prentice Hall, 2002), 72. Some examples include the Nile turned to blood as an attack on Hapi (the Nile god), the frogs as an attack on Heket (goddess of childbirth whose symbol was a frog), and the death of the firstborn as an attack on Osiris (the judge of the dead and patron god of the pharaoh).

17. YHWH's declarations seem to be the answer to Pharaoh's first dismissive words to Moses and Aaron, "Who is this Lord whom I'm supposed to obey by letting Israel go? I don't know [*yāda'*, acknowledge] this Lord" (Exod 5:2).

18. Wright, *The Mission of God*, 275.

19. Although the earlier translators of the Hebrew OT texts into Greek and Latin took this name to mean the Red Sea that lies south and east of Egypt (and many modern English translations still say the same), the title appears over twenty times in the OT and seems to be a general designation for the kind of reed-filled marshes found in northern Egypt's Nile River delta region. "Reed Sea" (*yam sûp*) appears five times in the book of Exodus alone: 10:19; 13:18; 15:4, 22; 23:31.

20. Perhaps furthering the notion of the exodus as the creation of the people, Achtemeier and Achtemeier (*The Old Testament Roots*, 32) note that texts elsewhere in the OT refer to YHWH becoming a "father" to Israel in the exodus (e.g., Deut 32:6, 10, 18; Isa 63:16; 64:8; Jer 3:19; Hos 11:1).

5. The Formation of God's People

1. Recall that the OT story has described earlier covenants made by YHWH with Noah and all living beings (Gen 9) and Abraham (Gen 15; 17), and later will describe a covenant made with David (2 Sam 7).

2. See the discussion of the origins and sources of the Pentateuch in chapter 3.

3. Timothy Green (*The God Plot*, 128) uses the analogy of the double portion of inheritance given to the oldest son in ancient Israel for the meaning of Israel as a "most precious possession." The oldest son received a larger portion not as a sign of exclusive favoritism but because he bore the responsibility to provide for the family as a whole after the father's death.

4. Ibid., 129–30.

5. This identity and role for Israel will appear explicitly in texts from the middle section of Isaiah (the portion often called "Second Isaiah"). For example, see Isaiah 42:1-9; 49:1-7.

6. Wright, *The Mission of God*, 225, 324–25.

7. The canonical story places the people at Sinai from three months after the exodus (Exod 19:1) to eleven months later (Num 10:11).

8. Wright, *The Mission of God*, 226–27.

9. Perhaps these views stem from an undue emphasis upon or inadequate understanding of NT texts that seem to downplay the importance of the Jewish law (e.g., Rom 7:6; Gal 3:13; Heb 8:13).

10. Notice that Psalm 119, which is the longest psalm in the book of Psalms, is an extensive celebration of the goodness of the divine law. Achtemeier and Achtemeier (*The Old Testament Roots*, 48–68) note that many of the criticisms of the Jewish law that appear in NT texts, some of which seem to suggest that the law *was* thought of as a mean to earn salvation, arose from a change in the interpretation of the law that happened in postexilic Judaism. In that later context, some groups within Judaism came to view the law as the means to establish (and not just maintain) the people's relationship with God.

11. Two collections of such political treaties have been of special interest: one collection from the Hittite kingdom (dating from the 1500s–1200s BCE) and another from the Assyrian Empire (ca. 600s BCE). For a discussion with ancient Near Eastern text examples, see Hays, *Hidden Riches*, 161–89.

12. For a discussion with ancient Near Eastern text examples, see ibid., 121–45.

13. I thank Brent A. Strawn for distinguishing the terminology of "on purpose" and "for a purpose."

14. Goheen, *A Light to the Nations*, 3.

15. John Calvin, *Institutes of the Christian Religion* II.vii.6-12

16. Another listing of the Ten Commandments appears in Deuteronomy 5:6-21, with some minor variations. For a recent in-depth study, see Patrick D. Miller, *The Ten Commandments*, Interpretation: Resources for the Use of Scripture in the Church (Louisville: Westminster John Knox, 2009).

17. This command to wholehearted trust and obedience that begins the formation in the wilderness will also notably appear as the fundamental demand in the final book of that wilderness journey (Deut 6:4-5) and the final charge to the people in the first book recounting their life in the promised land (Josh 24:14-15).

18. Brueggemann, *Theology of the Old Testament*, 184–85.

19. Ironically, the interlude in chapters 32–34, in which the Israelites build and worship a golden calf, illustrates the people's ongoing struggle to trust in YHWH's presence and provision. They give in to fear and mistrust, even while Moses is on Mount Sinai receiving YHWH's instructions for the people.

20. The CEB usually translates "the glory of the Lord" as "the Lord's glorious presence."

21. Later in the OT story, this same *glory* (presence) will be said to fill the Jerusalem temple that stands at the center of the people's life and worship (1 Kgs 6–8).

22. Green, *The God Plot*, 134.

23. Ibid., 138 (italics in original).

24. Ibid.

25. See Jacob Milgrom, *Leviticus 1–16: A New Translation with Introduction and Commentary*, AB 3 (New York: Doubleday, 1991).

26. Note the overall charge given to priests in Leviticus 10:10-11 to "distinguish between the holy and the common, and between the unclean and the clean" and to "teach the Israelites all the rules."

27. Later in the OT, the prophet Ezekiel uses this very image of the people's impurity causing YHWH to withdraw his holy, life-giving presence from Jerusalem to explain why the people suffered destruction and exile (Ezek 8–11).

28. Some of these stories that also appear in Exodus 15:22–18:27 on the way from Egypt to Sinai may have originated as different versions of the same tradition. See the discussion of the nature of the Pentateuch in chapter 3.

29. Green, *The God Plot*, 41.

30. Examples of the formation and preparation of the new generation in the final chapters of Numbers include Joshua's appointment as Moses's successor (27:12-23), regulations for proper offerings and festivals in the land (chs. 28–29), and instructions for how to divide and manage the land (chs. 34–35).

31. See Richard D. Nelson, *Deuteronomy*, OTL (Louisville: Westminster John Knox, 2002).

32. Deuteronomy is particularly similar to a seventh-century BCE Assyrian treaty known as the Vassal Treaty of Esarhaddon, a treaty imposed on subject kingdoms by the Assyrian emperor Esarhaddon to ensure their loyalty to his son after the emperor's death.

33. There is debate over the best translation of the Shema. The other major alternative to what is quoted here is "The LORD our God, the LORD is one."

34. Green, *The God Plot*, 70.

6. The Life of God's People (Part 1)

1. The books recounting this part of Israel's existence seem closer to what modern readers would think of as history-type works (with chronological references, accounts of monarchies and dynasties, etc.), and there is a substantial amount of related ancient written and archaeological sources from outside the Bible (e.g., Assyrian and Babylonian texts, material remains of cities, etc.). See Moore and Kelle, *Biblical History and Israel's Past*, chs. 3–8.

2. See Thomas Römer, *The So-Called Deuteronomistic History: A Sociological, Historical and Literary Introduction* (London: T and T Clark, 2007).

3. The classic formulation of the theory also suggested that the composer incorporated the already existing law code in Deuteronomy 4:44–30:20, with some added materials before and after, as a theological introduction to the Deuteronomistic History.

4. A common view has been to propose at least one compositional stage during the Judean monarchy (seventh century BCE) and at least one later during the Judean exile (sixth century BCE) and perhaps the subsequent postexilic period as well.

5. The "Instruction" mentioned here likely refers to some version of Deuteronomy 4:44–26:19.

6. See Hays, *Hidden Riches*, 161–89.

7. Here, and in nearly every conquest account in Joshua, the stories emphasize that the Israelites achieve victory through YHWH's miraculous acts (see 10:10-14; 11:6-8; 13:6) rather than human military strategy or action (the battle against Ai in ch. 7 is an exception).

8. See Mark S. Smith, *The Early History of God: Yahweh and the Other Deities in Ancient Israel*, Biblical Resource Series, 2nd ed. (Grand Rapids, MI: Eerdmans, 2002).

9. Green, *The God Plot*, 83.

10. See Dennis T. Olson, "The Book of Judges," *New Interpreter's Bible*, vol. 2 (Nashville: Abingdon Press, 1998), 721–888.

11. Matthew Schlimm, *This Strange and Sacred Scripture: Wrestling with the Old Testament and Its Oddities* (Grand Rapids, MI: Baker Academic), 62.

12. See John J. Collins, *Does the Bible Justify Violence?* (Minneapolis: Fortress, 2004), 17–20.

13. See Susan Niditch, *War in the Hebrew Bible: A Study of the Ethics of Violence* (New York: Oxford, 1993).

14. For a comprehensive survey of approaches within Christian theological perspectives, see Eric A. Seibert, "Recent Research on Divine Violence in the Old Testament (with Special Attention to Christian Theological Perspectives)," *CBR* 15 (2016): 8–40.

15. Ibid.

16. Several recent interpreters have considered the particular problem of how the conquest stories fit with a missional reading of Israel in the OT: Moberly, *Old Testament Theology*, 53–74; Brueggemann, *Theology of the Old Testament*, 496–98; Christopher J. H. Wright, *Deuteronomy*, NIBC 4 (Peabody, MA: Hendrickson, 1996), 108–20.

17. However, Joshua 11:20 says YHWH caused the Canaanites to attack Israel.

18. And significant debate remains about whether there is historical and archaeological evidence for the kind of Canaanite conquest portrayed by these texts. See Moore and Kelle, *Biblical History and Israel's Past*, 96–144.

19. See also Wright, *Deuteronomy*, 110–14. He concludes that the notion of God's people waging war to eliminate so-called pagan peoples is no longer applicable today precisely because the original rationale of preserving a "national distinctiveness" for Israel no longer applies to the intentionally "multinational community of the followers of Jesus" (ibid., 114).

20. The divine calling in Genesis 12:1-3 didn't imply that particular individuals or groups wouldn't undergo judgment or curse but only that the families of the earth *on the whole* would receive blessing through Abraham and Sarah's descendants.

21. I thank Samuel M. Powell for this analogy.

22. The book of Ruth follows Judges in the Protestant canon. It doesn't advance the larger storyline but explores various themes set against the backdrop of the judges' era. In the Hebrew canon, Ruth appears in a different location in the final canonical section (the Writings).

23. For a description of this imperial discourse and its relationship to Israel's story, see David Janzen, *The Necessary King: A Postcolonial Reading of the Deuteronomistic Portrait of the Monarchy*, HBM 57 (Sheffield: Sheffield Phoenix, 2013). Notice the connection with the portrayal of God in Genesis 1 as a sovereign who orders chaos and thus brings forth life (see ch. 3 in this book).

24. Ibid.

25. Green, *The God Plot*, 87.

26. Moses's speech to the people outside the land foreshadowed the possibility that they would insist on having a king (see Deut 17:14-20).

27. Goheen, *A Light to the Nations*, 55–56 (see 2 Sam 7:9-11).

28. Wright, *The Mission of God*, 233, 343–47.

29. For example, Wright (ibid., 345–47) notes the royal theology language in Psalms 2 and 72 that envisions the universal rule of the son of David and that all nations will be blessed through his rule.

30. Author's translation (the CEB reads, "Don't be upset about this"). Notice the similar terminology to "knowing good and evil (*ra'*)" in Genesis 3:5. The divine perspective appears in the following verses: "But what David had done was evil (*ra'*) in the LORD's eyes" (11:27).

31. Green, *The God Plot*, 84.

32. Ibid. The text suggests that these calves were intended to represent the presence of YHWH much like the ark of the covenant in the southern kingdom's capital city of Jerusalem (see v. 28). Yet, the act violates YHWH's demand for a single place of worship (Deut 12) and becomes known throughout the rest of 1–2 Kings as the "sins of Jeroboam."

33. For the standard introduction elements of northern and southern kings, compare, for example, 2 Kings 13:1-2 and 14:1-4.

34. Hezekiah's prayer for deliverance explicitly refers to the larger OT story of YHWH's redemptive mission and Israel's wider significance within it that appeared at the entrance into the land in Joshua (4:24), YHWH's covenant with David (2 Sam 7:25-27), and Solomon's dedication of the temple (1 Kgs 8:43): "So now, LORD our God, please save us from Sennacherib's power! Then all the earth's kingdoms will know that you, LORD, are the only true God" (2 Kgs 19:19).

35. The Babylonian destruction of Jerusalem likely occurred in July 586 BCE. The Babylonian Exile portrayed by the biblical narrative spanned from 586 to 539 BCE, but without clearly defined beginning and ending points.

36. See the final story in 2 Kings 25:27-30 that tells of Judah's King Jehoiachin living in Babylon under the authority of the Babylonian king.

37. See the description of the Deuteronomistic History at the beginning of this chapter.

38. Green, *The God Plot*, 94–95.

7. The Life of God's People (Part 2)

1. Charles Dickens, *A Christmas Carol: The Original Manuscript* (Oxford: Benediction Classics, 2012), 3.

2. See Moore and Kelle, *Biblical History and Israel's Past*, 334–95.

3. I thank Timothy Green for this analogy.

4. The attention to the experience of exile in other places throughout the OT has led scholars to suggest that it was the main time of writing and editing for much of the biblical literature and that it resulted in new understandings of the people's social and theological identity. See Brad E. Kelle, "An Interdisciplinary Approach to the Exile," in *Interpreting Exile: Displacement and Deportation in Biblical and Modern Contexts*, SBLAIL 10, ed. Brad E. Kelle, Frank Ritchel Ames, and Jacob L. Wright (Atlanta: Society of Biblical Literature, 2011), 5–38.

5. The biblical texts assign various lengths to the time of the exile, indicating that there was not just a single beginning and ending point (e.g., Jer 29:10-14 says seventy years). The narratives in the OT Historical Books describe the length as about half a century from the destruction of Jerusalem during the reign of the Judean king Zedekiah (2 Kgs 25:21; 2 Chr 36:17-21) to the reign of Cyrus the Persian (2 Chr 36:22-23; Ezra 1:1-4), roughly 586–539 BCE.

6. See Marc Zvi Brettler, *The Creation of History in Ancient Israel* (London: Routledge, 1995), 20–47.

7. For instance, this telling focuses almost entirely on Judah and Jerusalem (with virtually no mention of the northern kingdom of Israel), especially emphasizing that the temple was the defining center of Israel's life throughout its history and that the people's primary identity has always been a worshipping community rather than a political community. Even the great monarchs David and Solomon were primarily noteworthy because of what they did to inspire and execute the building of YHWH's temple and establish the people's proper worship (1 Chr 10:1–2; Chr 9:31).

8. Similarly, the prophet Ezekiel portrays the exile in priestly terms as serving the larger purpose of removing the sinful people so that the land could be cleansed and they could then be restored as a holy people to live on a holy land (see Ezek 36).

9. Wright, *The Mission of God*, 99 (italics original).

10. See Moore and Kelle, *Biblical History and Israel's Past*, 396–464.

8. The Voices of Israel's Poets, Sages, and Prophets

1. Many of the individual psalms in the book of Psalms are attributed to King David and could be read in conjunction with the narratives from 1–2 Samuel that tell David's part of the larger OT story. Likewise, most of the prophetic books identify the individual prophets and their words with particular historical

moments in Israel and Judah's past (e.g., see Isa 1:1; Hos 1:1) and could be read alongside the stories in 1–2 Kings that portray those parts of the main storyline.

2. Sarah Koenig, "The Witness of Israel's Poets and Sages: Job–Song of Songs," in Wall and Nienhuis, *Compact Guide*, 65–66.

3. The book of Lamentations has similar content to Psalms but appears among the prophetic books in the canon.

4. See Mark R. Sneed, *The Social World of the Sages: An Introduction to Israelite and Jewish Wisdom Literature* (Minneapolis: Fortress, 2015) and Richard J. Clifford, *The Wisdom Literature*, IBT (Nashville: Abingdon Press, 1998).

5. For examples with comparative discussions, see Hays, *Hidden Riches*, 297–337.

6. See Carol A. Newsom, *The Book of Job: A Contest of Moral Imaginations* (Oxford: Oxford University Press, 2009).

7. Reasons for prayers of thanks and praise or pleas for help in the book of Psalms include the celebration of YHWH's sovereignty and saving deeds, rescue from times of trouble, the people's victory in battle, difficulties associated with illness, guilt over sin, oppression by enemies, undeserved suffering, and more.

8. The book of Psalms likely reached its final form in the postexilic period, with the last section (Pss 120–150) only becoming fixed in the first century BCE.

9. Other important types of psalms in the book include royal psalms (focusing on Israel's king; Pss 2; 18; 45), wisdom psalms (giving teaching to the community; Pss 37; 49), Zion psalms (celebrating Jerusalem as YHWH's city; Pss 46; 48), and entrance liturgies (functioning in processions to the temple; Pss 15; 24).

10. About 60 percent of the psalms in the book are prayers for help (laments), many of which express the worshipper's feeling of God's absence and some of which blame God directly for undeserved suffering in the worshipper's life (see Ps 88).

11. See Goheen, *A Light to the Nations*, 57; Kaiser, *Mission*, 31–37.

12. Bo Lim, "The Witness of Israel's Prophets: Isaiah–Malachi," in Wall and Nienhuis, *Compact Guide*, 80.

13. Green, *The God Plot*, 99.

14. For a standard introduction to the prophetic books, including their composition history, see Odil H. Steck, *The Prophetic Books and Their Theological Witness* (St. Louis: Chalice, 2000).

15. In the Protestant canon, Lamentations appears between Jeremiah and Ezekiel because of an early Jewish tradition that associated the book with the prophet Jeremiah.

16. The book of Daniel has not traditionally been associated with the grouping of the twelve Minor Prophets because it seems to represent a type of apocalyptic writing. Although the grouping of the Minor Prophets as a whole loosely moves from before to after the exile, each individual book may contain material from all three periods that was included as the book took shape over time. And some of the books don't allow precise association with any particular period (Joel, Jonah).

17. See Achtemeier and Achtemeier, *The Old Testament Roots*, 89–114.

18. The association of these prophets with the time before the exile comes primarily from the introductory verses (superscription) of each book. The books themselves likely contain material from later eras, as well, inserted as the prophet's words were passed on and the collection was formed.

19. The gender categories employed in this ancient prophetic marriage metaphor (see also Ezek 16; 23) pose significant difficulties for contemporary readers. The prophet's metaphors of an adulteress woman to represent the sinful people and a faithful husband to represent God depict women and their experiences in negative ways, and the text itself contains images of domestic and sexual violence against the woman as part of the metaphor (e.g., Hos 2:3-4, 9-10).

20. Green, *The God Plot*, 114.

21. Ibid., 118.

22. See John N. Oswalt, *The Holy One of Israel: Studies in the Book of Isaiah* (Eugene, OR: Cascade Books, 2014), 88–93.

23. These kinds of oracles appear in prophetic books associated with all three eras before, during, and after the exile.

24. Brueggemann, *Theology of the Old Testament*, 502.

25. Oswalt, *The Holy One of Israel*, 91. While Israel remains passive in the Oracles against the Nations, there are some exceptions in other judgment speeches where YHWH equips his people to take an active role against the nations (e.g., Mic 4:13).

26. See ibid., 88–89.

27. Wright, *The Mission of God*, 240.

28. Oswalt, *The Holy One of Israel*, 91.

29. Scholars today generally consider the speeches in Isaiah 40–55 (sometimes called "Second Isaiah") to be from a different prophet (or prophets) than the eighth-century prophet Isaiah, whose words and actions are presented in the book's first thirty-nine chapters.

30. Green, *The God Plot*, 173, 169.

31. Oswalt, *The Holy One of Israel*, 91.

32. Standard OT introductory textbooks usually label Isaiah 40–55 as "Second Isaiah" (or "Deutero-Isaiah") and propose that the poetic prophecies originated among a prophet (or prophetic group) proclaiming YHWH's messages to the exiles near the end of the Babylonian period (ca. 539 BCE).

33. Standard OT textbooks usually label Isaiah 56–66 as "Third Isaiah" and identify its origins among the Persian-period Jerusalem community after 539 BCE.

9. The End Is the Beginning

1. Green, *The God Plot*, 218.

2. Some English translations (e.g., NRSV) read the Hebrew of this verse as a statement about what the prophet will do among the people ("he will turn the hearts..."). The CEB renders the statement as a command given to the people, but also as an action they will take in light of the work of the prophet among them.

3. For the use of this image with other elements of the OT as narrative, see Green, *The God Plot*, 41.

4. The four Gospels, for example, go over the same story of Jesus's life and teachings in different ways.

5. For a recent interpretation of the NT writings in light of the mission of God, see Flemming, *Why Mission*.

6. For discussion of this legacy, see Brueggemann, *Theology of the Old Testament*, 730. While the NT writers read the OT in light of Jesus, they didn't (for the most part) cast Israel as a failed or irrelevant community (see Rom 11).

7. Wright, *The Mission of God*, 122.

8. Flemming, *Why Mission*, xx.

9. Jesus was preceded by the prophetic announcements of John the Baptist. However, although John preceded Jesus (see Mark 1; Luke 1), the Gospel of Matthew that opens the NT introduces Jesus first through his genealogy and birth (chs. 1–2) and only then refers back to John the Baptist's prior ministry (ch. 3).

10. The Greek word *Christ* is a title that translates the Hebrew word for "Messiah" ("anointed one") used in the OT (e.g., Isa 45:1).

11. Flemming, *Why Mission*, xix.

12. Lodahl, *The Story of God*, 125.

13. Ibid., 128.

14. Ibid., 130.

15. Wright, *The Mission of God*, 213.

16. Ibid., 66–67.

17. Flemming, *Why Mission*, xxiii.

18. Brueggemann, *Theology of the Old Testament*, 712.

19. Ibid., 720.

Scripture Reference Index

34446832R00158

Made in the USA
San Bernardino, CA
02 May 2019